Planet Earth

The illustrated story of our wild and wonderful World

Published in the United States and its territories, Canada,
and the Philippine Islands by

HAMMOND World Atlas
Part of the Langenscheidt Publishing Group

36-36 33rd Street, Long Island City, NY, 11106
VP, Publisher Chuck Lang
Publishing Director Karen Prince

Planet Earth is a reprint of five books, previously published as the
Atlas In The Round series, including: Dinosaurs, Explorers, Natural
Disasters, and The Weather Atlas; written by Alastair Campbell,
Keith Lye, John Malam, Clare Oliver, and Charlie Watson.

Produced for HAMMOND WORLD ATLAS CORPORATION by

ILEX

The Old Candlemakers
West Street
Lewes
East Sussex BN7 2NZ
www.ilex-press.com

Publisher: Alastair Campbell
Creative Director: Peter Bridgewater
Managing Editor: Chris Gatcum
Editor: Ellie Wilson
Art Director: Julie Weir
Design Assistant: Emily Harbison

Printed and bound in Hong Kong

ISBN-13: 978-084-371834-8

Planet Earth

The illustrated story of our wild and wonderful World

Alastair Campbell
and Keith Lye

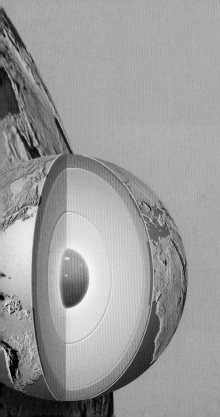

HAMMOND

Contents

Chapter 1: The Beginning

Chapter 2: The Physical Earth

Chapter 3: The Angry Earth

Chapter 4: Discovery And Exploration

Chapter 5: The World Today

Life On Earth

Our home, Planet Earth, is unlike any other planet in the Solar System. It may even be unique in the Universe, because it has the ideal conditions for the development of complex life forms. Our planet has much surface water, which is essential for life. But if Earth were closer to the Sun, it would be too hot to retain its surface water. And if it was farther away, then it would be too cold and any surface water would be locked in ice sheets.

The Earth was formed about 4.5 billion years ago. The first known signs of life—single-celled organisms called stromatolites—date back 3.5 billion years. Some organisms which are similar to those ancient ones can still be seen in Shark Bay in western Australia. The appearance of these life forms was important because they produced oxygen, a gas in the atmosphere that makes life on land possible.

From these simple beginnings, many complex life forms have evolved. Most of these plant and animal species are now extinct and we know of their existence from evidence found in rocks, called fossils. For example, the dinosaurs successively lived on Earth through the long Mesozoic Era, but they became extinct 65 million years ago.

Dinosaurs dominated the land during the Mesozoic Era, which lasted 196 million years. Some grew to gigantic size. But following the extinction of the dinosaurs, mammals, which had long been around in the Mesozoic Era as burrowing animals, began to flourish. Many kinds of mammals emerged in the Cenozoic Era, which continues to the present day, but most of them are also extinct, despite the great variety that live on our planet today. Towards the end of the Cenozoic Era human-like creatures began to appear. Modern humans finally evolved and they have dominated the world in the last 100,000 years.

Right *Organisms called stromatolites (which date back to 3.5 billion years ago) can be found in Shark Bay, western Australia.*

Below *The Giant Panda that lives in China is an endangered species. If not protected, this black-and-white bear could become extinct like the dinosaurs.*

Right *The Bengal tiger is also an endangered species that, like the Panda, needs to be protected.*

Far left *Triceratops, from the Cretaceous Period, lived 70 million years ago.*

Left *The dinosaur Dacentrurus, lived 155 million years ago, during the Jurassic Period in the Mesozoic Era.*

Studying The Earth

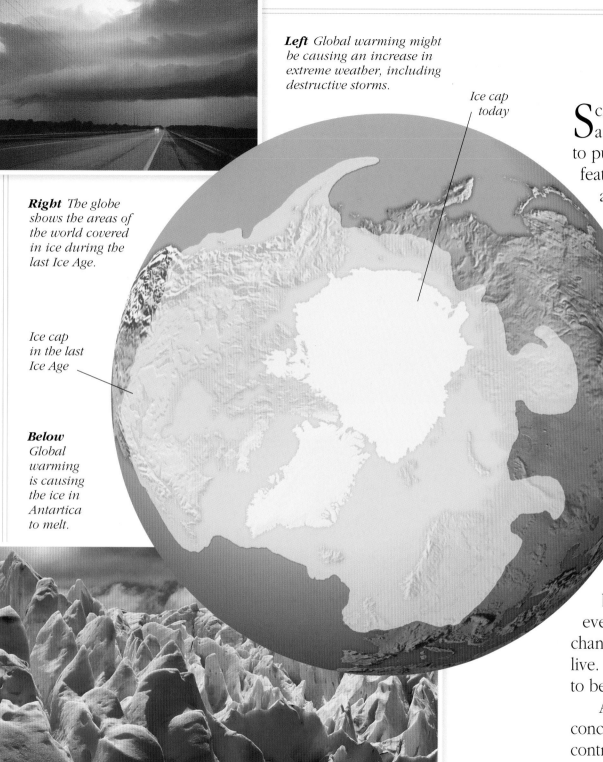

Ice cap today

Ice cap in the last Ice Age

Scientists have explained many of the Earth's mysteries. There was a time when people thought that earthquakes were sent by God to punish people. Today, science teaches us that they are a natural feature of our changing world. Most of the world has been explored and mapped, and modern transport enables us to travel to remote areas that were unknown to explorers only a few hundred years ago. Yet many mysteries remain.

Scientists study the weather and climate. They try to find out why climates have changed many times in the past. For example, only 11,000 years ago, much of the northern half of Planet Earth was buried under thick ice sheets. Yet by 10,000 years ago, it was probably warmer than it is today. The ice melted and large areas of land were flooded.

Today, scientists are interested in another problem. Since the late 18th century, fossil fuels (coal, oil and natural gas) have been burned in factories or in car engines. These fuels release a gas called carbon dioxide into the air. The amount of carbon dioxide in the Earth's atmosphere has been steadily increasing. Carbon dioxide is one of the gases (methane is another) that retains heat from the Sun. This creates a "greenhouse effect," heating our planet. This is called global warming.

Global warming is causing climates to change. It may also be the reason for an increasing number of extreme weather events, such as destructive storms and droughts. Global warming changes habitats—places where special groups of plants and animals live. This is causing organisms that cannot adapt to the new conditions to become extinct.

Around the world, the governments of many countries are concerned about global warming. They are working together to try to control and reduce the rate of global warming. More than ever before, people around the world realize that they depend on each other.

Chapter 1:
The Beginning

The story of how life has evolved on Planet Earth is long and complex. But scientists have pieced together an outline history of life on Earth. Until recently, the origins of the Universe were a mystery, but today scientists believe it was formed 13.7 billion years ago.

The Big Bang

Before the time of the Italian scientist Galileo (1564-1642), people thought that the Earth lay at the center of the Universe and that all the heavenly bodies rotated around it. But we now know that the Earth is a planet that orbits (rotates around) the Sun in the Solar System. The Sun is a medium-sized star, one of about 100 billion stars in the Milky Way galaxy. The Milky Way is only one of around 100,000 billion galaxies in the observable Universe. It is about 100,000 light-years across, (a light-year is the distance traveled by light in a year—about 5.88 trillion miles or 9.46 trillion km).

Around 50 years ago, scientists disagreed about the origins of the Universe. Some scientists thought it had always existed and that it had no beginning. But today most scientists believe that the Universe did have a beginning. They think that it was created 13.7 billion years ago in a massive explosion called the "Big Bang." In the first millionth of a second after the explosion, the new Universe expanded from a point of infinite mass and density into a huge fireball about 18.6 billion miles (30 billion km) across.

The Universe was a strange place after the Big Bang. The temperature in the first second of its existence was amazingly hot, and may have reached 10 billion degrees. The Universe then consisted mainly of radiation. Scientists have measured small variations of what is called the cosmic microwave background (CMB) radiation. CMB radiation left over from the creation of the Universe was discovered by accident in 1964. Scientists used measurements of these variations to work out the date of the Big Bang. All these ideas are theories, based on research, and discoveries might lead the scientists to modify the theories.

Left *People who lived centuries ago once believed that the Earth was flat. We now know that it is a round planet that orbits the sun in the Solar System.*

Right *Our Sun is a star in the Milky Way galaxy which is one of around 100,000 billion other galaxies in the Universe that we can observe.*

The New Universe

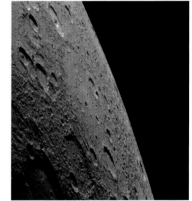

Scientists believe that it took about 300,000 years before the Universe was cool enough for atoms to form. They were mostly hydrogen atoms—hydrogen is still the most abundant material in the Universe. It took 200 million years before the first stars were formed, as particles of matter were drawn together in early galaxies. Stars were born and destroyed. Each set of new stars used material from the debris left behind by extinct stars. Around five billion years ago, a star began to form on the outskirts of the Milky Way galaxy. Around it was enough matter left over to create the planets which rotate around it. The Sun and the Solar System were born.

Much of our recent knowledge of the early Universe comes from the Hubble Space Telescope, which was named after the American astronomer Edwin Powell Hubble (1889-1933), who studied galaxies and discovered that they were all moving away from each other. The Hubble Space Telescope is a reflecting telescope which was built as an observatory to circle the Earth in space. Free of the Earth's atmosphere, it has produced amazing pictures of deep space. Because the pictures show galaxies at the time when light left them, they give us snapshots of the early Universe.

Above A close up photograph of Saturn's Moon reveals craters on its surface.

What is the future of the Universe? Scientists are divided on this issue. Some think that it will go on expanding for ever, with galaxies moving further and further apart. Others suggest that gravity may eventually halt the expansion. If that were to happen, the galaxies would fall back to form a single point of infinite mass and density. A Big Bang would then create a new Universe, starting the cycle all over again. This suggests that our Universe may have been created from the remains of an older Universe, just as new stars were created by destroyed ones.

Above The Hubble Space Telescope takes pictures from space which help scientists to learn more about the Universe.

Right This picture of many stars was taken in space by the Hubble Telescope. It allows scientists to study the stars more accurately.

The Solar System

The Solar System consists of the Sun and the heavenly bodies that orbit around it, including the planets, the Moon, asteroids, comets, meteorites, dust, and gas. Scientists think that it began to form around five billion years ago from a rotating disk of gas and dust, (the remains of extinct stars). Much of this material collected together to form the Sun, which contains 99.8 percent of the mass of the Solar System. The remaining material formed the other bodies that orbit around the Sun.

The Solar System had a violent early history, with newly formed, extremely hot bodies smashing into each other. Scientists think that around 4.4 billion years ago, about a million years after our Earth formed, our planet had a twin, whose orbit was close to that of the Earth. The twins crashed into each other and the bulk of the smaller body was absorbed by its larger twin. This created a new body of much the same size as today's Planet Earth. But a lot of debris was thrown into space. Eventually, this material collected together to form the Moon.

Right Mayan ruins in what is now Mexico's Yucatán Peninsula, where the comet that is thought to have killed the dinosaurs landed 65 million years ago.

Right Saturn is a heavenly body, a planet, that orbits around the Sun.

Left Jupiter is the largest planet in the Solar System.

Collisions still occur. In 1994, a comet crashed into the giant planet Jupiter. It created huge fireballs that scarred the planet and remained visible for months afterwards. Another major collision occurred about 65 million years ago when a huge asteroid, thought to be six miles (10 km) wide crashed into Planet Earth in the area of what is now Mexico's Yucatán Peninsula. The explosion was probably the reason why the dinosaurs became extinct. Huge collisions are now less common, but shooting stars still light up the night sky. These sudden streaks of light are the trails of meteors burning up as they enter the Earth's atmosphere. Small fragments of meteors reach Earth, helping scientists to understand the materials that make up our Solar System.

Above Saturn has many moons which orbit around it, unlike Earth, which has one.

The Solar System

The Solar System contains eight major planets. On average, Planet Earth lies 93 million miles from the Sun. Venus, the hottest planet with temperatures reaching 885 °F (475 °C), and Mercury are closer to the Sun than the Earth. Beyond the Earth lies a fourth rocky planet, Mars. Scientists think simple life forms may have lived on Mars. Mars has polar ice caps but its surface lacks water and is freezing cold. Beyond Mars lie four giant planets, which are made up largely of gas. The largest is Jupiter, whose mass is almost three times as much as the other planets combined. Beyond Jupiter lies Saturn, famed for its rings, Uranus, and Neptune.

Above A spiral galaxy similar to the Milky Way galaxy which is home to our Solar System.

Another body, called Pluto, lies beyond Neptune. Pluto lies in the Kuiper Belt and it was once regarded as the smallest planet. In 2003, astronomers discovered another slightly larger body, called Eris, beyond Pluto. In 2006, the International Astronomical Union decided to reclassify Pluto and Eris as "dwarf planets." In the same category, they placed Ceres, the biggest known asteroid in the asteroid belt between Mars and Jupiter. Ceres has a diameter of 567 miles (913 km). Astronomers think there may be a million or so asteroids in this belt which exceed 0.6 miles (1 km) across. Comets are small icy bodies that also orbit the Sun. Halley's Comet is famous because it can sometimes be seen from Earth. It orbits the Sun once every 76 years.

The Earth's position in the Solar System has made life possible. It benefits from being neither too close nor too far away from the Sun. It has an atmosphere which is held by gravity, and this protects the planet from the Sun's harmful ultraviolet radiation and from meteorites.

Above Traveling to space is now possible and astronauts have even walked on the Moon.

Right Planets in order from the Sun: Mercury; Venus; Earth; Mars; Jupiter; Saturn; Uranus; Neptune.

Continents On The Move

Maps of the world in a modern atlas show us the shapes of the continents and oceans as they appear today. You might think they have always looked like this, and that they have always been in the same positions on the Earth. In fact, the continents have been shaped and moved around over Earth's surface by powerful forces from deep inside the planet.

Many millions of years ago all land on Earth belonged to one huge super-continent. It has been given the name Pangea, meaning "All Earth." During the Mesozoic Era, Pangea broke up into smaller pieces. They are today's continents. It has taken millions of years for the continents to reach their present-day positions. They are still moving, slowly altering the world as it appears from space.

Below *Earth's continents and oceans as they appear today.*

*Continents move because the Earth's top layer, or crust, is divided into pieces called plates. The continents are attached to the plates, and the plates slide on top of Earth's mantle—a layer of semi-molten rock. The places where plates meet can be seen, such as along the San Andreas Fault, USA, **above**.*

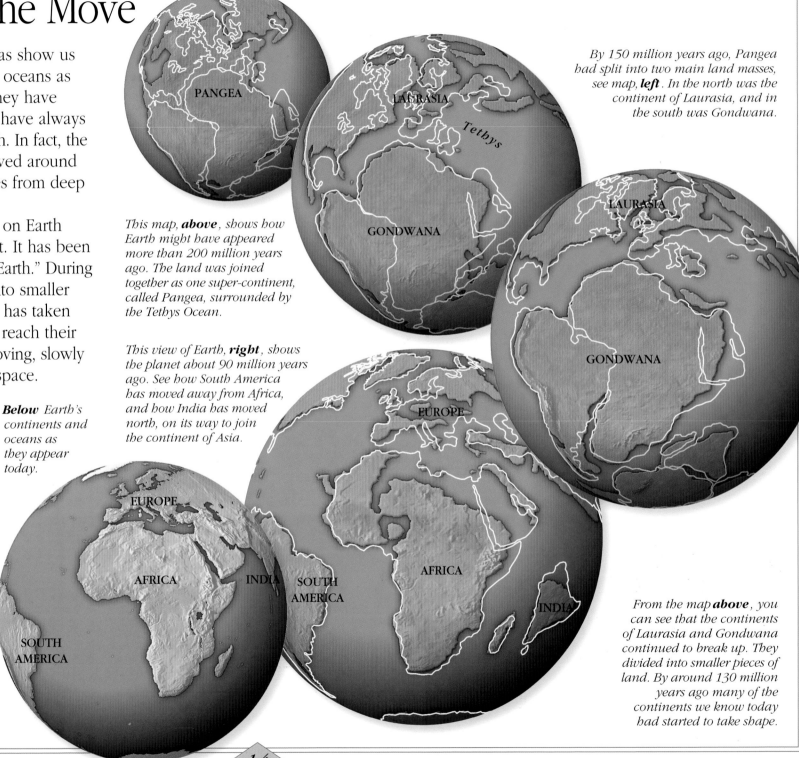

*By 150 million years ago, Pangea had split into two main land masses, see map, **left**. In the north was the continent of Laurasia, and in the south was Gondwana.*

*This map, **above**, shows how Earth might have appeared more than 200 million years ago. The land was joined together as one super-continent, called Pangea, surrounded by the Tethys Ocean.*

*This view of Earth, **right**, shows the planet about 90 million years ago. See how South America has moved away from Africa, and how India has moved north, on its way to join the continent of Asia.*

*From the map **above**, you can see that the continents of Laurasia and Gondwana continued to break up. They divided into smaller pieces of land. By around 130 million years ago many of the continents we know today had started to take shape.*

Above *The globes show the plates that form the Earth's hard outer layers.*

Below *The Earth contains a solid inner core, made up mainly of iron, and a viscous outer core. The core is about 4,190 miles (6,740 km) across. Around the core is the rocky mantle, which is about 1,800 miles (2,900 km) thick. The crust averages 3.7 miles (6 km) thick under the oceans and 22 miles (35 km) thick under the continents.*

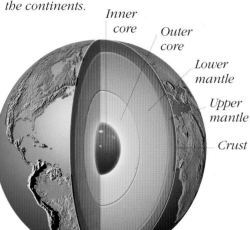

- Inner core
- Outer core
- Lower mantle
- Upper mantle
- Crust

Some plates move sideways alongside each other. For most of the time, the jagged plate edges are locked together. But friction finally breaks the rocks, causing the plates to move suddenly. This causes earthquakes.

Sea level | Ocean floor | Ocean ridge | Ocean trench

Magma rising through the crust to form a volcano

Direction of plate movement

Rising magma

Direction of plate movement

Plate descends and melts, producing magma

Hidden beneath the oceans are mountain ranges, called ocean ridges. Deep valleys in the middle of the ridges form the edges of plates which are moving apart. When plates move apart, molten magma from the mantle rises and plugs the gaps. When two plates collide, one plate sinks down beneath the other alongside the ocean trenches, the deepest places in the oceans. The edge of the descending plate melts and some of the molten rock rises and erupts out of volcanoes on the Earth's surface.

The Restless Earth

The Earth's outer layers, including the crust and the top, rigid layer of the mantle, are split into huge plates. The plates, which are about 62 miles (100 km) thick, rest on the mostly solid mantle. But the mantle also contains some molten material which moves around in slow currents. These currents move the plates and the continents resting upon them. Plates move apart along ocean ridges and collide along ocean trenches. Sometimes, when plates push against each other, the rocks between them are squeezed up into mountain ranges. Some plates move alongside each other. They are separated by long faults (cracks) in the Earth's surface.

Plates move occasionally in violent jerks, causing earthquakes. On average, plates move by only 0.8–4 inches (2–10 cm) a year. This sounds slow, but over the course of millions of years, plate movements change the face of the Earth.

When molten magma emerges through holes in the ground, called volcanoes, it is called lava. When some volcanoes erupt, they explode solid bits of lava high into the air. Other volcanoes erupt streams of runny lava. Most volcanoes lie near the plate edges in the ocean trenches. Some lie in the middle of plates, above heat sources in the mantle.

Birth Of A Volcano

Right *Cross section of an erupting volcano, showing lava bursting from the main vent and side vents, called dykes. Explosive pressure is created by the accumulation of magma, gases, and superheated steam beneath the Earth's surface. Once the magma escapes, it hardens to form the volcano sides, creating the typical cone shape.*

Fiery cloud

Plume of ash and lava

Main vent

Side vent

Dyke

Magma chamber

Batholith (dome of volcanic rock)

Lava flow

Below *The Hawaiian island of Mauna Loa, the world's largest active volcano, stands 5.5 miles (9 km) above the seabed.*

Volcanoes occur when hot, liquid rock (called magma) pushes up through a weak spot in the Earth's surface. Most volcanoes form as a bubble of magma in a chamber below the Earth's surface. As the chamber fills, the pressure builds up to eruption point. The sort of eruption depends on the sort of rock the magma contains, and the amount of gas. The eruption might be very frothy, turning to ash as soon as it escapes, or viscous and hot, running down the sides of the volcano as lava. Lava flows can reach temperatures of 2,200 °F (1,200 °C). Ash is just as dangerous, forming clouds that race along at 300 mph (500 kph) and reach an incredible temperature of 900 °F (500 °C). Volcanoes can spring up anywhere on the Earth's crust, even under the sea. They can climb all the way from the deep seabed to poke above the waves as islands.

Above *17th-century German scholar Athanasius Kircher attempted to explain how volcanoes worked.*

Right *Mount Pelée on Martinique exploded in 1902 with a surge of hot gases, called a pyroclastic flow.*

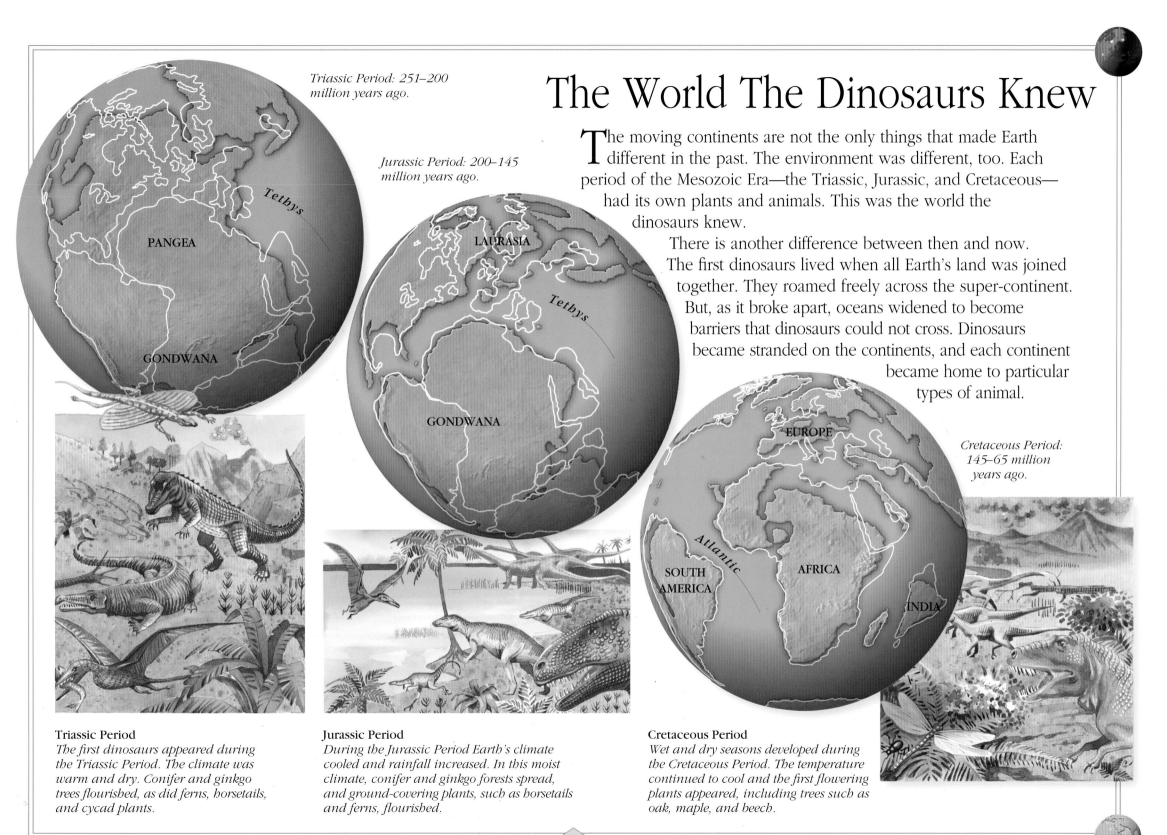

Triassic Period: 251–200 million years ago.

Jurassic Period: 200–145 million years ago.

The World The Dinosaurs Knew

The moving continents are not the only things that made Earth different in the past. The environment was different, too. Each period of the Mesozoic Era—the Triassic, Jurassic, and Cretaceous—had its own plants and animals. This was the world the dinosaurs knew.

There is another difference between then and now. The first dinosaurs lived when all Earth's land was joined together. They roamed freely across the super-continent. But, as it broke apart, oceans widened to become barriers that dinosaurs could not cross. Dinosaurs became stranded on the continents, and each continent became home to particular types of animal.

Cretaceous Period: 145–65 million years ago.

Triassic Period
The first dinosaurs appeared during the Triassic Period. The climate was warm and dry. Conifer and ginkgo trees flourished, as did ferns, horsetails, and cycad plants.

Jurassic Period
During the Jurassic Period Earth's climate cooled and rainfall increased. In this moist climate, conifer and ginkgo forests spread, and ground-covering plants, such as horsetails and ferns, flourished.

Cretaceous Period
Wet and dry seasons developed during the Cretaceous Period. The temperature continued to cool and the first flowering plants appeared, including trees such as oak, maple, and beech.

Dinosaurs At A Glance

Dinosaurs were the dominant members of the animal kingdom during the Mesozoic Era. However, they were not the only animals that lived on Earth during this long period of the planet's prehistoric past. Dinosaurs shared the world with creatures that flew in the sky and others that swam in the sea. None of these other animals were dinosaurs.

What makes a dinosaur a dinosaur? To be classified as a dinosaur an animal must have lived between 251 million and 65 million years ago, which was the time of the Mesozoic Era. It must have lived on land and walked on legs held straight out beneath its body. It must have been a reptile and unable to fly. An animal with all these characteristics was a dinosaur.

Some dinosaurs, such as this Saltasaurus, *had long tails*

Sight
Carnivores had better sight than herbivores. They needed good sight to see their prey. Some dinosaurs may have been able to see in the dark.

Like other carnivores, Deinonychus *probably had good eyesight*

A carnivore's tooth

Teeth
Carnivores had curved, blade-like teeth with serrated edges—the ideal meat-cutters. Herbivores had straight peg-like teeth for stripping leaves from branches, and also flatter teeth for chewing and grinding.

A herbivore's tooth

Dinosaurs may have had distinctive skin colors and patterns

Diet
Dinosaurs can be divided into three groups depending on the type of food they ate.

Giganotosaurus

Carnivores were meat-eaters. Predators caught and killed their prey. Scavengers ate meat from animals killed by others.

Triceratops

Herbivores were plant-eaters. They ate leaves, stems, fronds, and fruits. Stomach stones helped them digest their food.

Skin
Dinosaur skin was covered in overlapping scales, like today's reptiles. Some dinosaurs had bony plates, nodules, and spikes embedded in their skin. Others grew feathers over part or all of their bodies.

Feathered dinosaurs
Some dinosaurs may have had feathers, particularly small, agile carnivores such as this Caudipteryx. *These so-called "dinobirds" were unable to fly, but it was probably from them that modern birds evolved.*

Dinosaurs had legs held beneath their bodies

Avimimus

Omnivores had a mixed diet. They ate both meat and plants, as well as fish and eggs.

Dinosaur Families

The animal kingdom is divided into groups, such as reptiles, birds, mammals, and insects. Dinosaurs were reptiles. People who study dinosaurs look for tell-tale features in their fossils. By recognizing the features it is then possible to divide dinosaurs into families. A dinosaur "family tree" can be made, showing the families and how they are related to each other. The dinosaurs within each family share the same features.

Hip structure

One of the keys to studying dinosaurs lies in the shape of their hip bones. Dinosaurs either had hips with bones shaped like lizards or like birds. Depending on their hip shape, all dinosaurs are divided into either lizard-hipped (saurischian) or bird-hipped (ornithischian) dinosaurs.

Right *A simplified "family tree." Dinosaurs trace their origins back to a common ancestor. As they evolved, they branched out. One branch, birds, continues to the present day.*

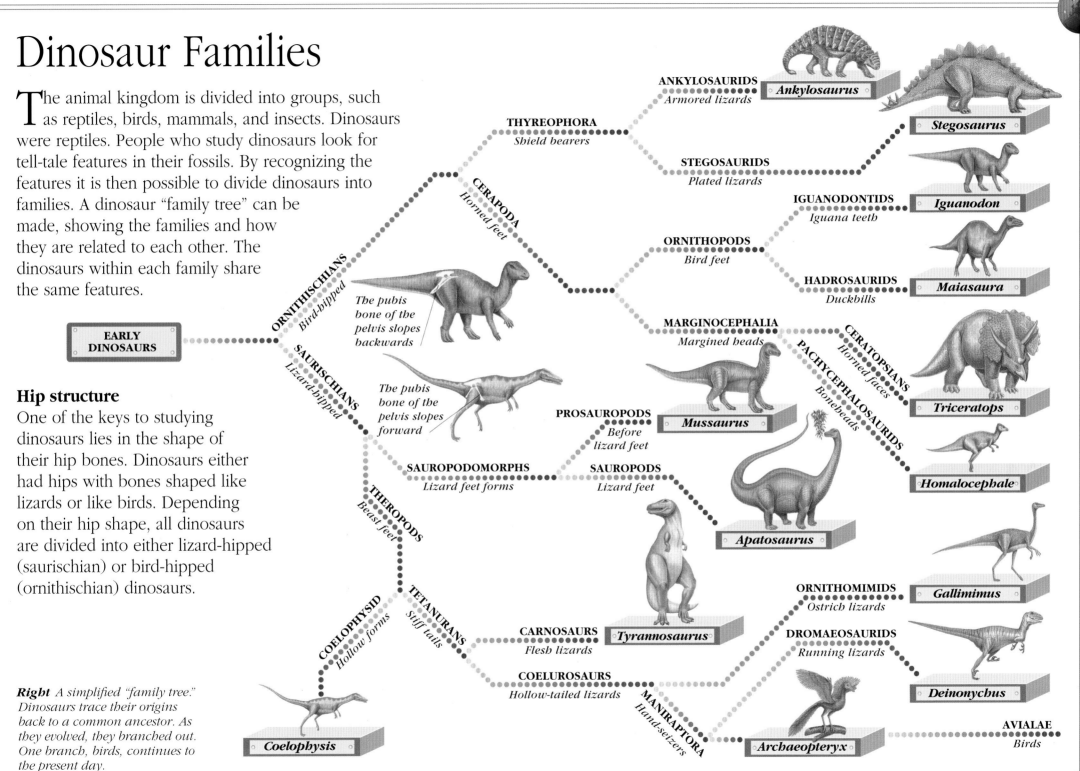

EARLY DINOSAURS

ORNITHISCHIANS
Bird-hipped

The pubis bone of the pelvis slopes backwards

SAURISCHIANS
Lizard-hipped

The pubis bone of the pelvis slopes forward

CERAPODA
Horned feet

THYREOPHORA
Shield bearers

ANKYLOSAURIDS
Armored lizards
Ankylosaurus

STEGOSAURIDS
Plated lizards
Stegosaurus

ORNITHOPODS
Bird feet

IGUANODONTIDS
Iguana teeth
Iguanodon

HADROSAURIDS
Duckbills
Maiasaura

MARGINOCEPHALIA
Margined heads

CERATOPSIANS
Horned faces
Triceratops

PACHYCEPHALOSAURIDS
Boneheads
Homalocephale

PROSAUROPODS
Before lizard feet
Mussaurus

SAUROPODOMORPHS
Lizard feet forms

SAUROPODS
Lizard feet
Apatosaurus

THEROPODS
Beast feet

COELOPHYSID
Hollow forms
Coelophysis

TETANURANS
Stiff tails

CARNOSAURS
Flesh lizards
Tyrannosaurus

COELUROSAURS
Hollow-tailed lizards

ORNITHOMIMIDS
Ostrich lizards
Gallimimus

DROMAEOSAURIDS
Running lizards
Deinonychus

MANIRAPTORA
Hand-seizers

AVIALAE
Birds
Archaeopteryx

Dinosaurs In North America

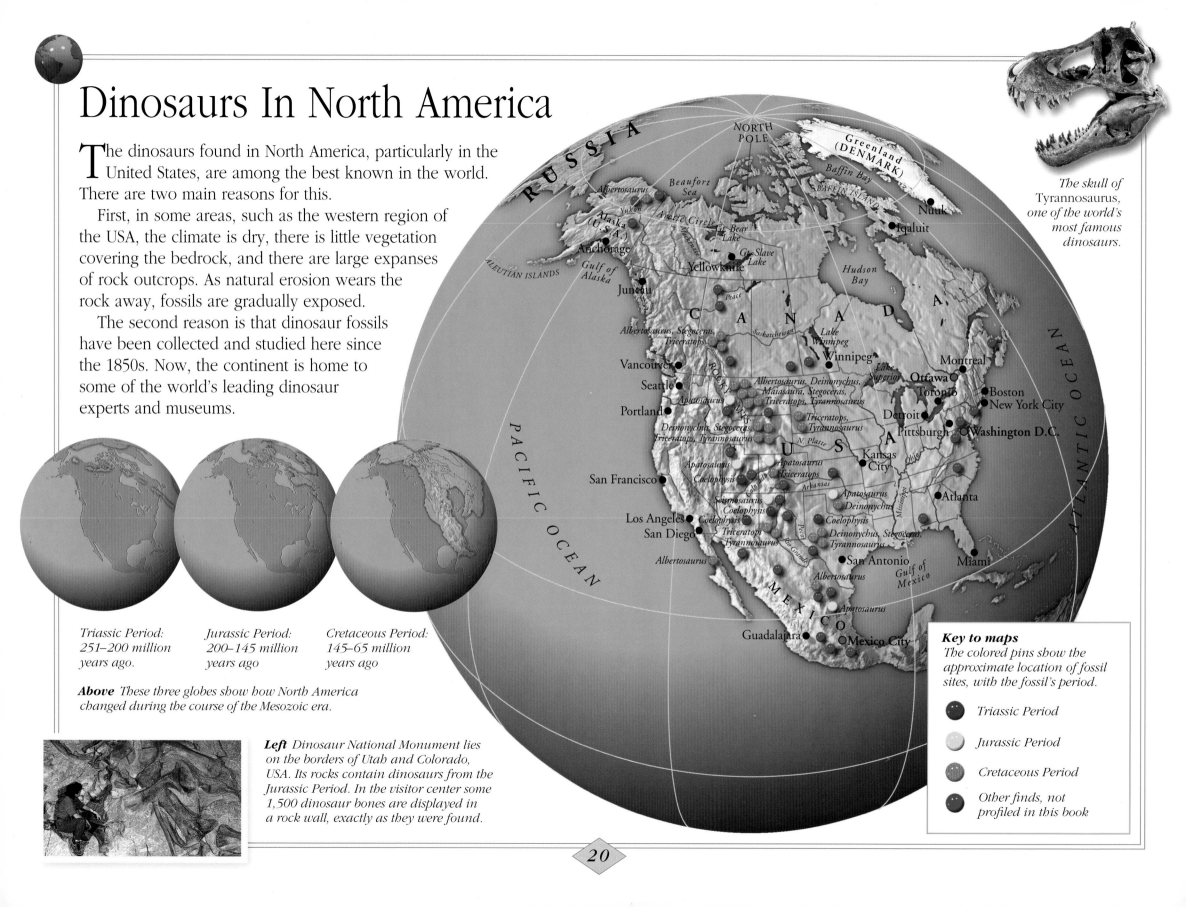

The dinosaurs found in North America, particularly in the United States, are among the best known in the world. There are two main reasons for this.

First, in some areas, such as the western region of the USA, the climate is dry, there is little vegetation covering the bedrock, and there are large expanses of rock outcrops. As natural erosion wears the rock away, fossils are gradually exposed.

The second reason is that dinosaur fossils have been collected and studied here since the 1850s. Now, the continent is home to some of the world's leading dinosaur experts and museums.

The skull of Tyrannosaurus, one of the world's most famous dinosaurs.

Triassic Period: 251–200 million years ago.

Jurassic Period: 200–145 million years ago

Cretaceous Period: 145–65 million years ago

Above *These three globes show how North America changed during the course of the Mesozoic era.*

Left *Dinosaur National Monument lies on the borders of Utah and Colorado, USA. Its rocks contain dinosaurs from the Jurassic Period. In the visitor center some 1,500 dinosaur bones are displayed in a rock wall, exactly as they were found.*

Key to maps
The colored pins show the approximate location of fossil sites, with the fossil's period.

Triassic Period

Jurassic Period

Cretaceous Period

Other finds, not profiled in this book

ALBERTOSAURUS *al-bur-toh-sore-us*

Length: *30 ft (9 m)* **Weight:** *2 tons*

Lived: *70 million years ago (Late Cretaceous)*

Albertosaurus ("Alberta Lizard") was a strongly built meat-eater, and was a relative of *Tyrannosaurus*. It had many of the features common to other tyrannosaurids ('tyrant lizards'). It had a massive head, its jaws were packed with long, sharp teeth, its body was compact and its hind legs contained strong muscles so it may have been a fast mover. Like other members of its family, its arms were small and each hand had two fingers. Perhaps it used these tiny limbs to grip prey while it bit and kicked its victim.

- *It preyed on small, slow-moving animals which it chased at up to 19 mph (30 km/h).*

- *As its eyes were on the sides of its head it might have had difficulty seeing anything straight in front of it.*

- *To make up for poor eyesight, it may have had a very good sense of smell.*

The flexible tail helped to balance its heavy body

Short, compact body

Teeth had serrated edges to cut through meat

Short arms, each with two fingers on the hand

Three big clawed toes on each foot

Albertosaurus *from:* Canada, Mexico, USA (Alaska, Montana).

The long, whip-like tail could be flicked at an attacker

Massive, pillar-like legs, with hind legs longer than front legs

A small head on a long, flexible neck

Apatosaurus *from:* Mexico, USA (Colorado, Montana, Oklahoma, Utah).

APATOSAURUS *ah-pat-oh-sore-us*

Length: *69 ft (21 m)* **Weight:** *30 tons*

Lived: *150 million years ago (Late Jurassic)*

A giant plant-eating dinosaur, *Apatosaurus* ("Deceptive Lizard") was a slow-moving animal. It may have spent much of the time eating in order to keep its huge body alive. Leaves, which it could take from the tops of trees, and horsetails and ferns on the ground were probably its main sources of food. In the front of its mouth were teeth shaped like pegs. There were no teeth at the back of its mouth. By combing its teeth through vegetation it could strip away the soft parts it wanted to eat, leaving tougher parts behind. The tongue pushed food to the back of its mouth, ready to swallow whole.

- *It swallowed stones, called gastroliths, which crushed plant material inside its stomach into a digestible pulp.*

- *It used to be called* Brontosaurus *("Thunder Lizard").*

COELOPHYSIS *see-loh-fie-sis*

Length: *10 ft (3 m)* **Weight:** *88 lb (40 kg)*

Lived: *220 million years ago (Late Triassic)*

A small, agile creature, *Coelophysis* ("Hollow Form") was a meat-eater that might have lived and hunted in packs. Its leg bones were almost hollow—hence its name—which would have reduced its weight. With a lightweight body, *Coelophysis* could have run faster and further than its rivals. It probably ate small vertebrates, fish, and insects.

- *Hundreds of* Coelophysis *skeletons have been found in one place in New Mexico, USA. They may have been a herd that drowned when a river flooded and trapped them.*

- *A* Coelophysis *skeleton with the bones of a baby* Coelophysis *inside it suggests this dinosaur might have been a cannibal.*

A long, slim head, large eyes and many small, sharp teeth

Coelophysis *from:* USA (Arizona, New Mexico, Texas, Utah).

◉ DEINONYCHUS *die-non-ick-us*

Length: *10 ft (3 m)*   **Weight:** *176 lb (80 kg)*

Lived: *110 million years ago (Early Cretaceous)*

Deinonychus ("Terrible Claw") earned its name from the large, sickle-shaped claw on the second toe of each foot. In an adult these claws were 5 inches (13 cm) long. When it walked or ran, it held the claws upright, to prevent them rubbing on the ground and wearing down. It was when the meat-eating *Deinonychus* went in search of prey that it put its deadly claws to use. With their sharp points and edges, these blade-like claws would have sliced deep into a victim's body. *Deinonychus* might have hunted in packs, stalking a creature much larger than itself until rushing in for the kill. It may have held onto its prey to weaken it.

● *Its jaws were packed with sharp teeth. Since they pointed backwards this would have made it difficult for a victim to pull free of them without causing itself greater injury.*

Deinonychus *from:* USA (*Montana, Oklahoma, Texas, Wyoming*).

Large eyes for good vision

Short arms

Perhaps its skin was patterned to camouflage it

"Terrible claw"

Maiasaura *from:* USA (*Montana*).

Long head

Strong fingers were used to hollow out a nest in the soil

The young may have recognized a parent by distinctive body markings and by calls

◉ MAIASAURA *may-ah-sore-ah*

Length: *30 ft (9 m)*   **Weight:** *3 tons*

Lived: *80 million years ago (Late Cretaceous)*

More is known about *Maiasaura* ("Good Mother Lizard") than many dinosaurs. This is because hundreds of well-preserved specimens have been found at a nest site, from eggs and babies to juveniles and adults. With so much material to study, it has been possible to work out the lifecycle of *Maiasaura* from birth to death. Its lifestyle has been investigated, too. It was a hadrosaurid ("duck-billed") dinosaur. Members of this family had wide, flat beaks. There were no teeth at the front of the mouth, but there were many small cheek teeth. It was a plant-eater that lived in very large herds.

● *It was named "Good Mother" because it cared for its young. Babies were born in well-made nests and parents brought food to them.*

● *A fully grown adult* Maiasaura *ate about 200 lb (90 kg) of vegetation every day.*

◉ SEISMOSAURUS *size-moh-sore-us*

Length: *131 ft (40 m)*   **Weight:** *30 tons*

Lived: *150 million years ago (Late Jurassic)*

Seismosaurus ("Earth-Shaking Lizard") was one of the largest dinosaurs. A giant plant-eater, it was a member of the diplodocid ("double-beam") family. This means that some of its tail bones had pairs of bony projections ("beams") on either side of them. Perhaps these bones gave added support to the animal's long, flexible tail. Like other sauropods (long-necked, long-tailed plant-eaters) *Seismosaurus* had stomach stones (gastroliths) in its belly. Without chewing teeth, these stones crushed its food to a pulp, making it easier to digest.

● *Only one* Seismosaurus *has been found. In its stomach was a pile of nearly 250 gastroliths, each about 2 inches (5 cm) in size.*

● *A fully grown, healthy* Seismosaurus *probably had few enemies—a creature so big would have been difficult to attack.*

'Double-beam' bones in this part of its tail

Front legs shorter than back legs

A long, flexible neck, able to reach to the tops of tall conifer and ginkgo trees

Pillar-like legs

Seismosaurus *from:* USA (*New Mexico*).

Stegoceras *from:*
Canada, USA
(*Montana, Texas,*
Wyoming).

The bone of its skull
was almost 2½ inches
(6 cm) thick

Long,
stiff tail

Short arms

STEGOCERAS *steg-oh-ser-as*

Length: *6 ft (2 m)*   **Weight:** *121 lb (55 kg)*

Lived: *70 million years ago (Late Cretaceous)*

A pachycephalosaurid ("bone-headed") dinosaur, *Stegoceras* ("Horny Roof") had many things in common with other members of its family. It was a plant-eater, whose large, thick-boned skull was its most distinctive feature. It was once thought it used its skull to head-butt

other animals—but this might have done it more harm than good. Perhaps it used its head to push and shove an opponent, to decide who was the stronger of the two. Animals often use displays of strength to determine who should be the leader of a group.

• *Its small size and long hind legs suggest*
that Stegoceras *was a fast mover, able*
to sprint away from danger.

• *The back of its skull was covered*
with bony knobs and bumps.
This feature is called a skull shelf.

Long hind legs,
each with four
toes

 TYRANNOSAURUS *tie-ran-oh-sore-us*

Length: *40 ft (12 m)*   **Weight:** *8 tons*

Lived: *70 million years ago (Late Cretaceous)*

Tyrannosaurus ("Tyrant Lizard") was one of the largest of all meat-eating predatory dinosaurs. It had a range of features which gave it many advantages over creatures less fortunate than itself. It had the power of speed, able to stride after its prey at up to 23 mph (36 km/h). It probably had a keen sense of smell, and good eyesight. But its jaws were its most dangerous assets. They were controlled by strong muscles that gave *Tyrannosaurus* a powerful bite. When it bit into its prey, its long knife-like teeth—each up to 7 inches (18 cm) long—sliced deep into the victim's flesh. It then shook its head from side to side, tearing off a chunk of meat.

• *When it walked or ran, it held its body level with the ground and its tail*
straight out behind it for balance.

• *Like modern meat-eating animals,* Tyrannosaurus *probably gorged itself on*
its prey, then went for several days before needing to eat again.

Tyrannosaurus *from:*
USA (*Montana, New*
Mexico, South Dakota,
Texas, Wyoming).

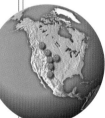

Triceratops *from:*
Canada, USA
(*Colorado, Montana,*
New Mexico, South
Dakota, Wyoming).

Bone neck frill
edged with
bony nodules

In short bursts
of speed it may
have reached
30 mph
(48 km/h)

TRICERATOPS *try-ser-a-tops*

Length: *30 ft (9 m)*   **Weight:** *5 tons*

Lived: *70 million years ago (Late Cretaceous)*

The plant-eating *Triceratops* ("Three-horned Face") belonged to the ceratopsid ("horn-faced") group of dinosaurs. These were some of the last dinosaurs to live on Earth, and *Triceratops* was one of the most striking of them. Its bulky body was carried near to the ground on four short legs. From the back of its skull grew a wide frill of solid bone—a shield that protected its unarmored body. On the front of its skull were three long horns, each of which could pierce the skin of a meat-eating predator. If it was threatened, it might have used its neck frill and horns in a show of aggression to scare its attacker away.

• *On a fully grown adult* Triceratops, *the horns*
that grew on its brow were up to 3 ft (1 m) long.

• *Its jaws ended in a large bony beak that*
would have been used to nip and tug at
vegetation, such as the tough fronds
of cycads and palm trees.

New teeth formed as worn
ones fell out with old age,
or were broken

Heavily built
hind legs and
three-toed feet

Like other
tyrannosaurids
it had short arms
and two fingers
on each hand

Dinosaurs In South America

Until the 1950s little had been done to discover which dinosaurs had lived on the continent of South America. Since then, many important discoveries have been made. Scientists now know that dinosaurs lived in South America for about 165 million years—almost the whole of the Mesozoic Era.

Some 50 types of dinosaur are now known from the continent, including one of the world's oldest-known dinosaurs, *Eoraptor*, and one of the world's largest meat-eaters, *Giganotosaurus*.

More species of dinosaur have been found in Argentina than in any other part of South America. This is because most work has been done here. However, dinosaurs lived across the continent and as more work is done they should be found in other countries.

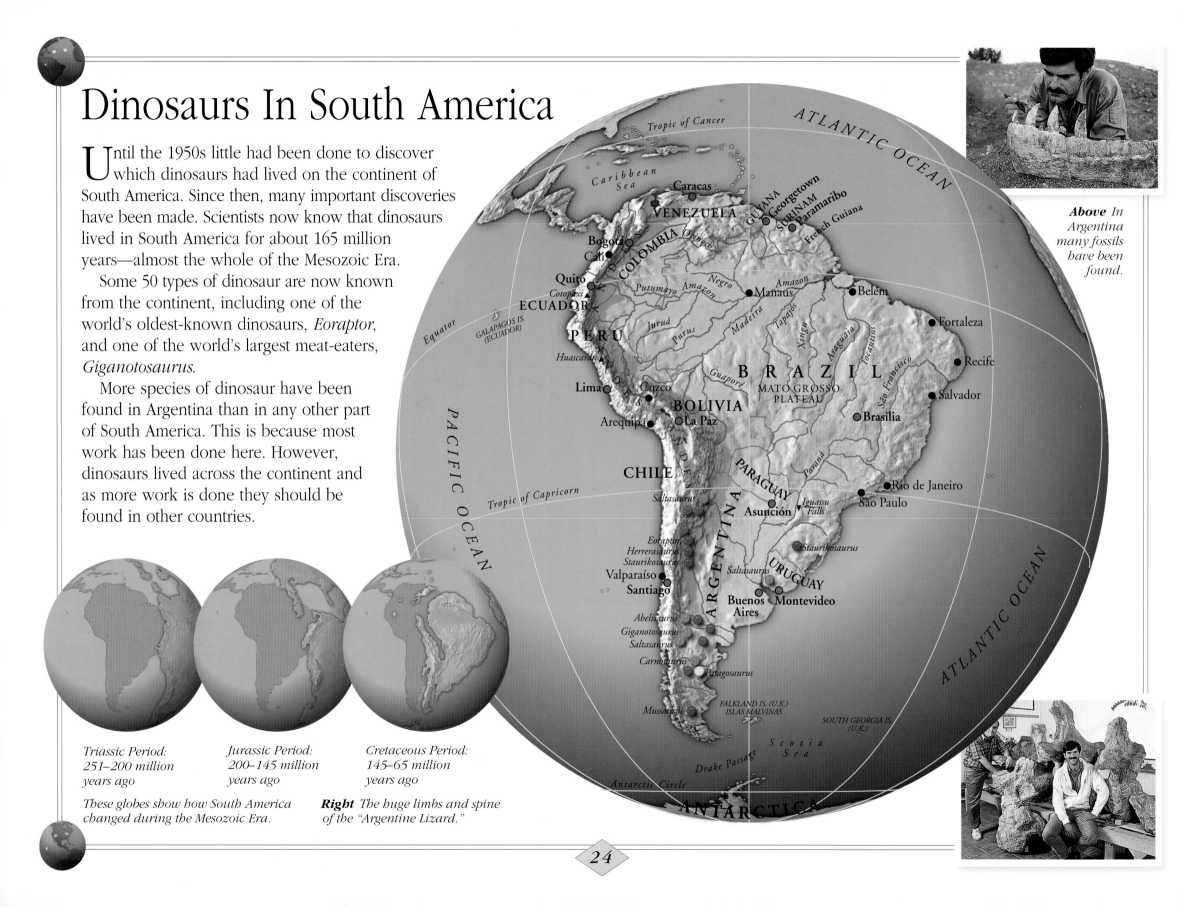

Above In Argentina many fossils have been found.

Triassic Period: 251–200 million years ago

Jurassic Period: 200–145 million years ago

Cretaceous Period: 145–65 million years ago

These globes show how South America changed during the Mesozoic Era.

Right *The huge limbs and spine of the "Argentine Lizard."*

Map labels:

Tropic of Cancer · ATLANTIC OCEAN · Caribbean Sea · Caracas · VENEZUELA · GUYANA · Georgetown · SURINAM · Paramaribo · French Guiana · Bogotá · COLOMBIA · Orinoco · Cali · Quito · ECUADOR · Cotopaxi · Putumayo · Amazon · Negro · Amazon · Manaus · Belém · Equator · GALAPAGOS IS. (ECUADOR) · Juruá · Purus · Madeira · Tapajós · Xingu · Araguaia · Tocantins · Fortaleza · PERU · Huascarán · ANDES · BRAZIL · Guaporé · São Francisco · Recife · Lima · Cuzco · MATO GROSSO PLATEAU · Salvador · BOLIVIA · Arequipa · La Paz · Brasília · PACIFIC OCEAN · Paraná · CHILE · PARAGUAY · Rio de Janeiro · Tropic of Capricorn · Saltasaurus · ARGENTINA · Asunción · Iguassu Falls · São Paulo · Eoraptor · Herrerasaurus · Staurikosaurus · Staurikosaurus · Saltasaurus · URUGUAY · Valparaíso · Santiago · Buenos Aires · Montevideo · Abelisaurus · Giganotosaurus · Saltasaurus · Carnotaurus · Patagosaurus · Mussaurus · FALKLAND IS. (U.K.) ISLAS MALVINAS · SOUTH GEORGIA IS. (U.K.) · Scotia Sea · Drake Passage · Antarctic Circle · ANTARCTICA · ATLANTIC OCEAN

24

Abelisaurus *from:* Argentina.

Only the 35 inch-long (90 cm) skull of Abelisaurus has so far been found.

Small eyes

Short snout

Long, slender teeth

 ABELISAURUS *ah-bell-i-sore-us*

Length: *23 ft (7 m)*	Weight: *1.5 tons*

Lived: *70 million years ago (Late Cretaceous)*

Some dinosaurs are found only in South America and nowhere else on Earth. This is particularly true of the dinosaurs that lived there during the Cretaceous Period. By this time South America had moved far enough away from other land to become a continent in its own right. Dinosaurs that lived there evolved as distinct species, related to dinosaurs elsewhere in the world, but no longer identical to them. One of these was *Abelisaurus* ("Abel's Lizard"), whose "distant cousin" was the two-legged meat-eater *Albertosaurus*, from North America.

● *A feature that identifies* Abelisaurus *as a distinct species, different from other large meat-eaters, is a partially closed-off eye socket (the hole in the skull where the eyes sit is partly filled with bone).*

● Abelisaurus *has been called "old-fashioned." This is because some of its features, such as its eye socket, are quite primitive. They are found in dinosaurs that died out before* Abelisaurus *lived in other parts of the world.*

● **EORAPTOR** *ee-oh-rap-tor*

Length: *3 ft (1 m)*	Weight: *6½ lb (3 kg)*

Lived: *228 million years ago (Late Triassic)*

Discovered in 1991, in northwest Argentina, *Eoraptor* ("Dawn Thief") was then the world's oldest-known dinosaur. It lived right at the beginning of the Age of Dinosaurs. It was a small dinosaur that moved swiftly around on two long, slender hind legs. A meat-eater that may have been both a hunter and a scavenger, its long jaws were packed with many small, serrated teeth. The area where its fossils have been found was a river valley during the Triassic Period. It perhaps hunted the area's fish and insects.

● *Because some of its bones were hollow,* Eoraptor *had a very lightweight body.*

● *It had about 70 bones in its backbone and the legs were twice as long as the arms.*

Eoraptor *from:* Argentina.

Lightly built body

Long snout

Short arms with five fingers

Long, thin legs with three-toed feet

● **CARNOTAURUS** *car-no-tor-us*

Length: *21 ft (6.5 m)*	Weight: *1 ton*

Lived: *95 million years ago (Middle Cretaceous)*

Like other dinosaurs from South America, *Carnotaurus* ("Meat Bull") was unlike those from elsewhere in the world. It, too, had followed its own course of evolution, developing unique characteristics not shared by other dinosaurs. Without a doubt, its most distinctive feature was a pair of bony horns that grew from its skull, just above its small eyes. Perhaps they were used in head-butting contests against other members of its species. A meat-eater that walked on two legs, *Carnotaurus* may not have been as fearsome as its name suggests. Even though its large head looks formidable, its jaws and teeth were rather weak.

● *The single specimen found so far is remarkable because an impression of the creature's skin has been well preserved. It shows that its body was covered with disk-shaped scales.*

● *Like other meat-eaters its arms were short—but those of* Carnotaurus *were shorter than those of most others.*

Horns above eyes

Thin teeth

Slender lower jaw

Distinctive skin composed of non-overlapping scales

Carnotaurus *from:* Argentina.

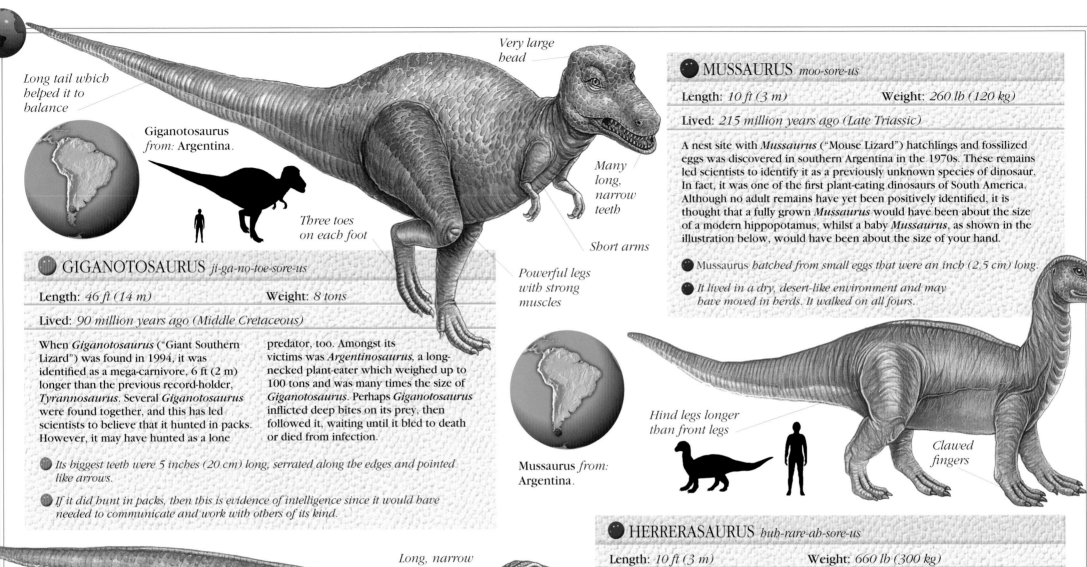

Long tail which helped it to balance

Very large head

Giganotosaurus from: Argentina.

Many long, narrow teeth

Three toes on each foot

Short arms

Powerful legs with strong muscles

GIGANOTOSAURUS *ji-ga-no-toe-sore-us*

Length: *46 ft (14 m)*   **Weight:** *8 tons*

Lived: *90 million years ago (Middle Cretaceous)*

When *Giganotosaurus* ("Giant Southern Lizard") was found in 1994, it was identified as a mega-carnivore, 6 ft (2 m) longer than the previous record-holder, *Tyrannosaurus*. Several *Giganotosaurus* were found together, and this has led scientists to believe that it hunted in packs. However, it may have hunted as a lone predator, too. Amongst its victims was *Argentinosaurus*, a long-necked plant-eater which weighed up to 100 tons and was many times the size of *Giganotosaurus*. Perhaps *Giganotosaurus* inflicted deep bites on its prey, then followed it, waiting until it bled to death or died from infection.

● *Its biggest teeth were 5 inches (20 cm) long, serrated along the edges and pointed like arrows.*

● *If it did hunt in packs, then this is evidence of intelligence since it would have needed to communicate and work with others of its kind.*

MUSSAURUS *moo-sore-us*

Length: *10 ft (3 m)*   **Weight:** *260 lb (120 kg)*

Lived: *215 million years ago (Late Triassic)*

A nest site with *Mussaurus* ("Mouse Lizard") hatchlings and fossilized eggs was discovered in southern Argentina in the 1970s. These remains led scientists to identify it as a previously unknown species of dinosaur. In fact, it was one of the first plant-eating dinosaurs of South America. Although no adult remains have yet been positively identified, it is thought that a fully grown *Mussaurus* would have been about the size of a modern hippopotamus, whilst a baby *Mussaurus*, as shown in the illustration below, would have been about the size of your hand.

● Mussaurus *hatched from small eggs that were an inch (2.5 cm) long.*

● *It lived in a dry, desert-like environment and may have moved in herds. It walked on all fours.*

Hind legs longer than front legs

Clawed fingers

Mussaurus from: Argentina.

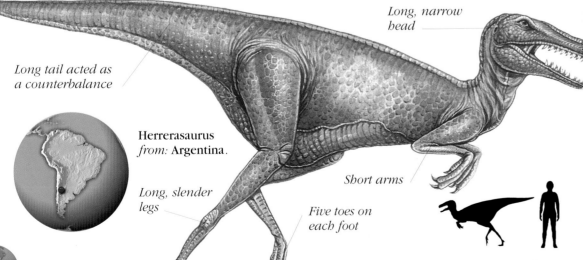

Long, narrow head

Long tail acted as a counterbalance

Herrerasaurus *from:* Argentina.

Long, slender legs

Short arms

Five toes on each foot

HERRERASAURUS *huh-rare-ah-sore-us*

Length: *10 ft (3 m)*   **Weight:** *660 lb (300 kg)*

Lived: *220 million years ago (Late Triassic)*

Herrerasaurus ("Herrera's Lizard") was one of the first dinosaurs. It lived during the earliest period of the Mesozoic Era, and was at home among ferns and conifer trees. A meat-eater, *Herrerasaurus* was a fast-moving predator. Its long legs gave it the ability to chase prey, such as *rhynchosaurs* (plant-eating reptiles) that were the predominant animals on land. Though small, *Herrerasaurus* had similar features to the larger carnivores that lived after it. Like them, it had strong jaws packed with backward-pointing sharp teeth, small arms and a long tail. These features helped to make it one of the most successful dinosaurs of its time.

● *The first* Herrerasaurus *specimen was discovered in 1958 by a farmer called Victorino Herrera, after whom it was named. Others have been found since.*

● *Because* Herrerasaurus *was an early dinosaur, some of its features, such as its leg and feet bones, were primitive compared with those of later dinosaurs.*

PATAGOSAURUS *pa-ta-go-sore-us*

Length: *65 ft (20 m)*   **Weight:** *15 tons*

Lived: *165 million years ago (Middle Jurassic)*

From Patagonia—the southern tip of Argentina—comes *Patagosaurus* ("Patagonian Lizard"). Very few large plant-eating dinosaurs have been found in South America, which makes *Patagosaurus* something of a rarity. It lived at a time when South America was still connected in part to western Europe and Africa. Dinosaurs could travel between these regions, but as the continents drifted apart the land bridge disappeared beneath the ocean. *Patagosaurus* is similar to a dinosaur from Europe, *Cetiosaurus*. They may have had the same ancestor, which is evidence that the land was once joined.

○ *The very large and slow-moving* Patagosaurus *would have made an easy target for predators. It may have used its long tail to lash out at them.*

○ *Like other giant plant-eaters,* Patagosaurus *walked on all fours. It had a long neck and, for reasons of safety, may have lived in herds.*

Small skull · Backbone · Ribs · Hip · Shoulder joint · Elbow joint · Wrist joint · Ankle joint · Knee joint

Patagosaurus *from:* Argentina.

SALTASAURUS *sal-ta-sore-us*

Length: *40 ft (12 m)*   **Weight:** *20 tons*

Lived: *80 million years ago (Late Cretaceous)*

This dinosaur is notable for its unusual skin. *Saltasaurus* ("Salta Lizard"), named after the region of Argentina where it was found, was a giant plant-eater. It had many features in common with others of its kind, such as a long, flexible neck, pillar-like legs, and a slender tail. But, unlike other giant herbivores, *Saltasaurus* had armor-plated skin. Bony plates and nodules studded its back, giving it protection from the teeth and claws of predators. Huge plant-eaters may have survived in South America because they had evolved this form of self-defense.

○ *The bony plates were oval and measured about 4 inches (10 cm) across.*

○ *The smaller nodules between the plates were pea-sized.*

Long neck

Armor-plated skin · Long, whip-like tail · Pillar-like legs

Saltasaurus *from:* Argentina, Uruguay.

Staurikosaurus *from:* Argentina, Brazil.

STAURIKOSAURUS *stor-ik-oh-sore-us*

Length: *7 ft (2 m)*   **Weight:** *66 lb (30 kg)*

Lived: *225 million years ago (Late Triassic)*

A predatory meat-eater, *Staurikosaurus* ("Cross Lizard") is one of South America's first dinosaurs. It was named after the Southern Cross, a well-known group of stars visible in the skies of the Southern Hemisphere. *Staurikosaurus* lived at the same time as *Herrerasaurus*, another early carnivore from South America with which it has some features in common. Like *Herrerasaurus*, *Staurikosaurus* shows signs of being slightly primitive because some of its bones (particularly those in its legs and feet) were not as well developed as the ones that later carnivores had.

○ *Its hands had five fingers and its feet had five toes. This feature identifies it as an early dinosaur, since later carnivores had three or four fingers and toes.*

Long tail · Long legs · Short neck

27

Dinosaurs In Europe

The study of dinosaurs began in Europe. As long ago as the 1600s it was known that fossilized bones found in quarries came from ancient animals. No one knew what the animals looked like, or how old they were. As more bones were found, scientists realized they came from creatures unlike any living animals. In 1822, an English scientist, James Parkinson, gave a name to one of these ancient animals. He called it *Megalosaurus* ("Great Lizard"), and it was the first dinosaur to be named. In 1842, Richard Owen, another Englishman, said that the animals belonged to a previously unknown group. He named the group "Dinosauria," from the Greek words *deinos*, meaning "terrible" and *sauros*, meaning "lizard."

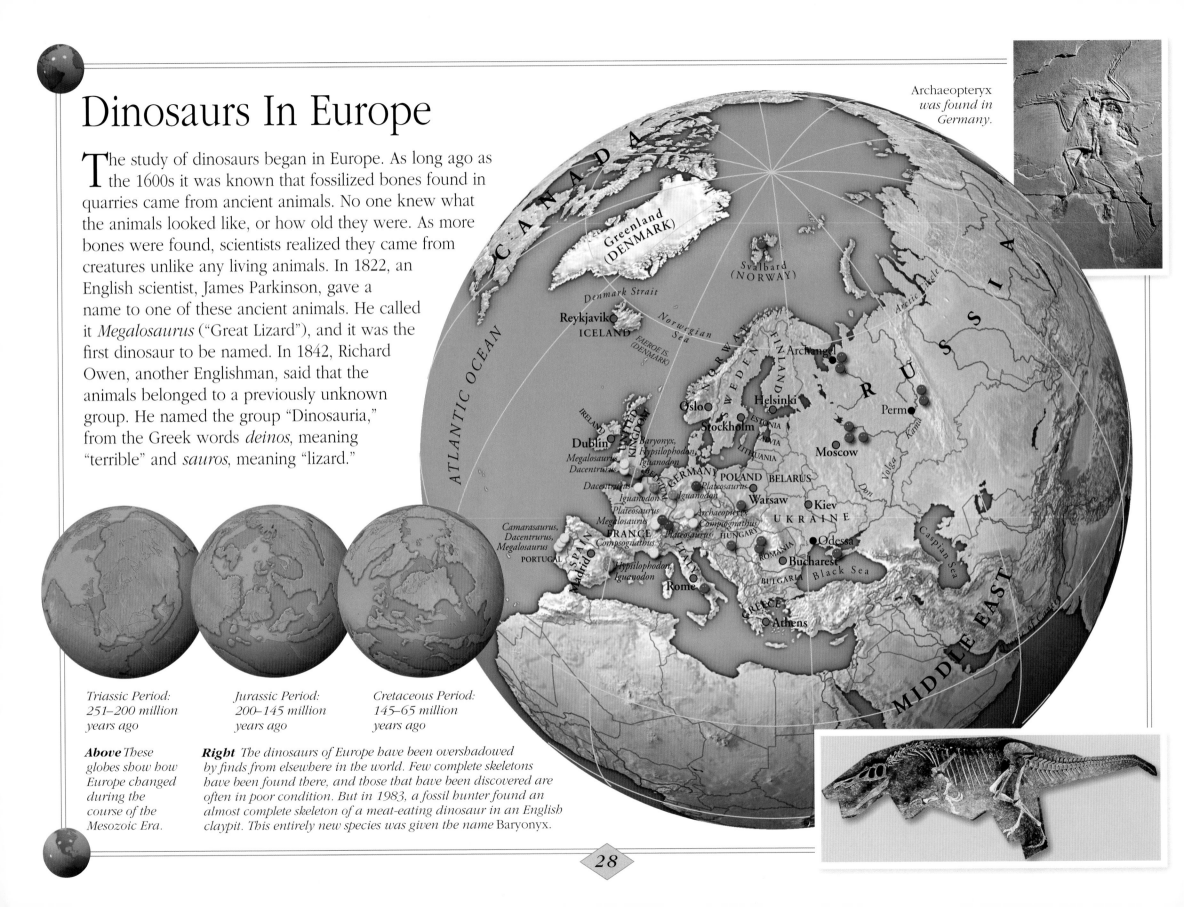

Archaeopteryx was found in Germany.

Triassic Period: 251–200 million years ago

Jurassic Period: 200–145 million years ago

Cretaceous Period: 145–65 million years ago

Above These globes show how Europe changed during the course of the Mesozoic Era.

Right The dinosaurs of Europe have been overshadowed by finds from elsewhere in the world. Few complete skeletons have been found there, and those that have been discovered are often in poor condition. But in 1983, a fossil hunter found an almost complete skeleton of a meat-eating dinosaur in an English claypit. This entirely new species was given the name Baryonyx.

28

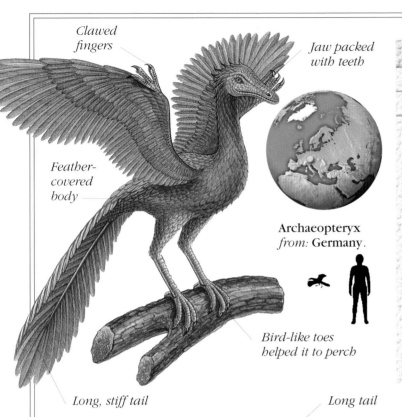

Clawed fingers

Jaw packed with teeth

Feather-covered body

Archaeopteryx *from:* Germany.

Long, stiff tail

Bird-like toes helped it to perch

ARCHAEOPTERYX *ar-key-op-ter-iks*

Length: *2 ft (60 cm)*   **Weight:** *6½ lb (3 kg)*

Lived: *150 million years ago (Late Jurassic)*

One of the world's most remarkable ancient creatures flapped its primitive wings among the sparse Jurassic vegetation of western Europe. This was *Archaeopteryx* ("Ancient Wing"), whose discovery in 1861 caused a major discussion among scientists which continues to this day. *Archaeopteryx* had feathers and a wishbone, two features associated with birds. But it also had features found in reptiles, such as teeth, a flexible neck, clawed fingers, long legs, and a long, bony tail. Fewer than 10 *Archaeopteryx* specimens have been found, all from a region in southern Germany. It is thought that *Archaeopteryx* is a link between dinosaurs and birds. It seems to be a stage in the origin of modern birds, a so-called "dinobird"—not quite a true bird, but no longer a dinosaur either.

- *Its wing muscles were weak, so it may have been unable to fly far. It may have used its wings to help it glide from tree to tree.*

- *Its clawed fingers probably helped it to grip and climb trees.*

CAMARASAURUS *kam-are-ah-sore-us*

Length: *60 ft (18 m)*   **Weight:** *20 tons*

Lived: *150 million years ago (Late Jurassic)*

A well-known giant plant-eater from North America, *Camarasaurus* ("Chambered Lizard") has also been found in Europe. Its name comes from the fact that the bones in its spine were not solid. Instead, they had air spaces, or chambers, in them. These hollow backbones reduced the weight of the animal's skeleton, perhaps making it easier for the bulky *Camarasaurus* to move about. When looked at under a microscope, the teeth of an adult *Camarasaurus* appear scratched. This shows it probably ate coarse vegetation. Teeth from a young *Camarasaurus* are not scratched, which suggests it ate softer plants than its parents.

- *Some scientists think that* Camarasaurus *could raise itself up on its back legs using its tail for support. If this is true, then maybe it did this to scare a predator away.*

- Camarasaurus *walked on all fours. Its limbs were all about the same length.*

Long tail

BARYONYX *bar-ee-on-iks*

Length: *33 ft (10 m)*   **Weight:** *2 tons*

Lived: *125 million years ago (Early Cretaceous)*

It is the long curved thumb claws which gave *Baryonyx* ("Heavy Claw") its name. What makes this meat-eater from England notable is that the remains of its last meal were found within its stomach area. Fish scales from *Lepidotes* (a fish that grew to about 3 ft [1 m] in length) found inside *Baryonyx*'s rib-cage tell us something about its diet. Even without this tell-tale evidence other clues point to it being a fish-eater. For example, it had a long snout with a spoon-shaped tip, and its upper jaw was S-shaped in side view. Modern fish-eating crocodiles have jaws just like this. *Baryonyx* may have been a scavenger too, using its long snout to reach into the bodies and tug at the rotting flesh of animals that had been dead for some time.

- *Each thumb claw was 14 inches (35 cm) long.*

- *Its jaws contained 96 small, sharp teeth. This is far more teeth than most other meat-eating dinosaurs had.*

- *It had long front limbs and, unlike other meat-eaters, it may sometimes have walked on all fours.*

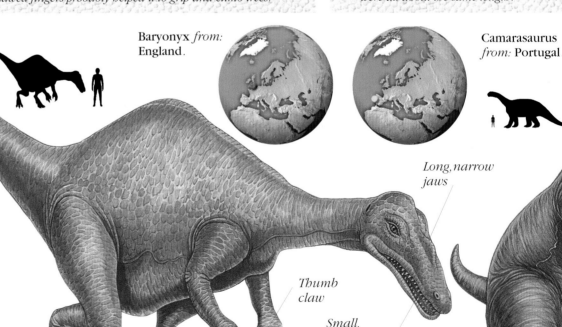

Baryonyx *from:* England.

Camarasaurus *from:* Portugal.

Long, narrow jaws

Thumb claw

Small, sharp teeth

Long front limbs

Heavy, thick-set legs

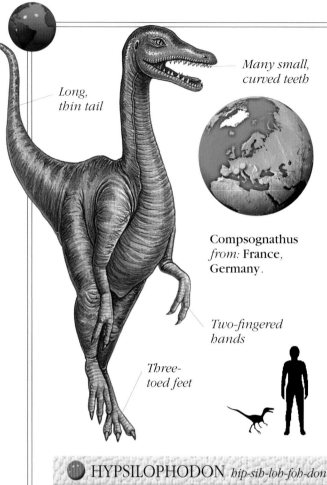

Long, thin tail

Many small, curved teeth

Compsognathus *from:* France, Germany.

Two-fingered hands

Three-toed feet

COMPSOGNATHUS *komp-so-nay-thus*

Length: *3 ft (1 m)*	Weight: *6½ lb (3 kg)*

Lived: *145 million years ago (Late Jurassic)*

A tiny dinosaur, about the size of a present-day turkey, *Compsognathus* ("Elegant Jaw") was a meat-eater that hunted small reptiles, mammals, and insects. It lived among wooded islands and lagoons. Within the rib-cage of one specimen the bones of a small lizard, *Bavarisaurus*, have been found, and it is this evidence that tells us something about the diet of *Compsognathus*. The presence of the lizard also tells us something else. Small lizards are fast-movers, never straying far from shelter. As *Compsognathus* was able to catch one, then it must have been an agile, speedy dinosaur. It must also have had good eyesight, able to see its victim amongst the rocks, ferns, and other hiding places.

- *Compsognathus lived at the same time and in the same place as the first bird, Archaeopteryx. Because they were a similar size to each other, and had near-identical skeletons, it can be difficult to tell them apart.*

- *Its small teeth were spaced apart, making them better for nipping at its victims rather than slicing into them, as the teeth of larger meat-eaters were designed to do.*

DACENTRURUS *day-sen-troo-rus*

Length: *16½ ft (5 m)*	Weight: *1 ton*

Lived: *155 million years ago (Late Jurassic)*

One of the few armored dinosaurs from Europe, little is known about *Dacentrurus* ("Pointed Tail"). It is named after the spikes on its tail. Pairs of spikes also grew on its back and neck. It is similar to a dinosaur from East Africa, *Kentrosaurus*. Dinosaurs like *Dacentrurus* and *Kentrosaurus*, whose bodies were protected by spikes and bony plates, are known as stegosaurs ("roof lizards"). These were large plant-eaters that walked slowly on all fours. Their body armor was for self-defense. If *Dacentrurus* was attacked, its spikes would have made it difficult for a predator to get close to it without injuring itself. And if *Dacentrurus* whipped its tail from side to side, it might have been able to drive a meat-eater away.

Pairs of spikes from neck to tail

- *Dacentrurus was originally called Omosaurus ("Shoulder Lizard") because it was thought spikes grew from its shoulders.*

HYPSILOPHODON *hip-sih-loh-foh-don*

Length: *7½ ft (2.3 m)*	Weight: *154 lb (70 kg)*

Lived: *120 million years ago (Early Cretaceous)*

A small, graceful dinosaur, the fossilized bones of many *Hypsilophodon* ("High-ridged Tooth") have been found together. This is taken as evidence that *Hypsilophodon* lived in herds rather than on its own. It was a plant-eater, nipping and tugging at soft vegetation with its horny beak. Inside its mouth were about 30 teeth, wide and sharp like chisel blades. As it grazed on leaves, horsetails, and palm fronds, it stuffed them into its cheek pouches. Then, as it chewed, its teeth chopped and crushed the vegetation until it was small enough to swallow. *Hypsilophodon* moved quickly on its two back legs— its arms and hands were probably used for grasping its food.

- *As its teeth wore down and fell out, new ones grew in their place.*

- *The long legs of Hypsilophodon indicate that it was a fast runner. With no other means of self-defense, speed was how it looked after itself. It could soon outrun a predator.*

Hypsilophodon *from:* England, Spain.

Horny beak

Pillar-like heavy legs

Grasping hands

Long, stiff tail

Long, slender legs

Dacentrurus *from:* England, France, Portugal.

IGUANODON *ig-wa-no-don*

Length: *33 ft (10 m)*   **Weight:** *5 tons*

Lived: *130 million years ago (Early Cretaceous)*

Iguanodon ("Iguana Tooth") is one of the world's best-known dinosaurs, whose remains have been found in several parts of western Europe, as well as in North America. A large herbivore, *Iguanodon* was a herd animal that grazed on low-growing vegetation, such as horsetails and ferns. At the front of its mouth was a bony, toothless beak that nipped off the soft, succulent parts of plants. Inside its mouth its tongue pushed food into its roomy cheek pouches, ready to be chewed to a digestible pulp by its sharp, serrated teeth. A notable feature of *Iguanodon* was a long, sharp spike that grew on each thumb. Perhaps this was how it defended itself in an attack, rearing up on its back legs and stabbing at its foe with its thumb spikes. Males may have used their thumb spikes in leadership contests.

- *In 1878, at Bernissart, Belgium, coal miners found a mass grave of about 30 Iguanodon. It is thought the animals had fallen down a deep ravine, or been caught by a flash flood.*

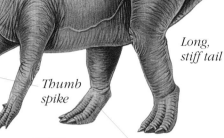

Long, stiff tail

Thumb spike

Wide, cow-like hoof

Iguanodon *from:* **Belgium, England, Germany, Spain**.

MEGALOSAURUS *meg-al-oh-sore-us*

Length: *30 ft (9 m)*   **Weight:** *1 ton*

Lived: *170 million years ago (Middle Jurassic)*

The first dinosaur ever to be given a name (before the word "dinosaur" had even been invented), *Megalosaurus* ("Great Lizard") was a powerful meat-eater. In spite of its important place in the history of dinosaur studies, *Megalosaurus* is not at all well known, because no complete specimen has yet been found. It is usually compared with other large carnivores, from which scientists imagine that it was both a hunter and a scavenger. One of its principal victims may have been *Iguanodon* which lived at the same time and in the same place as *Megalosaurus*.

- *Megalosaurus had long, curved teeth with serrated edges for slicing easily through skin and bone.*

- *A similar looking dinosaur from North America,* Torvosaurus *("Savage Lizard") is thought to be a close relative of* Megalosaurus.

Powerful legs with three toes

Megalosaurus *from:* **England, France, Portugal**.

PLATEOSAURUS *plat-ee-oh-sore-us*

Length: *23 ft (7 m)*   **Weight:** *2 tons*

Lived: *220 million years ago (Late Triassic)*

A large four-legged herbivore, *Plateosaurus* ("Flat Lizard") was one of Europe's first giant dinosaurs. In common with other massive plant-eaters, *Plateosaurus* shares several features with them. It was long-necked and had a small head; its back legs were longer than its front limbs; its body was bulky, and it most probably carried stones in its stomach which crushed its food to a pulp for rapid digestion. With its long neck it could have reached up to high-growing leaves, which its leaf-shaped teeth would have stripped from their branches. Perhaps it also ate plants that grew on the ground. *Plateosaurus* finds are common in some parts of Europe, suggesting that this giant herbivore was one of the most abundant dinosaurs of its day.

- *Plateosaurus was probably a herd animal. At Trossingen, Germany, many have been found in a mass grave, suggesting that a herd was killed in a single accident, such as a flood.*

- *It is called "Flat Lizard" because its teeth were flat-sided.*

- *It may have been able to rear up on its back legs to reach the very tops of tall trees.*

Tail vertebrae

Plateosaurus *from:* **France, Germany, Switzerland**.

Rib-cage

Neck vertebrae

Small skull

Five-fingered hands

Dinosaurs In Asia

Dinosaurs have been found across much of Asia. China and Mongolia are particularly rich in dinosaur fossils, and more than 100 different species of dinosaurs have been found here, which is more than anywhere else in the world. It is not only well-preserved skeletons that continue to be found in China and Mongolia— eggs and footprints are found too. Many great discoveries have been made in China, such as nesting sites of *Protoceratops* and *Oviraptor*. Feathered dinosaurs have also been found here, such as the remarkable *Caudipteryx*. The work of international expeditions in Asia is increasing the worldwide knowledge of dinosaurs. Asia also has some of the world's best dinosaur-only museums.

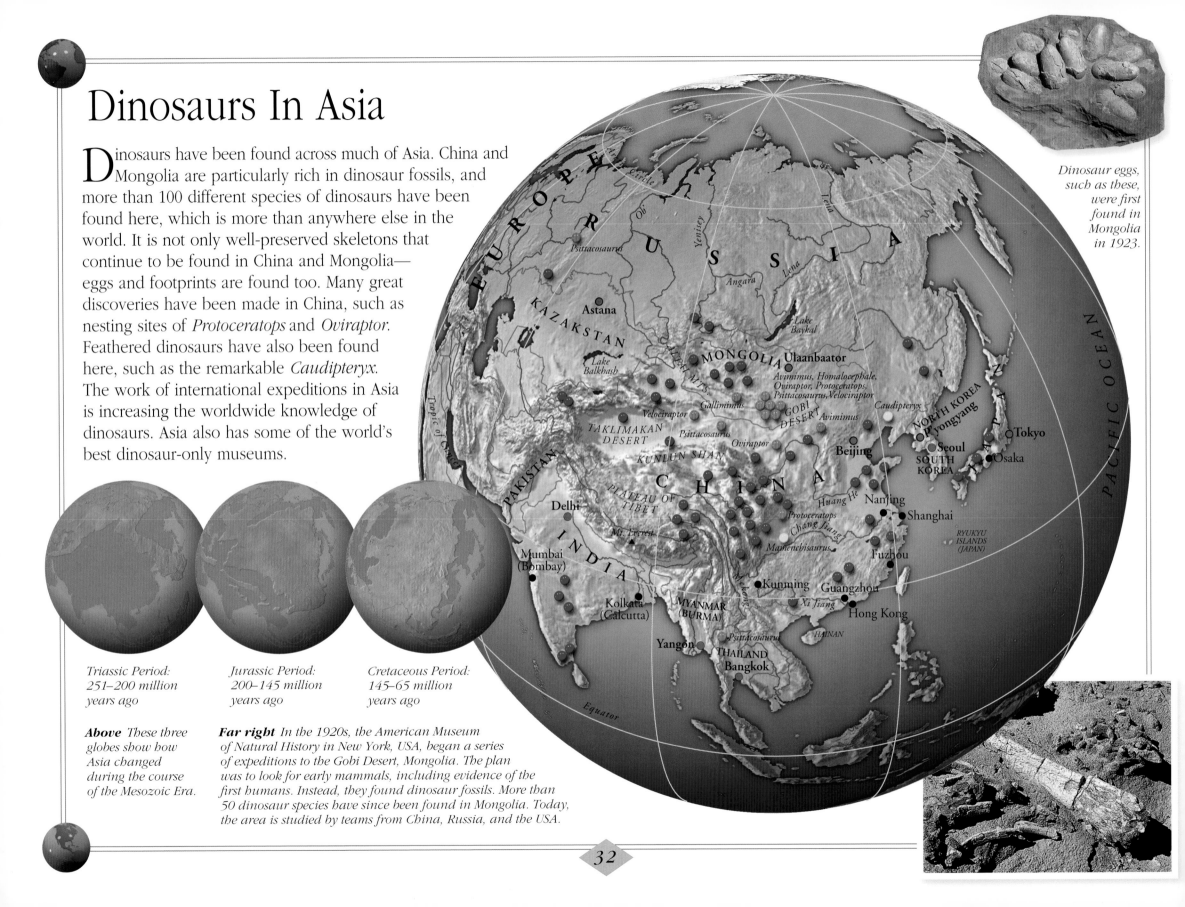

Dinosaur eggs, such as these, were first found in Mongolia in 1923.

Triassic Period: 251–200 million years ago

Jurassic Period: 200–145 million years ago

Cretaceous Period: 145–65 million years ago

Above *These three globes show how Asia changed during the course of the Mesozoic Era.*

Far right *In the 1920s, the American Museum of Natural History in New York, USA, began a series of expeditions to the Gobi Desert, Mongolia. The plan was to look for early mammals, including evidence of the first humans. Instead, they found dinosaur fossils. More than 50 dinosaur species have since been found in Mongolia. Today, the area is studied by teams from China, Russia, and the USA.*

AVIMIMUS *ay-vee-meem-us*

Length: *5 ft (1.5 m)*   **Weight:** *33 lb (15 kg)*

Lived: *80 million years ago (Late Cretaceous)*

The bird-like appearance of *Avimimus* ("Bird Mimic") is its most striking feature. But *Avimimus* was not a bird. It was a long-legged dinosaur that had some of the features we can see in birds. For example, its head was particularly bird-like, having large eyes, a toothless beak, and a large brain. Its arms also show bird-like qualities, particularly in the way it could fold them in toward its body, just like a bird folds its wings. Although no evidence has yet been found for feathers on *Avimimus*, Russian scientists who have studied it believe it may have been one of the first feathered dinosaurs. They think it grew feathers on its arms. If this is true, then when *Avimimus* stretched its arms, they would have looked like little wings.

- *Avimimus could not fly. Its arms were much too short for any kind of flight.*

- *Avimimus was probably an omnivore, a creature that has a diet of both plants and meat. It may have fed mainly on insects.*

Body may have had feathers

Bird-like head

Stiff, bony tail

Long legs

Short, folding arms

Avimimus *from:* China, Mongolia.

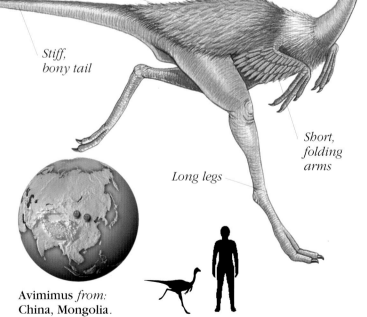

Teeth only at the front of the upper jaw

Short arms

Fan-like tail feathers

Long legs

Caudipteryx *from:* China.

CAUDIPTERYX *cor-dip-ter-iks*

Length: *3 ft (1 m)*   **Weight:** *6½ lb (3 kg)*

Lived: *130 million years ago (Early Cretaceous)*

Caudipteryx ("Tail Feather") was a feathered dinosaur, first found in China in the 1990s. When scientists from China and Canada studied it they thought it was an *Archaeopteryx*, or a close relative. However, as the fossil was cleaned and examined in great detail, they became aware that the animal was different from *Archaeopteryx*. In particular, its teeth were different. It was a new species of dinosaur—one of the so-called "dinobirds"—and it was named *Caudipteryx* after its eye-catching long tail feathers. Perhaps *Caudipteryx* fanned its tail feathers in courtship displays, when it was looking for a mate, as birds do today. These feathers could also have been used to improve the dinosaur's speed and balance as it ran.

- Caudipteryx *could not fly. Its arms were too short to act as wings, and, more importantly, its "flight" feathers were not the correct shape to get it airborne. True flight feathers (like those in birds) are slightly curved and uneven, whereas the ones that* Caudipteryx *had were straight and evenly shaped.*

- *Small stones inside its stomach crushed its food to a digestible pulp.*

GALLIMIMUS *gal-ee-meem-us*

Length: *20 ft (6 m)*   **Weight:** *1,100 lb (500 kg)*

Lived: *75 million years ago (Late Cretaceous)*

Gallimimus ("Chicken Mimic") was the largest of a group of dinosaurs called ornithomimids ("ostrich dinosaurs"). It was a speedy, two-legged animal that lived on a mixed diet of plants, insects, and small animals. Like other members of its group it had a bird-like, toothless beak, and large eyes. With its head held high in the air it was probably able to see for long distances. Its long neck would have come in useful when it poked around in undergrowth for food, and its strong clawed fingers were the ideal tools for scratching around on the ground.

- Gallimimus *could probably run at great speed. A modern ostrich can run at up to 43 mph (70 km/h), a speed which it is thought* Gallimimus *could easily equal.*

Long, stiff tail

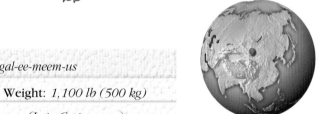

Gallimimus *from:* Mongolia.

Long, flexible neck

Long legs

Short, compact body

Grasping hand

Three clawed toes

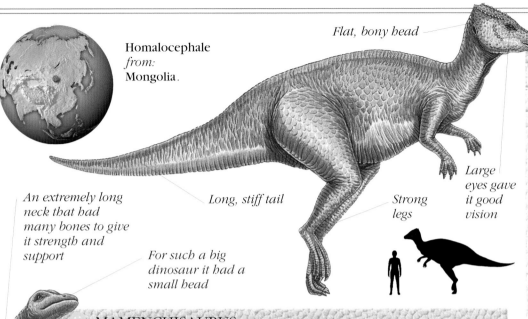

Homalocephale
from:
Mongolia.

Flat, bony head

An extremely long neck that had many bones to give it strength and support

Long, stiff tail

Strong legs

Large eyes gave it good vision

For such a big dinosaur it had a small head

HOMALOCEPHALE *hom-al-oh-seff-ah-lee*

Length: *10 ft (3 m)*	Weight: *95 lb (43 kg)*

Lived: *80 million years ago (Late Cretaceous)*

Homalocephale ("Even Head") belonged to a group of dinosaurs called pachycephalosaurids ("bone-headed"). These were small- to medium-sized plant-eaters with heavy bodies. Their distinctive feature was an exceptionally thick-boned skull, from which protruded bony knobs and short spikes. Unlike most other "boneheads," whose skulls were dome-shaped, *Homalocephale* had a flat, even-shaped skull, hence its name. There were bony nodules, ridges, and short spikes on the top and back of its skull, and also on its cheeks. This dinosaur had large eyes, and scientists believe it also had a good sense of smell. Both these factors would have been of great use to *Homalocephale*, since it had no means of self-defense other than being able to run from danger. With good eyesight and smell it could detect an approaching predator.

- Like other "boneheads," such as Stegoceras from North America, Homalocephale *may have used its bony head in pushing contests to determine who should be a group leader.*

- *It could walk on all fours.*

- *It lived in a dry, desert-like environment and may have moved in herds.*

- Homalocephale *was a browser that mostly ate leaves.*

MAMENCHISAURUS *mah-men-chee-sore-us*

Length: *82 ft (25 m)*	Weight: *27 tons*

Lived: *160 million years ago (Late Jurassic)*

A huge, long-necked herbivore, *Mamenchisaurus* ("Mamen Brook Lizard") is one of the largest of all Chinese dinosaurs. It was discovered in the 1950s, at a site in central China where so-called "dragon's bones" had been found over many years. When the bones of *Mamenchisaurus* were reassembled, the full size of this giant was revealed. It had one of the longest necks of all dinosaurs, measuring some 46 ft (14 m) in length. Why it needed such a long neck is still something of a puzzle, but scientists usually say it was to help it stretch up to leaves that grew at the top of tall trees.

- *"Dragon's bones" found in China may not all have come from dinosaurs. Some scientists think they are bones from ancient mammals, not reptiles.*

- Mamenchisaurus *had spoon-shaped teeth which were ideal for combing through vegetation, stripping leaves from their branches.*

Oviraptor
from:
China,
Mongolia.

OVIRAPTOR *oh-vee-rap-tor*

Length: *6 ft (1.8 m)*	Weight: *44 lb (20 kg)*

Lived: *80 million years ago (Late Cretaceous)*

When this bird-like dinosaur was discovered in the 1920s, it was found on top of a nest of eggs. At that time the eggs were thought to belong to *Protoceratops*. Because scientists thought the new dinosaur was stealing eggs from the nest of a *Protoceratops*, they named it *Oviraptor* ("Egg Thief"), but this idea is now known to be wrong. Far from stealing eggs, *Oviraptor* had been found lying on its own eggs, no doubt incubating them until they hatched. Long legs gave *Oviraptor* the power of speed, and strong, clawed hands helped it grasp its prey. Its toothless beak was moved by powerful muscles, and on top of its head grew a tall, bony crest. The purpose of the crest is unclear.

Crest

- Oviraptor *was a hunter, running down smaller animals which it killed with kicks and bites.*

Toothless beak

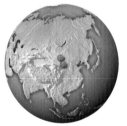

Front legs were shorter than its back legs

Mamenchisaurus
from: China.

PROTOCERATOPS *pro-toe-ser-a-tops*

Length: *6 ft (1.8 m)*   **Weight:** *400 lb (180 kg)*

Lived: *80 million years ago (Late Cretaceous)*

A squat herbivore, *Protoceratops* ("First Horned Face") has provided scientists with a wealth of valuable information. It was found in the Gobi Desert, Mongolia, in the 1920s. The spot turned out to be a nesting site where adults, juveniles, hatchlings, eggs, and nests were found. It was a major discovery because these were the first dinosaur eggs ever to be found. With only short legs (it was no taller than 2 ft [60 cm]), *Protoceratops* was a slow mover, but what it lacked in speed it made up for with a heavily protected, large-sized head. A wide frill of bone grew from the back of its skull, protecting the soft skin of its neck. Its snout ended in a powerful parrot-like beak which could as easily bite through twigs as it could through the arm or leg of a small predator out to attack it. Behind its beak were small teeth which chewed on food until ready to swallow.

● *Protoceratops laid its eggs in a spiral pattern inside its nest, which was a shallow hole scooped in the sand of its desert home. Eggs were like cylinders, 8 inches (20 cm) long and 7 inches (17.5 cm) around the middle.*

● *A newly hatched* Protoceratops *was 12 inches (30 cm) long. The young probably stayed close to their parents for several years, until they were strong enough to lead their own independent lives.*

Bony neck frill

Back legs were longer than front legs

Strong, parrot-like beak

Protoceratops *from:* China, Mongolia.

Psittacosaurus *from:* China, Mongolia, Russia, Thailand.

Long arms with grasping hands

Box-like head with powerful beak

PSITTACOSAURUS *sit-ak-oh-sore-us*

Length: *6½ ft (2 m)*   **Weight:** *176 lb (80 kg)*

Lived: *110 million years ago (Early Cretaceous)*

Psittacosaurus ("Parrot Lizard," after the parrot-like shape of its beak) was a small, lightly built, two-legged herbivore. It was one of the first dinosaurs to develop a distinctive beak, which it used in a slicing motion to chop through tough vegetation. Once inside its mouth, food was pushed into its cheek pouches by its strong tongue. After the leaves, palm fronds, and other plant material had been crushed by its teeth, the pulp was gulped down into its stomach, to be further broken down by the grinding action of stones, bacteria, and digestive juices.

● *Psittacosaurus was an early member of the ceratopsid ("horned face") group of dinosaurs. Its cheek bones were prominent, and it is possible that over millions of years they became the horns of dinosaurs such as* Triceratops.

● *A newly hatched* Psittacosaurus *was tiny—the size of a robin.*

Long legs

VELOCIRAPTOR *vel-o-see-rap-tor*

Length: *6 ft (1.8 m)*   **Weight:** *55 lb (25 kg)*

Lived: *70 million years ago (Late Cretaceous)*

A fast-moving, meat-eating dinosaur, *Velociraptor* ("Quick Predator") was one of the supreme hunters of its day. Similar to *Deinonychus* from North America, it had a large sickle-like claw on the second toe of each foot. Inside its long jaws were sharp, serrated teeth—the perfect shape for slicing meat. A lot is known about how and what it fought, since a *Velociraptor* has been found in Mongolia locked in battle with a *Protoceratops*. The right arm of the *Velociraptor* is gripped in the beak of the *Protoceratops*, while the *Velociraptor* seems to be clawing at the neck of its prey. It was probably kicking the *Protoceratops*, trying to rip its hide with its claws. *Velociraptor* was probably a pack animal, preying on old and weak animals.

● *Velociraptor had a large head and a big brain. It probably had a high degree of intelligence.*

● *Some scientists believe that small meat-eaters like* Velociraptor *had feathers.*

Tail held straight behind for balance as it moved at speed

Long sharp claw held off the ground when it moved

Strong arms

Velociraptor *from:* China, Mongolia.

Dinosaurs In Africa

Dinosaurs lived in Africa throughout the Mesozoic Era, and many fossil sites have been found there. Some of the first African dinosaurs were unearthed on the island of Madagascar in the 1890s. One hundred years later, in 1999, the world's oldest-known dinosaur was found there. This yet-to-be-named herbivore is at least 230 million years old. Elsewhere, the countries of North Africa, particularly Morocco, have produced many dinosaur fossils, such as the sail-backed *Spinosaurus*. From East Africa, a site in Tanzania has produced the bones of hundreds of dinosaurs. Southern Africa is known for *Lesothosaurus*. So far, little scientific work has been done in West Africa.

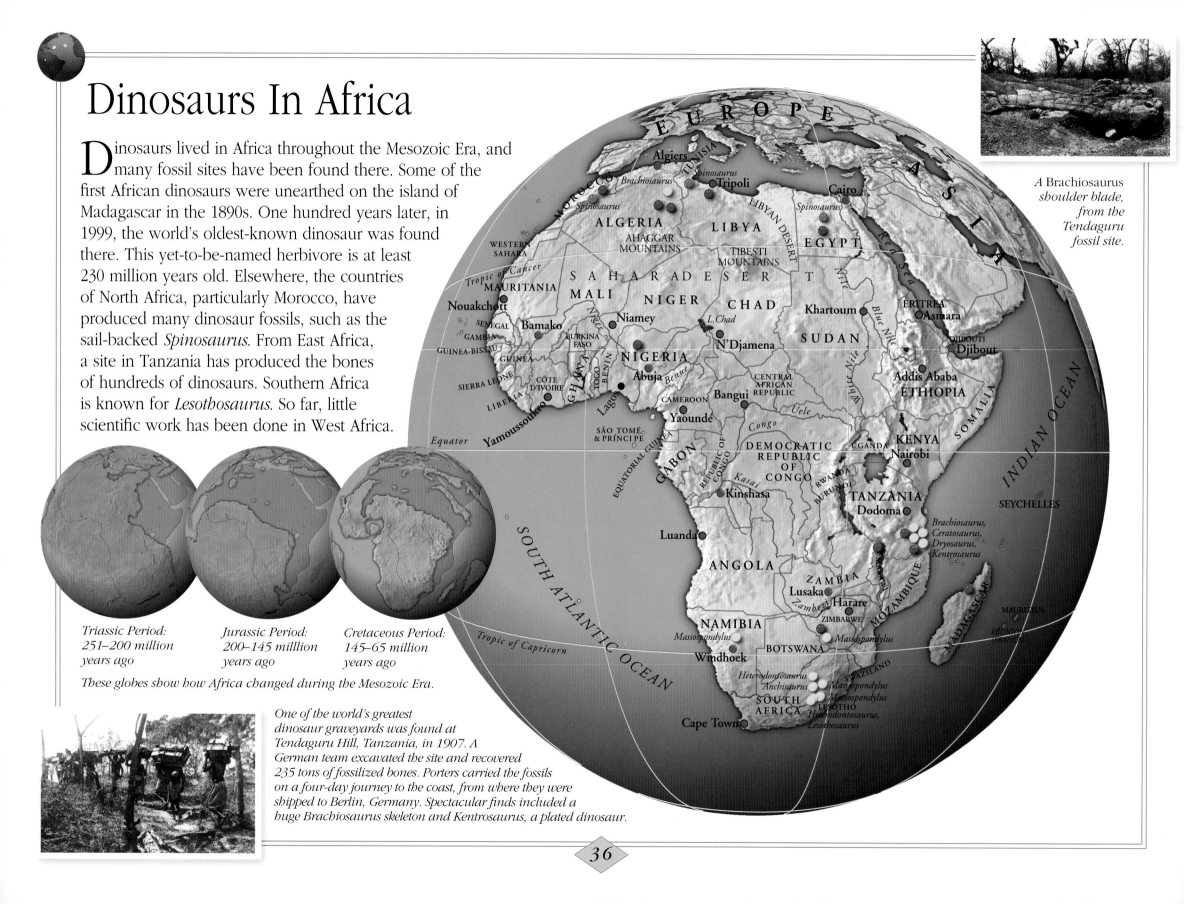

A Brachiosaurus shoulder blade, from the Tendaguru fossil site.

Triassic Period: 251–200 million years ago

Jurassic Period: 200–145 milllion years ago

Cretaceous Period: 145–65 million years ago

These globes show how Africa changed during the Mesozoic Era.

One of the world's greatest dinosaur graveyards was found at Tendaguru Hill, Tanzania, in 1907. A German team excavated the site and recovered 235 tons of fossilized bones. Porters carried the fossils on a four-day journey to the coast, from where they were shipped to Berlin, Germany. Spectacular finds included a huge Brachiosaurus skeleton and Kentrosaurus, a plated dinosaur.

ANCHISAURUS *an-key-sore-us*

Length: *8 ft (2.4 m)*   **Weight:** *60 lb (27 kg)*

Lived: *190 million years ago (Early Jurassic)*

This small dinosaur was given the name *Anchisaurus* ("Near Lizard") because its body was close to the ground. It was an early species of plant-eating dinosaur, and was an ancestor of the giant herbivores that lived later, such as *Brachiosaurus*. *Anchisaurus* was able to walk on its two back legs as well as on all fours. When feeding, it could rear up on its back legs, supporting its body by resting its tail on the ground. In this way it could reach leaves that grew high up. It also ate plants that grew on the ground. Its weak teeth nipped at soft, easy-to-chew plants.

○ Anchisaurus *also lived in North America. Its fossilized bones were found in northeast USA in 1818. It was the first dinosaur discovered in North America.*

Anchisaurus *from:* South Africa.

Long tail held off the ground

Four toes on each foot

Large nostrils on top of head

Small head

Blunt, shaped teeth

Five fingers on each hand

BRACHIOSAURUS *brak-ee-oh-sore-us*

Length: *82 ft (25 m)*   **Weight:** *30–50 tons*

Lived: *150 million years ago (Late Jurassic)*

A giant herbivore, *Brachiosaurus* ("Arm Lizard") is named after its long front legs. Scientists who studied it in the early 1900s noticed how they grew from its shoulders, as if they were arms. In spite of its name, *Brachiosaurus* was a four-legged dinosaur that walked slowly along, perhaps at no more than 2 mph (3 km/h). It may have lived in herds, feeding on low-growing ferns and cycads, and the tough needle-like leaves of conifer trees. With such a huge body to feed, *Brachiosaurus* would have needed a large amount of food—one estimate puts its daily food intake at 440 lb (200 kg) of plants every day. For a creature so big, *Brachiosaurus* had a small head and a tiny brain. Its weak jaws held 52 chisel-like teeth. To eat, *Brachiosaurus* probably combed its teeth back and forth through plants, stripping leaves from their branches.

○ *It is still a mystery why* Brachiosaurus *had nostrils on top of its head. They were large, which suggests a good sense of smell. Perhaps it was better at finding food by smell, rather than sight.*

Its neck was 30 ft (9 m) long

Long, stiff tail

Front legs longer than back legs

Nose horn

CERATOSAURUS *ser-a-toe-sore-us*

Length: *20 ft (6 m)*   **Weight:** *1 ton*

Lived: *150 million years ago (Late Jurassic)*

A fast-moving meat-eater, *Ceratosaurus* ("Horned Lizard") earned its name from the short horn that grew on the tip of its snout. Horny ridges also grew near its eyes. Given that its main weapon of attack was its long, dagger-like teeth, its head protrusions must have had another purpose. Males may have used them for display purposes, such as when they attracted mates. The horns on females may have been smaller than those on males. *Ceratosaurus* was probably a lone predator, like other large carnivores. It would have preyed on smaller animals, grasping them with its clawed hands then kicking and biting them.

○ Ceratosaurus *had a large head. When it ate, the bones of its skull moved sideways, letting it gulp down large chunks of meat.*

○ *When its teeth fell out—either through age, disease or damage—*Ceratosaurus *was able to grow new ones to replace them.*

Curved claws

Walked on back legs

Ceratosaurus *from:* Tanzania.

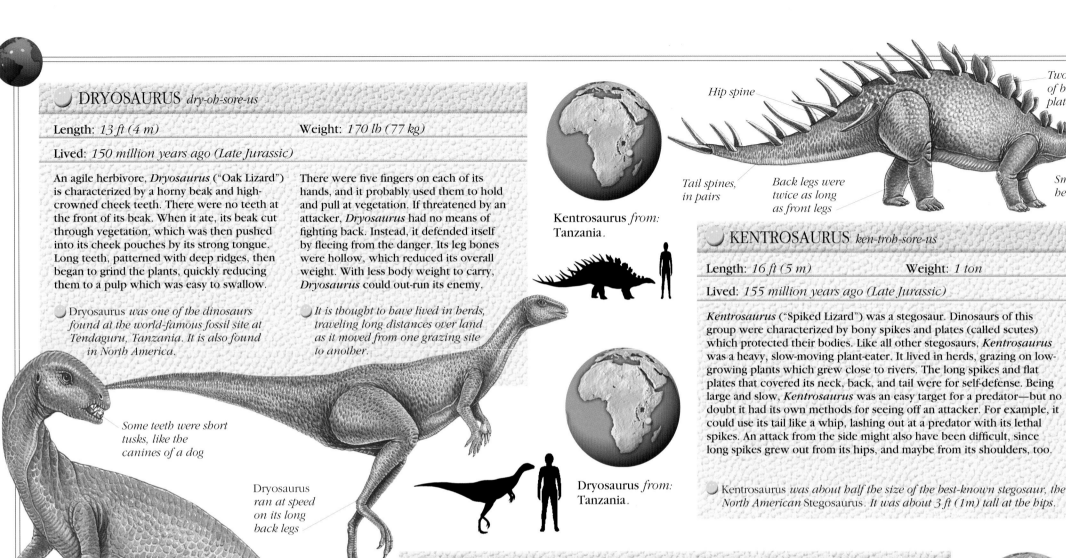

DRYOSAURUS *dry-oh-sore-us*

Length: *13 ft (4 m)*   **Weight:** *170 lb (77 kg)*

Lived: *150 million years ago (Late Jurassic)*

An agile herbivore, *Dryosaurus* ("Oak Lizard") is characterized by a horny beak and high-crowned cheek teeth. There were no teeth at the front of its beak. When it ate, its beak cut through vegetation, which was then pushed into its cheek pouches by its strong tongue. Long teeth, patterned with deep ridges, then began to grind the plants, quickly reducing them to a pulp which was easy to swallow.

There were five fingers on each of its hands, and it probably used them to hold and pull at vegetation. If threatened by an attacker, *Dryosaurus* had no means of fighting back. Instead, it defended itself by fleeing from the danger. Its leg bones were hollow, which reduced its overall weight. With less body weight to carry, *Dryosaurus* could out-run its enemy.

○ Dryosaurus *was one of the dinosaurs found at the world-famous fossil site at Tendaguru, Tanzania. It is also found in North America.*

○ *It is thought to have lived in herds, traveling long distances over land as it moved from one grazing site to another.*

Kentrosaurus from: Tanzania.

Dryosaurus from: Tanzania.

Some teeth were short tusks, like the canines of a dog

Dryosaurus ran at speed on its long back legs

Strong, grasping arms and hands

Long, stiff tail

Clawed toes

Hip spine

Two rows of bony plates

Tail spines, in pairs

Back legs were twice as long as front legs

Small head

KENTROSAURUS *ken-troh-sore-us*

Length: *16 ft (5 m)*   **Weight:** *1 ton*

Lived: *155 million years ago (Late Jurassic)*

Kentrosaurus ("Spiked Lizard") was a stegosaur. Dinosaurs of this group were characterized by bony spikes and plates (called scutes) which protected their bodies. Like all other stegosaurs, *Kentrosaurus* was a heavy, slow-moving plant-eater. It lived in herds, grazing on low-growing plants which grew close to rivers. The long spikes and flat plates that covered its neck, back, and tail were for self-defense. Being large and slow, *Kentrosaurus* was an easy target for a predator—but no doubt it had its own methods for seeing off an attacker. For example, it could use its tail like a whip, lashing out at a predator with its lethal spikes. An attack from the side might also have been difficult, since long spikes grew out from its hips, and maybe from its shoulders, too.

○ Kentrosaurus *was about half the size of the best-known stegosaur, the North American* Stegosaurus. *It was about 3 ft (1m) tall at the hips.*

HETERODONTOSAURUS *het-er-oh-dont-oh-sore-us*

Length: *4 ft (1.2 m)*   **Weight:** *55 lb (25 kg)*

Lived: *205 million years ago (Early Jurassic)*

This dinosaur is named after its unusual teeth. *Heterodontosaurus* ("Different-toothed Lizard") had three types of teeth—most dinosaurs only had one type. At the front of its lower jaw was a horny beak which made contact with a bony pad on the upper jaw. Either side of the bony pad were small, sharp teeth, then tusk-like teeth. At the back of its mouth

were close-packed chewing teeth. A small herbivore, *Heterodontosaurus* grazed on low-growing plants, nipping them off with its beak and front teeth. It may have used its tusks to puncture and rip through tough plants. These special teeth may have had a more important function—males may have used them in a mating display.

○ *It is thought that only males grew the tusk-like teeth. A Heterodontosaurus skull has been found that does not have these teeth, and this may have belonged to a female.*

○ Heterodontosaurus *was a lightly built dinosaur, able to run at speed on its two long back legs. It had long shins and feet, which mark it out as a running animal.*

Heterodontosaurus *from:* South Africa, Lesotho.

LESOTHOSAURUS *le-soo-too-sore-us*

Length: *3 ft (1 m)*	Weight: *66 lb (30 kg)*

Lived: *200 million years ago (Early Jurassic)*

Living in herds that scampered quickly across the hot, semi-desert plains of what is today Lesotho and South Africa, this small dinosaur was built for speed. Named after the country in which it was first found, *Lesothosaurus* ("Lesotho Lizard") was a lightly built animal. Its leg bones were hollow, an important weight-saving feature designed to help it run fast. *Lesothosaurus* was a herbivore that ate low-growing plants. Its small teeth were sharp, and shaped like arrowheads. As it chewed its food its upper and lower teeth interlocked. Over time they wore down and fell out, and new ones grew in their place. *Lesothosaurus* may have dug burrows, like some small lizards do today. Two *Lesothosaurus* have been found curled up together, as if they were sleeping inside a burrow. A burrow would have a been a safe place to rest, and hide from predators.

● If Lesothosaurus *turns out to be the same dinosaur as* Fabrosaurus, *it will have to be called by this other name.*

● *Some people think* Lesothosaurus *may have had a mixed diet, eating meat from insects and carrion as well as plants. It is thought to have lived in herds.*

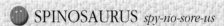

Long legs with four toes on each foot

Small head, large eyes

Short arms with five fingers on each hand

Lesothosaurus *from:* Lesotho, South Africa.

MASSOSPONDYLUS *mas-oh-spon-die-lus*

Length: *16½ ft (5 m)*	Weight: *1 ton*

Lived: *200 million years ago (Early Jurassic)*

Massospondylus ("Massive Vertebrae") is an early example of a long-necked, long-tailed herbivore. In spite of its length, it was not very tall, perhaps measuring little more than 3 ft (1 m) at the hips. It was only toward the middle of the Jurassic Period that the truly gigantic herbivores appeared, such as *Apatosaurus* and *Brachiosaurus*. But even in the early Jurassic Period, *Massospondylus* was showing signs of what was to come later. Its bulky body was supported on four sturdy legs, its tail was stiff, and its teeth seem suited to stripping leaves from branches. Stomach stones show that its food was crushed to aid its digestion. The stones found in a specimen from Zimbabwe came from a place 12½ miles (20 km) from where the animal's fossil was found. It may have lived in herds that traveled long distances.

● Massospondylus *was named in 1854 by Richard Owen, the creator of the word "dinosaur."*

● *This dinosaur has also been found in Arizona, USA.*

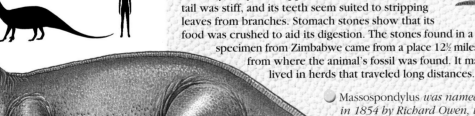

Small head

Long neck

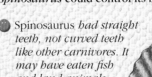

Massospondylus *from:* Lesotho, Namibia, South Africa, Zimbabwe.

Long, stiff tail

SPINOSAURUS *spy-no-sore-us*

Length: *49 ft (15 m)*	Weight: *4 tons*

Lived: *100 million years ago (Middle Cretaceous)*

A huge carnivore, *Spinosaurus* ("Spine Lizard") is named after the row of long bony spines which grew from its backbone. These spines were up to 6½ ft (2 m) long, and their purpose was to support a fan-like skin "fin" which ran the length of its back. Fossils of this strange-looking dinosaur have only ever been found in North Africa. The fin may have been brightly colored and used for display purposes, acting as a calling sign to others of its species. It may also have been used to scare off predators, especially if *Spinosaurus* could change it to a warning color by flushing it red with blood. Another theory is that it acted as a heat regulator, trapping heat on cool days and releasing heat on hot days. In this way *Spinosaurus* could control its body temperature.

● Spinosaurus *had straight teeth, not curved teeth like other carnivores. It may have eaten fish and land animals.*

Spinosaurus *from:* Egypt, Morocco, Tunisia.

Skin fin supported by bone spines

Teeth and jaw shape, like those of Baryonyx *from Europe, seem adapted for a diet of fish*

Dinosaurs in Australia and New Zealand

Triassic Period
251–200 million
years ago

Jurassic Period
200–145 million
years ago

Cretaceous Period
145–65 million
years aog

Very few dinosaurs have been found in Australia. It is the flattest of all the continents, and for much of the Mesozoic Era a large part of it lay under the sea. Dinosaur fossils that are found here tend to come from the eastern part of the continent, where there are fossil-bearing rocky outcrops. Although few dinosaur bones have been found in Australia, many trackways have been discovered. These footprints belong to both large and small dinosaurs, which is strong evidence that Australia was indeed home to many different dinosaur species. *Minmi*, a small armored dinosaur, and *Muttaburrasaurus*, which resembled *Iguanodon*, are two of the continent's better-known dinosaurs.

New Zealand has fewer known dinosaur species than Australia, and none have yet been named. They resemble the dinosaurs of Antarctica. Both New Zealand and Australia were once joined to Antarctica until they broke away about 40 million years ago.

LEAELLYNASAURA *lee-ell-en-a-sore-ah*

Length: *3 ft (1 m)*	Weight: *44 lb (20 kg)*

Lived: *105 million years ago (Early Cretaceous)*

Discovered at Dinosaur Cove, a fossil site in Victoria, southeast Australia, *Leaellynasaura* ("Leaellyn's Lizard") was a small, two-legged herbivore. It had similar features to other members of its group (*Leaellynasaura* was a hypsilophodontid), such as a horny beak and high-crowned cheek teeth. It may have been able to see in poor light, since it lived at a time when Australia was further south than it is today. Winters would have been longer, and daylight hours shorter. *Leaellynasaura* may have been specially adapted to these conditions.

The rock at Dinosaur Cove in which the bones of Leaellynasaura and other dinosaurs were found was so hard that gelignite was used to break it open.

Leaellynasaura
from: Australia.

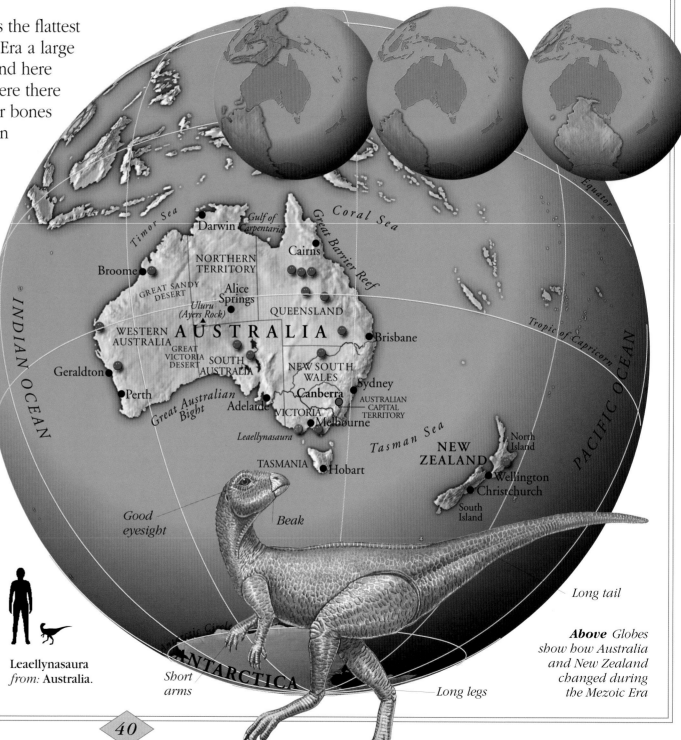

Good
eyesight

Beak

Short
arms

Long tail

Long legs

Above Globes
show how Australia
and New Zealand
changed during
the Mezoic Era

Dinosaurs In The Polar Regions

ANKYLOSAUR *an-kee-loh-sore*

Length: *33 ft (10 m)*   **Weight:** *5 tons*

Lived: *70 million years ago (Late Cretaceous)*

Ankylosaurs ("Fused-together Lizards") were a widespread family of armor-plated dinosaurs. They lived towards the end of the Mesozoic Era and are known from North America, Asia, and Australia. In 1986, the skull and some bony plates from an *ankylosaur* were found on James Ross Island, just off the coast of the frozen continent of Antarctica. It was the first dinosaur to be found on this continent. Although it has not been linked to any particular kind of *ankylosaur* (and so does not have a species name), it is clear that it had many features in common with other members of its group. It was a four-legged herbivore whose body was protected by bony plates and nodules.

This unnamed ankylosaur *was not alone on Antarctica. Remains of other plant-eaters and also meat-eaters have been found there.*

Unnamed ankylosaur *from:* **Antarctica.**

It seems odd to think of dinosaurs living in the polar regions—places with low temperatures and little daylight. Since the mid-1980s, fossils and footprints have been found in both areas, showing that dinosaurs did live within the polar regions.

Dinosaurs of the northern polar region include *Albertosaurus* from Alaska, USA, and *Stegosaurus* from Russia, while *Troodon* has been found in Alaska and Russia. Dinosaurs of the southern polar region have been found in Antarctica. Those from Australia and New Zealand are also polar dinosaurs, since these lands were once joined to Antarctica.

Long head with large eyes

Troodon *from:* **Canada, Russia, USA** *(Alaska, Montana, Wyoming).*

Long arms with long clawed fingers on its hands

Slender, long legs

TROODON *troo-oh-don*

Length: *7 ft (2 m)*   **Weight:** *88 lb (40 kg)*

Lived: *70 million years ago (Late Cretaceous)*

An eagle-eyed carnivore, *Troodon* ("Wounding Tooth") is known from sites below the northern polar circle in Canada and the USA. But it also lived within the polar region and has been found in Alaska, USA, and also in Russia. It was a sleek dinosaur, able to move at great speed to chase its prey, such as smaller reptiles and mammals. Its eyes were large, about 2 inches (5 cm) across, which suggests it had a good sense of vision. Some scientists believe it may have been a night hunter, able to detect its prey in the dark. For those that ventured to the far north, good vision would have been essential in the region's poor light.

In Montana, USA, Troodon *teeth have been found among the nests of plant-eaters, suggesting it ate eggs.*

Troodon *was named in 1856 on the evidence of one tooth.* Troodon *bones were not found until the 1980s.*

Death Of The Dinosaurs

There are almost 100 different theories about why dinosaurs died out. Some theories are far-fetched (aliens hunted them), some cannot be proved (a plague killed them all), and some are more plausible.

One idea popular with scientists is the impact theory. This states that a giant meteorite (a space rock) slammed into the Earth about 65 million years ago. The impact sent a huge volume of dust into the atmosphere, and it was blown around the globe. The dust stopped sunlight from reaching the ground and a period of darkness began. Plants died through lack of sunlight and, with nothing to eat, plant-eating dinosaurs starved to death. The meat-eaters then died as their food supplies disappeared.

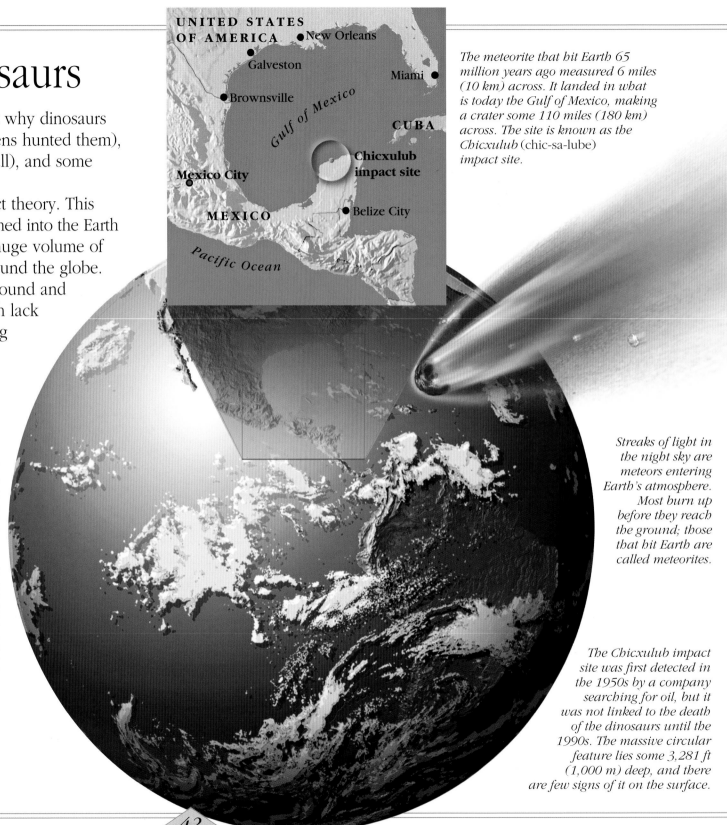

The meteorite that hit Earth 65 million years ago measured 6 miles (10 km) across. It landed in what is today the Gulf of Mexico, making a crater some 110 miles (180 km) across. The site is known as the Chicxulub (chic-sa-lube) impact site.

Streaks of light in the night sky are meteors entering Earth's atmosphere. Most burn up before they reach the ground; those that hit Earth are called meteorites.

The Chicxulub impact site was first detected in the 1950s by a company searching for oil, but it was not linked to the death of the dinosaurs until the 1990s. The massive circular feature lies some 3,281 ft (1,000 m) deep, and there are few signs of it on the surface.

Another theory states that dinosaurs died out because of volcanic eruptions. In this theory scientists say that volcanoes, erupting over thousands of years, pumped ash and carbon dioxide gas into the atmosphere. The climate changed (it either grew hotter or colder, no one is certain), and dinosaurs died because they could not adapt.

Discovering Dinosaurs

Collectors have been fascinated by fossils for hundreds of years, but it is only within the past two centuries that they've aroused the serious interest of scientists. Today, teams of paleontologists (the scientists who study dinosaurs and other ancient animals) go on expeditions to the places where they know they will find dinosaur remains. Because the continents have changed their shapes so much, both during the time the dinosaurs were alive and since, their fossils are only found in certain parts of the world. Once found, it takes a lot of effort to carefully excavate the fossils, pack them, and then transport them to a museum where they are prepared for display and study.

Brushing removes dust

Fossil hunters know what to look for. A bone weathering from a cliff or a curiously shaped stone may be the clues to a dinosaur fossil nearby. Fossils are freed from the ground with hammers and chisels. It's slow work and great care is taken not to damage the remains.

Bone being coated in plastered bandage.

Fossils packed in crates

The bones are made ready to transport to the museum. Each bone is coated in a thick layer of plaster-coated bandage or hard foam. When the plaster has set hard, the bone is carefully lifted and packed into crates.

As more of the dinosaur is exposed, the bones are cleaned, drawn and photographed. Every bone is given a number so that scientists will know how to rebuild the skeleton when it is in the museum.

Above *In the museum, the bones from the excavation are taken to the conservation department. There, the plaster jackets are removed. To make the bones strong enough to handle, cracks are repaired and missing pieces are filled in. Eventually, the skeleton is mounted on a metal frame, called an armature, and it goes on display. If the skeleton is not complete, the bones are kept in boxes in the museum's storeroom.*

A fully mounted dinosaur skeleton, like this Apatosaurus (**right**) *is an impressive sight. But even though many scientists have worked hard to create such a restoration, years of work still lie ahead. Scientific articles will be written about the fossil, and details about the animal's lifestyle will be worked out. It might have died millions of years ago, but its bones have a story to tell.*

Chapter 2:
The Physical Earth

Animals and plants have adapted to the most extreme climates. Climates have changed many times in the past, with ice ages and periods when it was hotter than it is today, but now all living things on Earth face a new threat—global warming, caused by human activity.

Measuring The Earth

Globes are models of the Earth, showing how our planet looks from a spacecraft. But globes also have names and lines drawn on them. One point marked on the top of a globe is the North Pole, while the point at the bottom is the South Pole. An imaginary line joining the North Pole to the center of the Earth and the South Pole is called the Earth's axis. The axis, around which the Earth rotates, is tilted by 23.5°. Most globes are mounted on stands and tilted, just like Planet Earth.

Halfway between the poles is another imaginary line running around the globe. This line is called the Equator. It divides the world into two equal halves, called hemispheres (the word "hemisphere" means half a sphere). The equator is a line of latitude, as are the other lines drawn around globes parallel to the Equator. Globes also show lines of longitude that run at right angles to the lines of latitude.

Globes show accurately areas, shapes, directions and distances on Earth. The surfaces of globes also contain networks of lines of latitude and longitude. Every place on Earth has its own latitude and longitude.

The Earth rotates on its axis once every 24 hours. When places on Earth face the Sun, it is day. When they turn away from the Sun, it is night.

Direction of rotation

The Earth's axis

Sunlight

The line of longitude known as prime meridian (0° longitude) runs through Greenwich, England. Time is measured east and west of the prime meridian. The Earth takes 24 hours to rotate once on its axis. Hence, 15° of longitude represents one hour. If you travel eastwards from the prime meridian, 180° represents a gain of 12 hours. But going westwards, 180° represents a loss of 12 hours. So, the world is divided into 24 time zones. The 180° line of longitude is called the International Date Line, marking a time difference of 24 hours. When you cross the line from west to east, you gain a day. When you return from east to west, you lose a day.

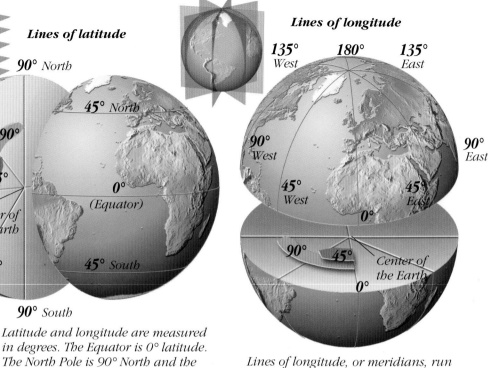

Lines of latitude

90° North
45°
90°
0°
45°
Center of the Earth
45°
90° South

45° North
0° (Equator)
45° South

*Latitude and longitude are measured in degrees. The Equator is 0° latitude. The North Pole is 90° North and the South Pole is 90° South. Latitude is measured by the angle made between the Equator and the place at the center of the Earth. The cutaway globe, **above**, shows that latitudes 45° North and South are measured by the 45° angle at the center of the Earth.*

Lines of longitude

135° West 180° 135° East
90° West   90° East
45° West   45° East
0°
90° 45° Center of the Earth
0°

Lines of longitude, or meridians, run at right angles to the lines of latitude, passing through the North and South Poles. They are measured from the center of the Earth, 180° east and 180° west of the prime meridian (0° longitude). Longitudes 45° West and East are shown on the globe above.

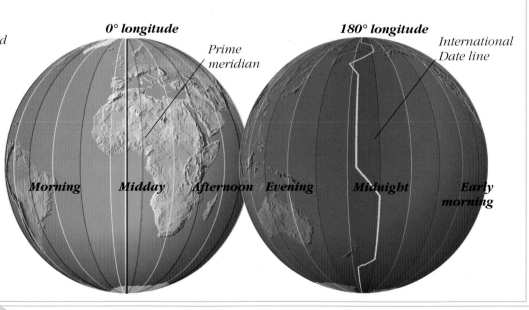

0° longitude   **180° longitude**

Prime meridian

International Date line

Morning   Midday   Afternoon   Evening   Midnight   Early morning

Weather And Seasons

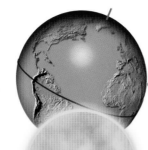

March 20 or 21: start of northern spring and southern autumn

June 20 or 21: northern summer and southern winter

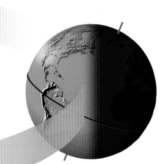

Sun

The Earth travels around the Sun, completing one journey in 365 days, 5 hours, 48 minutes, and 46 seconds. The diagram shows that when the northern hemisphere tilts towards the Sun, it gets more sunlight. As a result, it is summer. When the southern hemisphere tilts towards the Sun, it is summer in the southern hemisphere and winter in the northern hemisphere.

December 21 or 22: northern winter and southern summer

September 22 or 23: start of northern autumn and southern spring

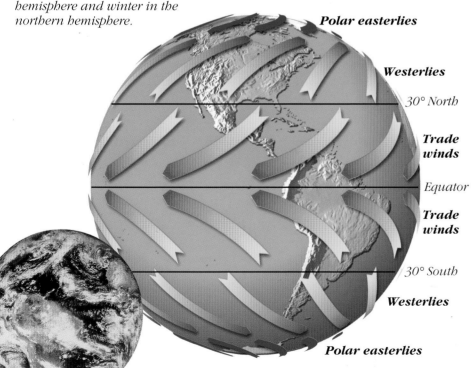

Polar easterlies

Westerlies

30° North

Trade winds

Equator

Trade winds

30° South

Westerlies

Polar easterlies

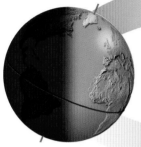

The Earth is surrounded by a layer of air, called the atmosphere. Weather is the changing day-to-day state of the atmosphere. For example, a weather forecaster may say that it will be dry in the morning, with rain in the evening. Because the Earth's axis is tilted, regions in the middle latitudes get four seasons every year—spring, summer, autumn, and winter. Some places do not have four seasons. They include regions in the low latitudes (near the Equator where it is always hot) or in the high latitudes (near the poles where it is always cold).

Storms are major weather systems. The most common storms are thunderstorms. Many form near the Equator and also where westerly winds meet polar easterlies. Other storms are hurricanes which form north and south of the Equator. These storms can be seen from space.

*The photograph of the Earth, **far left**, shows swirling clouds over our planet. The atmosphere surrounding the Earth is always on the move. The diagram of the world's main wind belts shows that, around the Equator, where the Sun's heat is strong, hot air is rising. In the upper atmosphere, this rising air spreads out north and south. The air sinks back to the surface around 30° North and 30° South latitude. At the surface, some of the descending air flows back towards the Equator, forming the trade winds. Some flows towards the poles, forming westerly winds. Circular storms called depressions form where the warm westerly winds meet cold easterly winds flowing from the polar regions.*

A huge circular storm, called a hurricane, photographed from a spacecraft.

The Air Around Us

We cannot see it, smell it, or taste it, but the air that surrounds us is vital for life. Without air, we would not be able to breathe in the life-giving gas, oxygen. Plants cannot survive without carbon dioxide, another gas that is a small but vital component of air.

The air also contains moisture. This occurs in the form of tiny droplets of water or ice crystals which make up clouds. But much of the moisture is in an invisible form, called water vapor. The air also contains tiny specks of volcanic ash, dust, pollen, salt, and soot.

Air has weight. This can be proved by removing air from a bottle with a vacuum pump and weighing it. The bottle with no air weighs less than the same bottle filled with air. The vast mass of air that surrounds our planet is called the atmosphere and its great weight presses down on the Earth's surface. Pressure caused by the weight of air varies. When warm air rises, air pressures fall. When cold air sinks down, air pressures start to rise.

1 TON

Air has weight, but it is much lighter than solids or liquids. However, the atmosphere, which stretches hundreds of miles above the Earth's surface, still weighs about 5,000 trillion tons. This means that directly above each one of us is a column of air that weighs nearly one ton. Amazingly, we do not feel this pressure. This is because we are supported on all sides by an equal pressure. In the same way, fish have adapted to survive in the great pressures that exist at the bottom of the oceans.

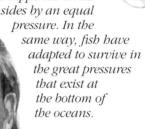

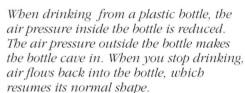

When drinking from a plastic bottle, the air pressure inside the bottle is reduced. The air pressure outside the bottle makes the bottle cave in. When you stop drinking, air flows back into the bottle, which resumes its normal shape.

Winds are currents of air which can be strong enough to push sailing boats forward at considerable speed.

Air contains nitrogen (78%), oxygen (21%), and argon (0.9%). There are traces of other gases, including all-important carbon dioxide (0.0335%).

The Atmosphere

The atmosphere is divided into five layers. The troposphere is the lowest layer. It contains four-fifths of the air in the atmosphere and most of the moisture. Almost all of the conditions we call weather occur in the troposphere.

The troposphere varies from about six miles (10 km) thick at the North and South Poles to 10 miles (16 km) thick at the Equator. When you fly up through the troposphere, temperatures fall by about 3.5 °F for every 1,000 ft (6.5 °C for every 1,000 m). Temperatures become stable at the top of the troposphere at around -67 °F (-55 °C). Strong winds, called jet streams, blow around the top of the troposphere and the lower stratosphere.

The stratosphere, where the air is much thinner, extends up from the troposphere to about 30 miles (48 km) above the ground. The stratosphere contains a layer of a gas called ozone.

Above the stratosphere are the mesosphere, thermosphere, and exosphere. Beyond 300 miles (480 km) above the Earth, the atmosphere fades into space.

Without the atmosphere's protection, the Sun's radiation would be deadly. Even so, sun-block must be used in outdoor activities.

High-flyers? Certain species of bird soar to heights of over seven miles (11.3 km) above Earth's surface!

Before it fades into space at an altitude of about 300 miles (480 km), the atmosphere's top three layers are: the mesosphere, the thermosphere, and the exosphere. Satellites can orbit at heights of between 155 miles (250 km) and 25,000 miles (40,000 km).

The stratosphere is above the troposphere and reaches a height of 30 miles (48 km). Manned balloons have reached the upper stratosphere.

The stratosphere's ozone layer protects people from most of the Sun's harmful ultraviolet radiation. Over-exposure to this can cause skin cancer.

Jet planes fly up to the tropopause (at the very top of the troposphere).

The troposphere is the bottom layer of the atmosphere, extending to a height of 6–10 miles (10–16 km).

Hang gliders fly comfortably at 500 ft (150 m).

Exosphere

Thermosphere

Mesosphere

Stratosphere

Ozone layer
10–20 miles
(15–30 km)

Troposphere

Satellites
22,295 miles
(35,880 km)

Meteors
62 miles (100 km)

High-altitude balloon
32 miles (40 km)

Highest flying bird
7 miles (11.3 km)

Jet airliners
6–10 miles
(10–16 km)

Open basket balloon
1000 ft
(305 m)

Hang glider
500 ft (150 m)

The Sun's Heat

The Sun's rays heat the atmosphere. They also heat the land and sea areas on the Earth's surface. Warmth from the surface, in turn, heats the atmosphere.

The surface is not heated in equal amounts. Around the Equator (an imaginary line that runs around the world exactly half-way between the North and South Poles), the Sun is high in the sky. As a result, the Sun's heat is intense. But near the poles, the Sun is always low in the sky. Here, the Sun's rays pass through a greater thickness of air and are spread over a larger area of land and sea. As a result, the atmosphere is heated less at the poles than it is at the Equator.

The amount of heating varies according to the seasons. As the Earth travels around the Sun, its axis (an imaginary line joining the North Pole, the center of the Earth, and the South Pole) is tilted. Summer in the northern half of the world occurs when the North Pole is tilted toward the Sun. Winter occurs when the northern parts of the world are tilted away from the Sun.

The world's peoples experience a variety of climates.

North Pole

Equator

South Pole

Near the North and South Poles, the Sun is low in the sky. As a result, it is very cold.

The Sun's higher position gives more warmth in those areas closer to the Equator.

On the Equator, the Sun is at its highest in the sky, so the heating effect is at its greatest.

The Sun's powerful rays heat different parts of the Earth's surface unequally.

*Seasons:
As the Earth moves around the Sun, first the northern half (northern hemisphere) leans toward the Sun. For the rest of the year, the southern hemisphere leans toward the Sun. When your part of the Earth leans toward the Sun, it is summer.*

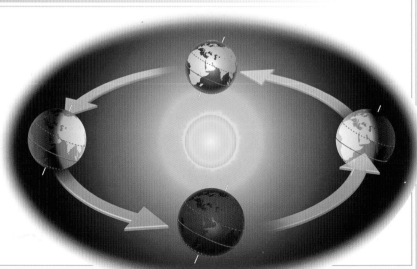

The Moving Atmosphere

Temperate areas are neither too hot nor too cold. They have clearly marked seasons.

Deserts occur around 30° North and 30° South of the Equator, in zones of high air pressure.

Polar regions around the North and South Poles are the coldest places on the planet.

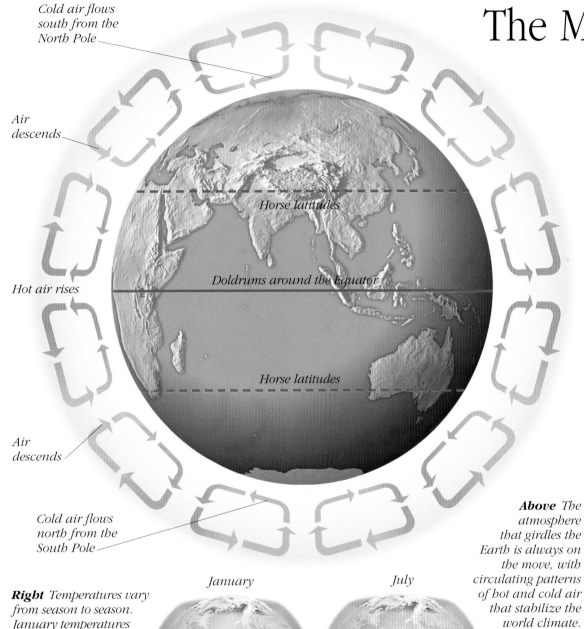

Cold air flows south from the North Pole

Air descends

Hot air rises

Air descends

Cold air flows north from the South Pole

Horse latitudes

Doldrums around the Equator

Horse latitudes

Right *Temperatures vary from season to season. January temperatures are low in the northern hemisphere, but it is summer in the southern hemisphere. In July, the maps show that temperatures are lower south of the Equator and higher in the north.*

January

Cooler

Warmer

July

Warmer

Cooler

Above *The atmosphere that girdles the Earth is always on the move, with circulating patterns of hot and cold air that stabilize the world climate.*

The lines on a globe that are parallel to the Equator are called lines of latitude. The Equator is 0° latitude. The two poles are 90° North and 90° South. Other lines of latitude are numbered between 0° and 90°.

Near the Equator, the Sun's rays heat the surface. The surface heats the air above it. Strong currents of warm air rise, creating a zone of low air pressure at ground level, called the Doldrums. As the air rises, it becomes colder. Finally, in the upper atmosphere, it spreads out north and south. Around 30° North and 30° South, the cool air sinks, creating "horse latitudes," a zone of high air pressure.

Some descending air flows back across the surface toward the Equator and some flows towards the poles. Cold air from the poles also flows toward the Equator. These movements of hot and cold air from region to region prevent our planet from becoming overheated or unbearably cold.

Winds are light in the Doldrums, where sailing ships are often becalmed.

Winds

Winds have a great impact on weather. In the northern hemisphere, a north wind lowers the temperatures, while a south wind raises them.

The main, or prevailing, winds are caused by those movements of the atmosphere described on page 51. When air sinks at the horse latitudes, around 30° North and 30° South, some air flows back toward the Equator and some flows toward the poles. The map of the world's prevailing winds shows that the air does not flow directly north or south. Instead, winds are deflected by the Earth's rotation—to the right of the direction in which they naturally flow in the northern hemisphere and to the left in the southern hemisphere.

The winds blowing from the horse latitudes toward the Doldrums are called trade winds. The winds blowing from the horse latitudes toward the poles are called westerly winds. Cold winds blowing from the poles toward the Equator are called polar easterlies.

Left The combination of strong winds and high tides can flood coastal areas.

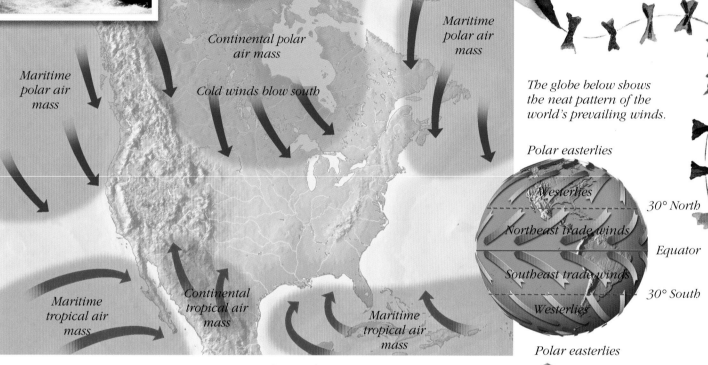

Maritime polar air mass

Continental polar air mass

Cold winds blow south

Maritime polar air mass

Maritime tropical air mass

Continental tropical air mass

Maritime tropical air mass

Using the wind to make a kite fly high can be fun—but wind also plays a vital role in shaping the world's weather.

The globe below shows the neat pattern of the world's prevailing winds.

Polar easterlies

Westerlies

Northeast trade winds — 30° North

Equator

Southeast trade winds

Westerlies — 30° South

Polar easterlies

Above *The map shows a good example of how winds help to determine climate. In winter, winds blow from cold air masses that form over the northern part of North America, to meet warmer winds coming up from the Equator. These stop the cold air from reaching the southern part of the United States, which never experiences the bitterly cold winters of the northern part. In between, the winter weather rarely reaches either extreme.*

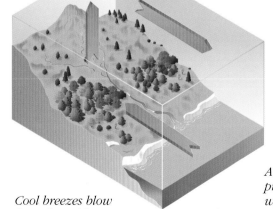

Cool breezes blow from the colder sea to the warmer land by day.

At night the process is reversed, with breezes blowing off cooling land toward the warmer sea.

Moisture In The Air

Clouds are classified according to their height above the ground. Clouds above 20,000 ft (6,100 m) are called high clouds and include cirrus, cirrostratus, and cirrocumulus. Medium clouds, at 8,200 ft (2,500 m), include altocumulus and altostratus. Nimbostratus, stratocumulus, cumulus, and stratus are all low clouds. Cumulonimbus (thunder clouds) start as low clouds, but they may grow into large, high clouds.

A
B
C
D
E
F
G
H
I
J

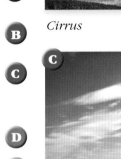

A Cirrus

B Cirrostratus

C Cirrocumulus

D Altocumulus

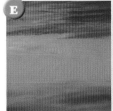

E Altostratus

F Cumulonimbus

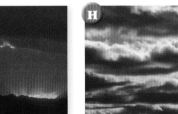

G Nimbostratus

H Stratocumulus

I Cumulus

J Stratus

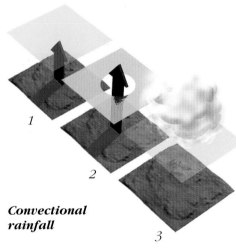

Condensation occurs when water vapor turns into water droplets. For example, droplets form when warm air comes into contact with a cold windowpane. Dew is similar. It forms in the early morning when beads of water form on plants and leaves.

Convectional rainfall

1 Warm air rises and cools.

2 As the air cools, the invisible vapor condenses.

3 Cumulus clouds are formed.

If you leave a saucer of water outside in warm weather, the water eventually disappears. The Sun's heat has turned the water into invisible water vapor. This process is called evaporation, a term used by scientists for changes that take place when a liquid or solid is converted into a gas or turned into a vapor.

Warm air can hold more water vapor than cold air. But, as the air cools, its capacity to hold water vapor is reduced. Cooling air eventually reaches a point when it is saturated—that is, it contains all the water vapor it can hold at that temperature. This is called the dew point. Further cooling means that the air starts to lose water vapor. The invisible vapor then turns back into visible water droplets or tiny ice crystals.

Clouds are formed in this way. When warm air rises from the ground, it gradually becomes cooled. Eventually, tiny droplets of water, or ice crystals, start to form around specks or other matter in the air. This process is called condensation. Clouds are formed from billions of water droplets or ice crystals.

On cold days, warm breath turns into a cloud of water vapor.

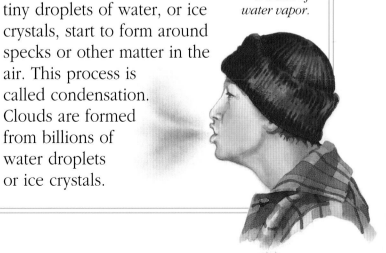

Rainfall

When clouds form, the water droplets are too light to fall to the ground. But when they collide inside clouds, they grow until they are heavy enough to form raindrops. Rain may also form from ice crystals. Ice crystals grow as cold droplets freeze around them. As they fall, ice crystals can melt and become raindrops.

Rain is formed in several ways. On warm days, the Sun evaporates moisture which is swept upwards by currents of warm air. As the air cools, clouds form and rain falls. This is called convectional rain. When wind from the sea passes over mountains, the air rises and cools. Clouds form and rain falls on the mountain slopes. This is called orographic rain.

Left People may seek shelter from the rain but life on Earth depends on rainfall.

Above Rainbows are formed when the Sun's rays pass through droplets of water, which split white light into the colors of the rainbow.

Above Heavy or prolonged rainfall sometimes causes floods, which can wash away buildings and cars. Disastrous floods can cause great loss of human life.

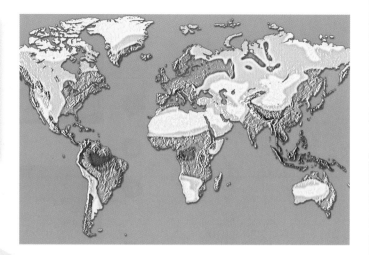

Above Annual rainfall varies greatly around the world. Some areas are deserts, while others have so much rainfall that floods are common. Dark blue areas have over 80 inches (2,030 mm) of rain; light blue, 20–40 inches (500–1,000 mm). Green areas have 10–20 inches (250–500 mm) of rain and yellow areas have under 10 inches (250 mm) a year.

Clouds form

Mountain range

Moist wind

Left Orographic rain occurs when moist winds from the sea cross over mountain ranges. The rising air is cooled, clouds form, and heavy rain or snow falls on the mountain slopes. Once they pass the crest of mountain ranges, the winds start to descend. The air then becomes warmer and moisture is evaporated. The leeward sides of ranges are therefore said to be in a rain shadow area which is dry.

Left Convectional rainfall is common near the Equator. Morning skies are often clear. Then intense heating of the ground causes warm, moist air to rise. High above the ground, the air cools and water vapor condenses into water droplets, forming massive thunderclouds. The droplets fuse to form raindrops and, in the late afternoon, heavy rain occurs. After the storm, the sky clears.

Snow, Hail, And Frost

Above *Hailstorms often cause great damage, as large hailstones are capable of denting cars.*

Above *Playing in the snow is fun, but snow can also cause transport problems.*

Above *The combination of snow, ice, and frost turns the countryside into a winter wonderland.*

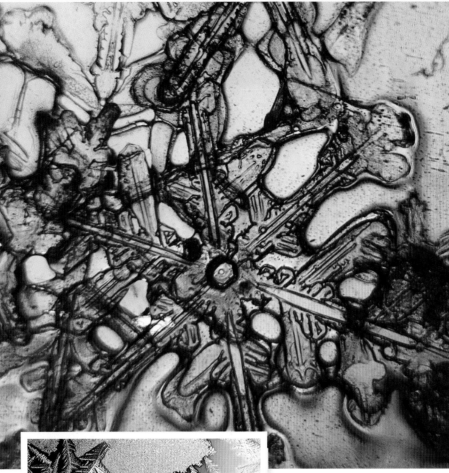

Above *A snowflake, shown here magnified under a microscope, is formed from around 100 ice crystals that are stuck together.*

Left *Beautiful fern-like patterns of frost are made up of frozen water droplets, often appearing on windows in icy weather.*

Water reaches the ground from the air in several forms including rain, snow, sleet, hail, and frost. They are all called precipitation.

Snow is formed in cold clouds when tiny ice crystals stick together until they form snowflakes. A snowflake which measures about one inch (2.5 cm) across may be formed from 100 crystals stuck together. Sleet is a mixture of snow and rain. Hail forms when ice crystals rise and fall in cold clouds. Water droplets freeze around them until they become large pellets of ice heavy enough to fall as hailstones. Hailstones can wreak great damage on crops and glass greenhouses.

There are three kinds of frost. The delicate patterns of frost seen on windowpanes are called hoar frost. Thick coatings of ice which form on cold surfaces are called glazed frost. The third kind of frost, rime, forms when extremely cold water droplets freeze on contact with cold surfaces.

Four inches (100 mm) of snow is almost the same as 0.4 inches (10 mm) of rainfall.

The Water Cycle

About 97 percent of the world's water is in the oceans. Sea water is far too salty for drinking or farming. But a natural process, called the water cycle, ensures that the land gets a regular supply of essential fresh water.

The cycle begins when the Sun evaporates water from the sea. Water vapor, which makes up only 0.001 percent of the world's water, is swept into the air where it condenses to form clouds. Winds blow the clouds over the land. Rain from clouds runs into rivers and sinks into the ground. In mountains, snow falls. But this snow eventually melts and adds to the fresh water supply.

Gravity ensures that most of the water that reaches land eventually finds its way back into the oceans, and the water cycle is completed.

The Sun makes water evaporate from both land and sea to form rain-bearing clouds.

Trees and plants cannot survive without fresh water from the water cycle.

Much of the water vapor in the water cycle comes from the oceans. Water also evaporates from rivers and lakes, and water vapor is released by plants through their leaves—a process called transpiration. Gravity ensures that most of the water from land areas makes its way back to the sea, where the cycle begins again.

Lakes and rivers are supplied by water brought to land by the water cycle.

Rain and snow fall on mountains

Winds carry clouds over the land

Clouds form

Transpiration from lakes and vegetation releases water vapor

Water seeps down to the sea through rocks

Moist air rises

Water returns to the sea in rivers

The sea begins the water cycle. Fresh water flows back from land to sea.

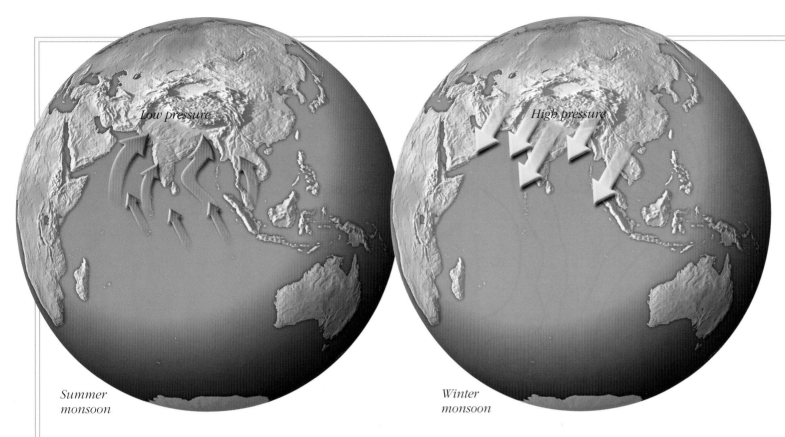

Low pressure

High pressure

Summer monsoon

Winter monsoon

Monsoons

Four main factors—temperature, wind, moisture, and air pressure—affect weather conditions in the troposphere. Changes in air pressure cause monsoons (seasonal reversals of wind directions). The best-known monsoon occurs in the Indian subcontinent.

In winter, the land in southern Asia is chilled and cool air sinks, creating a high pressure air mass. Northeasterly winds blow outwards from this mass. In spring, the land warms and hot air rises, creating a low pressure air mass. Southwesterly winds laden with water vapor from the oceans are then drawn into southern Asia. Summer winds formed in this way bring abundant rain to southern and southeastern Asia—rain vital to farmers who depend on it for their crops. But if the rains are too heavy, they can destroy crops and cause floods that drown people and animals.

Other monsoons occur in eastern Asia, northern Australia, parts of Africa, and the southwestern United States.

Above *The maps show how wind directions in southern Asia are reversed between summer and winter. The summer winds come from the sea and bring huge amounts of water to the land. In winter, dry winds blow off the land.*

Below *Trees cannot grow unless there is water in the soil which the plants can absorb through their roots.*

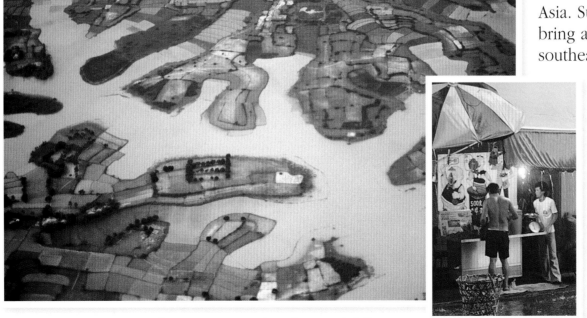

Above *Monsoon regions with wet summer winds get heavy rainfall and floods. Cherrapunji, in northeast India, gets more than 433 inches (11,000 mm) of rain a year.*

Business as usual, despite the torrential rains.

Sheltering from a sudden downpour.

Depressions

In some parts of the world, the weather is stable. In other places, it can often change from hour to hour. Changeable weather is caused by low air pressure systems, which are called depressions or cyclones. By contrast, high-pressure anticyclones usually bring stable weather.

Depressions are circular air systems. They form along the polar front, where warm westerly winds meet up with cold, dense air flowing from the poles. Warm and cold air do not mix easily. When warm air flows into waves in the polar front, it flows over the cold air. Cold air then follows along behind the warm air and a depression is born.

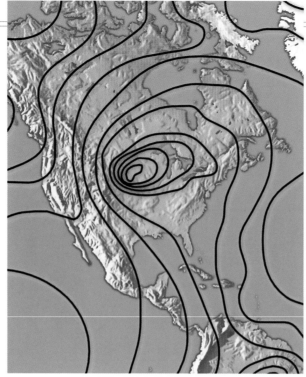

Above *On weather maps the circular lines, also called isobars, surround areas with equal air pressure. Depressions can be recognized because the lowest value of air pressure is found at their center.*

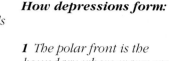

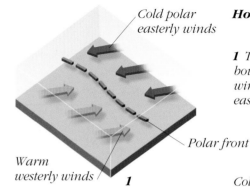

Warm westerly winds

Cold polar easterly winds

Polar front

1

How depressions form:

1 *The polar front is the boundary where warm westerly winds meet up with cold polar easterly winds.*

2 *Waves develop in the polar front. Warm air flows into these waves, forming two fronts. Cold fronts are shown by lines marked with tiny triangles. Warm fronts are shown as lines with semi-circles along them.*

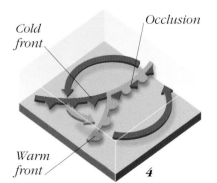

Cold front

Warm front

2

3 *A fully formed depression consists of dense cold air, with light warm air at the center. The cold air undercuts the warm air along the front. Along the warm front, the warm air flows above the cold air.*

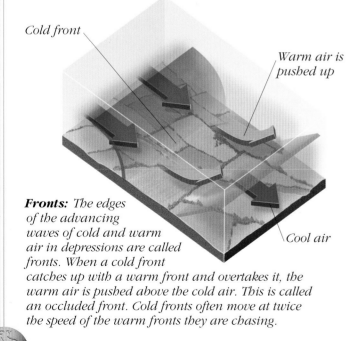

Cold front

Warm air is pushed up

Cool air

Fronts: *The edges of the advancing waves of cold and warm air in depressions are called fronts. When a cold front catches up with a warm front and overtakes it, the warm air is pushed above the cold air. This is called an occluded front. Cold fronts often move at twice the speed of the warm fronts they are chasing.*

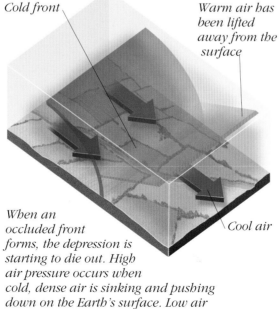

Cold front

Warm air has been lifted away from the surface

Cool air

When an occluded front forms, the depression is starting to die out. High air pressure occurs when cold, dense air is sinking and pushing down on the Earth's surface. Low air pressure occurs when warm air rises.

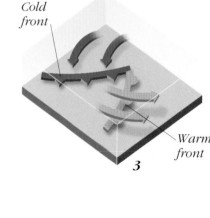

Cold front

Warm front

3

4 *The cold air eventually catches up with the warm front, forming an occlusion. An occlusion is shown by a line with alternating triangles and semi-circles.*

Cold front

Occlusion

Warm front

4

Stormy Weather

Stormy and changeable weather is the main feature of depressions. Ahead of the warm front, clouds form as warm, light air flows above the cold air ahead of it. The first clouds that appear when a warm front is advancing are high cirrus clouds. Later, the clouds are lower. They bring light, but persistent, rain or snow.

After the warm front has passed, temperatures increase and skies clear. But soon the cold front arrives. It travels about twice as fast as the warm front. When it arrives, temperatures fall. Cold air forms a wedge beneath the warm air, forcing it upwards. If the warm air contains a lot of water vapor, huge thunderclouds called cumulonimbus may form in the rising air along the cold front. But stormy weather and heavy rain or snow from these clouds do not last for long.

When a cold front catches up with a warm front, an occluded front is formed. Along an occluded front, warm air is pushed above cold air. Clouds continue to form and rain and snow still fall. But the weather along an occluded front is less extreme and long-lasting than along warm and cold fronts.

Left *Stormy weather and thunderstorms are features of cold and warm fronts.*

Above *Rain falling from banks of clouds that accompany fronts.*

Left *Storm clouds tower into the sky.*

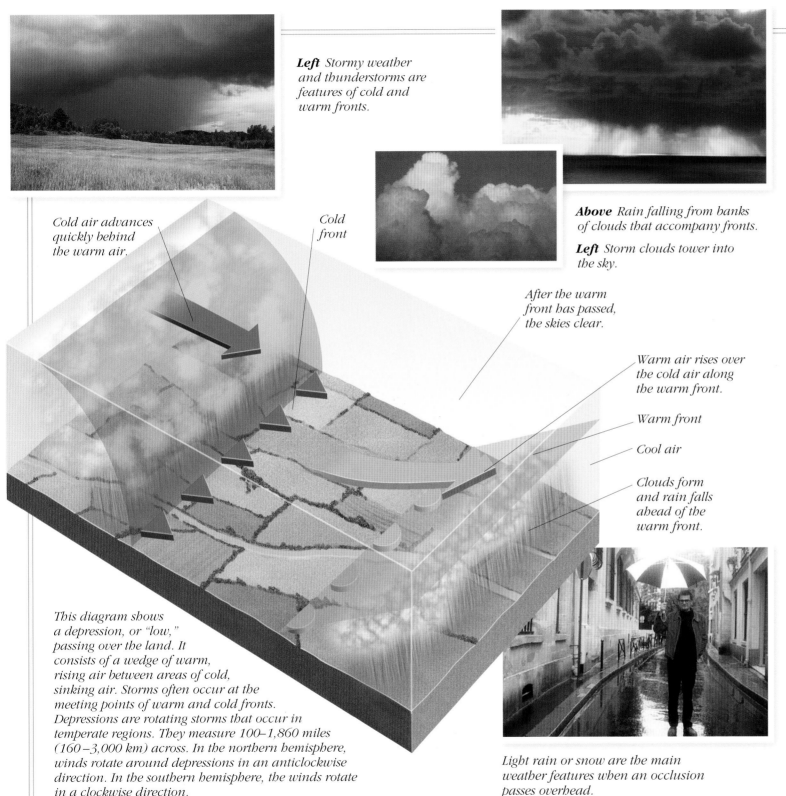

Cold air advances quickly behind the warm air.

Cold front

After the warm front has passed, the skies clear.

Warm air rises over the cold air along the warm front.

Warm front

Cool air

Clouds form and rain falls ahead of the warm front.

This diagram shows a depression, or "low," passing over the land. It consists of a wedge of warm, rising air between areas of cold, sinking air. Storms often occur at the meeting points of warm and cold fronts. Depressions are rotating storms that occur in temperate regions. They measure 100–1,860 miles (160–3,000 km) across. In the northern hemisphere, winds rotate around depressions in an anticlockwise direction. In the southern hemisphere, the winds rotate in a clockwise direction.

Light rain or snow are the main weather features when an occlusion passes overhead.

The calm before the storm.

Thunderstorms

On average, 45,000 thunderstorms occur around the world every day. Many of these happen in regions near the Equator, where strong currents of moist air rise upwards. Water vapor condenses to form cumulonimbus clouds. These are the breeding ground for lightning and thunder. Cumulonimbus clouds occur in temperate regions, on hot summer days or along cold fronts.

Lightning, which can start fires and kill people, is made up of huge electrical sparks. It occurs in one or more strokes. The forked lightning that follows a jagged path across the sky is called a return stroke. Return strokes travel at the speed of light, which is 186,282 miles/sec (299,792 km/sec).

Cumulonimbus clouds are an ominous sight.

Forked lightning strikes.

The sequence above shows one theory on why lightning occurs. The center of hailstones in clouds have a negative charge, while the outside is positively charged (**1**). When the hailstones break up, positive light outer fragments are swept up (**2**) while heavy negative cores fall to the base of the cloud (**3**). The charges are discharged as a huge electric spark (**4**). Lightning may be attracted from the cloud base to positively charged high buildings or the ground (**5**), and the return stroke generates further strikes (**6**).

Cumulonimbus clouds form

Warm, moist air rises

Above *Cumulonimbus clouds, which cause thunderstorms, form when warm, moist air rises. Lightning, which occurs in these clouds, heats up the air along its path. The hot air particles collide with cooler air, creating thunder. We see lightning before we hear thunder because light travels faster than sound. A thunderstorm does not always produce visible lightning.*

Hurricanes

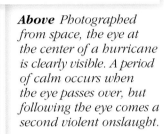

Above *Photographed from space, the eye at the center of a hurricane is clearly visible. A period of calm occurs when the eye passes over, but following the eye comes a second violent onslaught.*

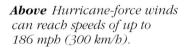

Above *Hurricane-force winds can reach speeds of up to 186 mph (300 km/h).*

Above *Hurricanes are capable of awesome destruction when they reach land.*

Thunderstorms are the most common storms, but hurricanes are the most destructive. Hurricanes batter Caribbean islands, Central America, and the eastern coasts of the United States. Hurricanes in eastern Asia are called typhoons. In southern Asia they are known as tropical cyclones, while in Australia they are called willy-willies.

Hurricanes develop in the trade wind belt, north and south of the Equator. They have a core, or eye, where pressure is low. Around the eye, warm air rises to create storm clouds and violent winds that rotate at up to 186 mph (300 km/h).

Hurricanes are much larger than thunderstorms, often measuring 120–310 miles (200–500 km) across. When they reach land, huge waves crash against the shore and cause serious flooding.

Hurricanes have a central eye around which are huge circular bands of cumulus and cumulonimbus clouds. The top clouds are made of ice, but lower clouds are composed of water droplets. The hurricane is powered by fast-rotating winds. Hurricanes form over the oceans. On average, 11 reach North America's shores every year. They bring fierce winds and torrential rain, but soon die out over the mainland.

It's hard to walk when hurricane winds blow.

Tornadoes

The most violent storms that form over land areas are called tornadoes. They are small weather systems, measuring only about 0.25 miles (0.4 km) across at ground level, but they can cause great destruction.

Also called twisters, tornadoes form when rotating funnels of cloud sink down from cumulonimbus clouds, as warm air rises and rotates around the funnel. Some funnels do not reach the ground. Some reach the ground, withdraw, and then come down again. Tornadoes are short-lived. Most of them last no more than an hour.

Air pressures are extremely low in the center of the tornadoes. The difference in air pressure in a tornado and the inside of a building can make the building explode. Tornadoes also tear trees out of the ground and lift cars and people into the air. When tornadoes develop over water, they form features called waterspouts.

The United States is hit by around 600 to 700 tornadoes a year, mostly in spring and early summer.

Tornadoes are frequent in the central and southern United States.

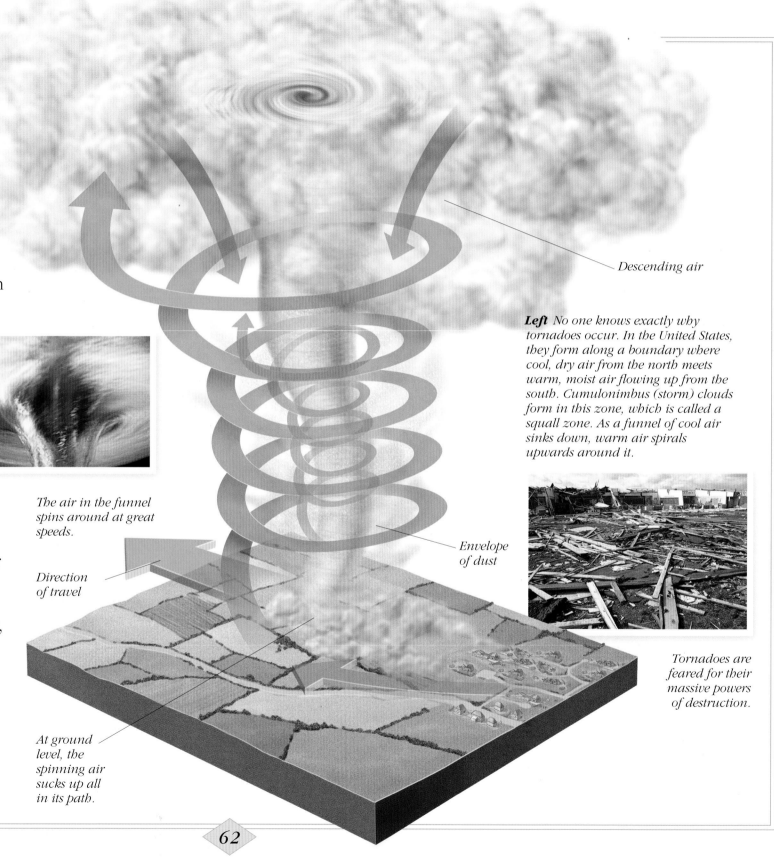

Descending air

Left *No one knows exactly why tornadoes occur. In the United States, they form along a boundary where cool, dry air from the north meets warm, moist air flowing up from the south. Cumulonimbus (storm) clouds form in this zone, which is called a squall zone. As a funnel of cool air sinks down, warm air spirals upwards around it.*

The air in the funnel spins around at great speeds.

Direction of travel

Envelope of dust

At ground level, the spinning air sucks up all in its path.

Tornadoes are feared for their massive powers of destruction.

Sandstorms And Blizzards

Above *Windblown sand shapes the scenery in deserts. Unless they are protected by metal, sand can cut down wooden telegraph poles, strip paint from cars, hollow out caves, and undercut boulders. Over countless years, sand has shaped the desert landscape by sculpting all sorts of weird and wonderful rock formations.*

Sandstorms and duststorms occur in deserts. During sandstorms, the wind lifts up grains of sand and bounces them across the surface. Sand grains are heavy, and they are seldom lifted more than 6.6 ft (2 m). But sandstorms are very unpleasant. Windblown sand affects desert scenery, because it acts like a natural sandblaster. Duststorms can be dangerous to aircraft because clouds of dust can be lifted to heights of 9,840 ft (3,000 m) or more.

Blinding blizzards occur in polar regions and also in temperate areas affected by cold Arctic air masses.

They are caused by strong, bitterly cold winds that whip up dry, powdery snow and ice from the surface. Wind speeds in blizzards reach 35–45 mph (56–72 km/h). They occur in northern North America and Russia.

North America and Siberia are also hit by icestorms. They happen when rain or wet (melting) snow freezes onto cold surfaces, such as roads or vehicles.

Left *Severe blizzards can cause serious disruption, even in cities. They can stop all traffic and cause businesses to close.*

Above *Windblown sand during sandstorms can be very painful, but usually the heads of adults remain above the level of swirling sand grains. Choking dust clouds, however, can be lifted to much greater heights (above right).*

Desert peoples are always ready to protect themselves from sandstorms.

Right *The hardy people who live near the poles are used to surviving in blizzard conditions.*

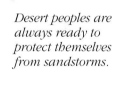

Heatwaves And Floods

Besides storms, other unusual weather conditions can also cause damage and loss of life. For example, some areas experience periods when temperatures soar way above the average. People feel uncomfortable, especially if the amount of water vapor in the air (humidity) is high. Heat can also lead to deaths —in 1980 an estimated 1,500 people died during a heatwave in the United States.

Periods of great heat are often accompanied by drought, when no rain falls for weeks or months. Droughts dry up the land and the plants on it. Dry plants burn easily, often causing forest fires. In Africa, long droughts kill the animals of nomadic herders, who then starve.

When droughts occur, people pray for rain. But too much rain can swell rivers until they overflow, causing terrible floods that destroy people and property. In Africa and Asia, after floods subside, people are at risk from diseases like cholera and malaria.

Excessive heat affects people badly, making them listless and irritable. In heatwaves, city and country dwellers alike seek the relief of a cold shower—in New York, the tops of fire hydrants are often torn off as the temperature rises, to provide cooling sprays of water. Heatwaves are especially unpleasant when the humidity is high. They often occur during anticyclones (high-pressure air systems), when the skies remain clear for long periods. The Sun's heat is then at its most intense.

*Coastal floods (**above**) are often caused by hurricanes, but most floods are caused by heavy rain. Rainwater may also mix with soil to form mudslides (**below**). Mudslides in Honduras and Nicaragua killed 10,800 people in 1998.*

Studying The Weather

Right *Aneroid barometers show changes in air pressure. Falling pressure often means that rain is on the way.*

Left *A sunshine recorder enables statistics to be kept on the hours when the Sun shines.*

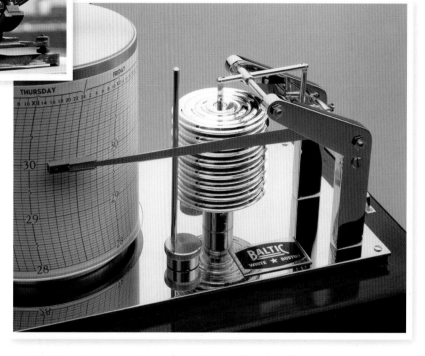

Above *A barograph uses a pen that records changing air pressures on a paper chart mounted on a rotating drum.*

Above *Thermometers are used to measure temperature. To avoid exposure to direct sunlight and record the correct air temperature, they are kept in shelters.*

*Hi-tech sensors (**above**) measure wind speed by its sound. Cup anemometers (**below**) rotate as the wind blows and record wind speeds. Vanes indicate wind direction.*

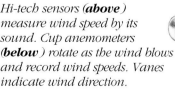

Above *A rain gauge measures rainfall. The inside is shaped like a funnel, with a tube to hold the water.*

The weather affects our lives in many ways. It determines the clothes we wear when we go out. Weather is also important to farmers and to people working in communications, industry, and transport. For example, a sudden frost or hailstorm can severely damage a farmer's crops, while icy roads are a hazard for truck drivers. The science of weather is called meteorology and the people who study it are meteorologists. Many of them work in weather forecasting.

Fir cones react to humidity. When the air is dry, the cone closes up. When it is humid, the cone quickly opens up.

To produce a forecast, different elements of weather must be measured. These include temperature, air pressures, wind speeds and directions, and rainfall. Around the world, meteorologists at weather stations on land or on ships at sea measure weather conditions.

Meteorologists collect and analyze information from weather stations. They must interpret all the complex information before predicting how weather patterns are likely to develop.

Cows can give clues about the weather— when they lie down, it may indicate storms are on the way.

Information From Space

The accuracy of weather forecasts has increased greatly in the past 50 years, because we now know much more about conditions in the upper atmosphere.

A major breakthrough came with the use of radio-sondes. A radio-sonde is a large hydrogen-filled balloon that carries instruments to measure temperatures and air pressures, with a radio to transmit the data back to the ground. When the balloon bursts at high altitude, the instrument pack floats down attached to a parachute.

Other information comes from weather satellites, which photograph cloud patterns over the Earth. They also measure the temperature and humidity in the upper atmosphere. Jet aircraft send back information about weather conditions in the upper troposphere and lower stratosphere, while radar locates bands of rain.

A weather satellite.

Left Some weather satellites are launched into space by rocket, while others are deployed by the USA's space shuttle.

Above Television cameras in satellites send back pictures of the Earth and its weather to ground stations. These pictures are analyzed to provide weather forecasters with information that can be captured in no other way. Some weather satellites circle the Earth from pole to pole. Others are positioned over the Equator to move around in unison with the rotating Earth.

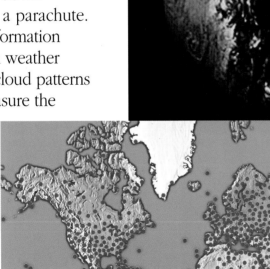

This map shows weather stations around the world where radio-sonde balloons are released.

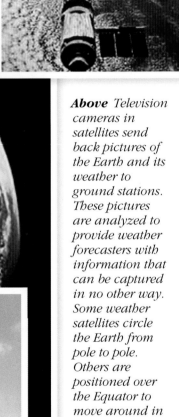

Left Weather balloons carry radio-sondes high into the upper atmosphere.

Weather Maps

Hundreds of weather stations around the world gather the information needed for accurate weather maps.

Warm fronts are identified on weather maps by orange semi-circles. Cold fronts are identified by blue triangles.

Occluded fronts can include both warm (orange) and cold (blue) air.

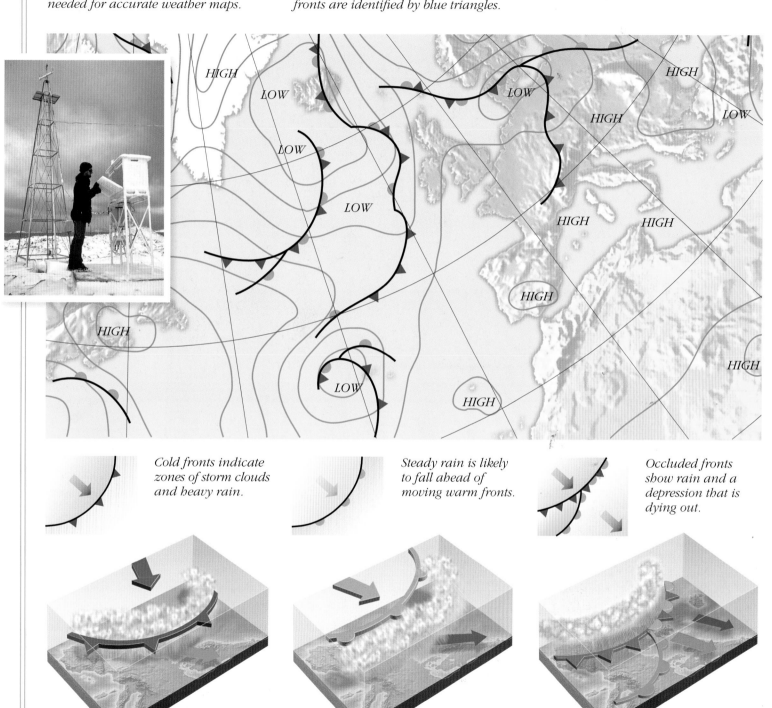

HIGH

LOW

HIGH

LOW

LOW

HIGH

LOW

LOW

HIGH

HIGH

HIGH

HIGH

LOW

HIGH

LOW

HIGH

At more than 7,000 weather stations around the world, meteorologists measure conditions in the air at ground level and often at various layers in the upper atmosphere. At some stations, they record information every 30 minutes. Other stations make measurements every six or 12 hours. Stations transmit this information to weather centers, where it is fed into computers that prepare weather maps.

Weather maps prepared by computers are called synoptic charts, because they give a synopsis, or summary, of weather conditions on the ground and at various levels in the atmosphere at a point in time.

These weather maps show isobars, which are circular lines indicating the positions of depressions and anticyclones. Other features can then be added to the maps, including temperatures, wind speeds and directions, precipitation, and cloud cover. The synoptic charts provide all the information that is needed for meteorologists to prepare the most accurate weather forecasts possible.

Cold fronts indicate zones of storm clouds and heavy rain.

Steady rain is likely to fall ahead of moving warm fronts.

Occluded fronts show rain and a depression that is dying out.

A vast array of data is used to predict changing weather patterns.

Weather Forecasting

Synoptic charts show how the weather has changed over the past few days. Armed with this knowledge, meteorologists produce prognostic charts. They give a prognosis (or forecast) of what the weather will be like in 24, 36, or 48 hours time. From these charts, meteorologists supply written forecasts to newspapers, radio, and TV stations. Some forecasts are short-range, covering the next 24–36 hours, while extended or long-range forecasts cover five days or more.

Computers are almost always used to produce forecasts, but meteorologists still have an important role to play. Often, they have recent information not available to the computer. They also have the experience to allow for local factors. Forecasting today involves an effective collaboration between skilled people and computers. Short-range forecasts now reach a high level of accuracy. But for all the sophisticated technology available to forecasters, mistakes do occur. For example, a storm may start in an area where there are few stations.

Left Weather maps on TV often use symbols that do not appear on prognostic charts. TV forecast maps are simplified to make them easy to understand at a glance.

Aircraft play a vital part in gathering information—with both special weather planes and commercial flights reporting data.

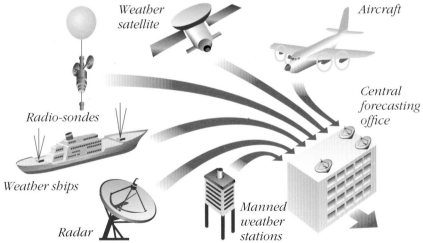

Above Information reaches the weather center from a vast number of sources. This is used to produce forecasts that are supplied to airports, the media, farmers, sailors, and many others affected by the weather.

Weather satellite

Aircraft

Radio-sondes

Central forecasting office

Weather ships

Radar

Manned weather stations

Above The importance of accurate forecasts to the modern world can be judged by the vast technical and human resources put into today's weather centers.

Climate

Kilimanjaro (**left** and **below**) is in Tanzania. It is Africa's highest peak. Mountains can produce a variety of vegetation, as shown below. Kilimanjaro lies near the Equator, and has several vegetation zones.

Alpine tundra

Snow and ice permanently cap Kilimanjaro

Upland moorland

Mountain rainforest

Savannah (tropical grassland)

Weather is the hour-to-hour state of the atmosphere, while climate is the usual, or average, weather of a place. Several factors influence climate. One is latitude, or how close you are to the Equator or to the poles.

Other factors are important. Because temperatures fall with height, by 1 °F for every 300 ft (7 °C for every 1,000 m), mountain tops on the Equator are cold. Mountains also affect rainfall. Slopes facing the wind (windward) are rainier than those sheltered from the wind (leeward).

Climate is also affected by the sea and ocean currents. A warm current called the Gulf Stream flows from the hot Caribbean Sea region to northwestern Europe. Winds that blow on to the shore across this warm current bring mild weather to some regions that would otherwise be much colder. The further you go from the sea, the more extreme the climate. In the heart of a continent, summers are normally hotter, and winters colder, than in coastal regions.

Gulf Stream

Mountains also affect rainfall. Slopes facing prevailing wind get more rain and snow than leeward slopes.

The Gulf Stream brings warm water to Europe's coasts.

The Gulf Stream warms the climate on the west coasts of northwest Europe. This allows semitropical plants to grow in places where it should be too cold for them to survive.

Climatic Regions

There are six main kinds of climate. Polar climates include areas covered by snow and ice. Treeless areas, called tundra, have a short summer when the snow melts and plants grow. Polar regions have little rain or snow.

Cold snowy climates have long winters. Forests of coniferous trees (trees with cones and, usually, hard, needle-like leaves) grow in this climate. Coniferous trees include fir and pine.

Mid-latitude or temperate climates have warm summers and cold to mild winters. Typical trees growing in this climatic zone include ash, beech, and oak. They shed leaves in fall and grow new ones in spring.

Dry climates have an average annual rainfall of less than 10 inches (250 mm). They include deserts and dry grasslands, such as the prairies of North America.

Tropical rainy climates are hot and wet. Dense rainforests grow in places with rain throughout the year. Other areas are wet, but they have a marked dry season. Such areas are often covered by savannah, or tropical grassland with scattered trees.

High mountains contain different zones of climates. Near the Equator, rainforests or savannah may flourish at the base, with polar conditions, where nothing grows, at the very top.

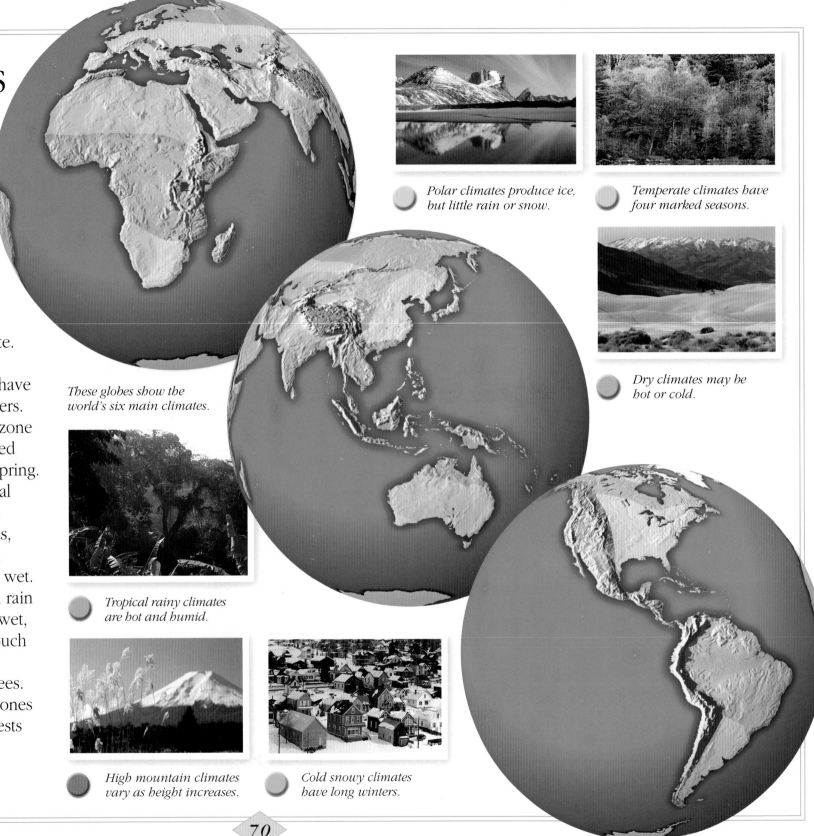

These globes show the world's six main climates.

Polar climates produce ice, but little rain or snow.

Temperate climates have four marked seasons.

Dry climates may be hot or cold.

Tropical rainy climates are hot and humid.

High mountain climates vary as height increases.

Cold snowy climates have long winters.

Have Climates Changed?

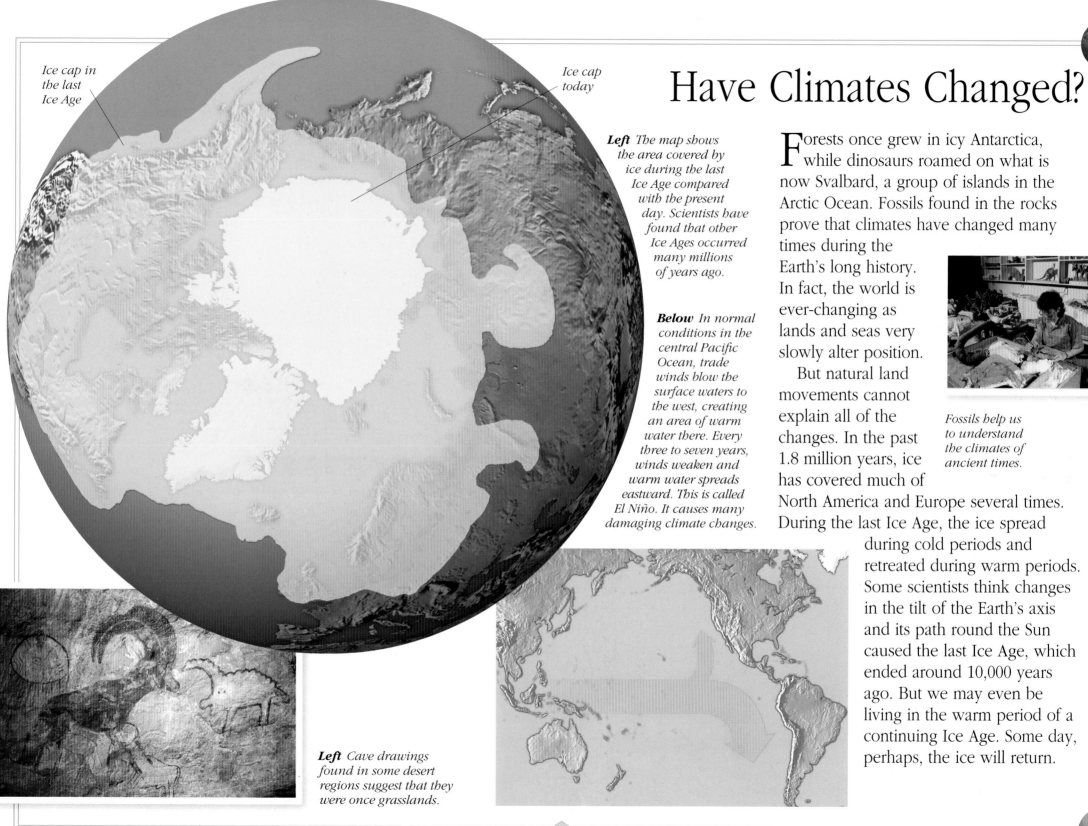

Ice cap in the last Ice Age

Ice cap today

Left *The map shows the area covered by ice during the last Ice Age compared with the present day. Scientists have found that other Ice Ages occurred many millions of years ago.*

Below *In normal conditions in the central Pacific Ocean, trade winds blow the surface waters to the west, creating an area of warm water there. Every three to seven years, winds weaken and warm water spreads eastward. This is called El Niño. It causes many damaging climate changes.*

Left *Cave drawings found in some desert regions suggest that they were once grasslands.*

Forests once grew in icy Antarctica, while dinosaurs roamed on what is now Svalbard, a group of islands in the Arctic Ocean. Fossils found in the rocks prove that climates have changed many times during the Earth's long history. In fact, the world is ever-changing as lands and seas very slowly alter position.

But natural land movements cannot explain all of the changes. In the past 1.8 million years, ice has covered much of North America and Europe several times. During the last Ice Age, the ice spread during cold periods and retreated during warm periods. Some scientists think changes in the tilt of the Earth's axis and its path round the Sun caused the last Ice Age, which ended around 10,000 years ago. But we may even be living in the warm period of a continuing Ice Age. Some day, perhaps, the ice will return.

Fossils help us to understand the climates of ancient times.

Air Pollution

Today, many people think our weather is being changed by human activity. Factories have been powered by wood, coal, oil, and natural gas. They once poured smoke into the air, and many cities suffered from smog (a word made from two words: smoky fog). Most factories now use smokeless fuels, but industry still pours gases into the air, causing air pollution. Some gases are dissolved in water droplets, making acid rain that kills trees and a large number of the living creatures found in rivers and lakes.

Pollution belches from an oil drilling platform at sea.

Chemicals called CFCs have caused a serious problem. They are used in refrigerators and spray cans, and have badly damaged parts of the ozone layer in the stratosphere. This allows more of the Sun's harmful ultraviolet rays to reach the ground.

Above *The burning of forests for agriculture causes major pollution—trees take carbon dioxide from the air, but forest fires create damaging carbon dioxide.*

Above *Vehicles are a major source of pollution.*

In some cities, car exhausts cause severe smog.

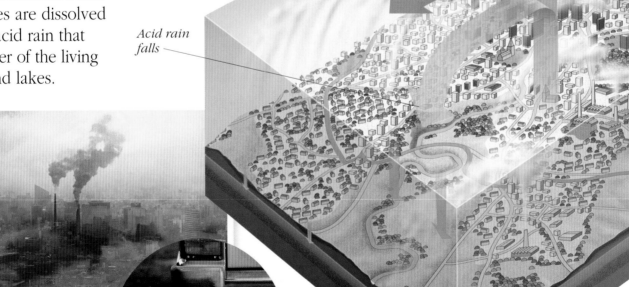

Clouds of moist air

Polluted air rises and mingles with moist clouds

Acid rain falls

Polluted rain soaks into the earth

Main sources of pollution in a developed area are general transport (50%), home heating (16%), industrial pollution (14%) and waste incineration (4%). Air pollution rises and mingles with water in the clouds to form destructive acid rain, and also returns to ground level where it adversely affects air quality for everyone.

Global Warming

Carbon dioxide traps heat rising from the ground, preventing it from escaping into space. This warms the Earth's atmosphere.

Warming increases the amount of water vapor in the air, which absorbs air pollution and leads to heavier rainfall.

Clouds can act as a form of insulation that will prevent heat escaping into space.

Before 1850, carbon dioxide made up 280 parts per million in the atmosphere. By 1990, it had risen to 345 parts per million and was still rising. Computers have predicted that, by 2100, temperatures around the world will have risen by as much as 1.8°F–7.2°F (1°C–4°C). Droughts, heatwaves, and floods will probably become more common.

Carbon dioxide is produced by burning wood, coal, oil, and vegetation.

In 2007, scientists on an international panel stated that planet Earth is warming at a faster rate. They said it was more than 90 percent certain that the warming is caused by factories and cars pumping carbon dioxide into the atmosphere.

Volcanoes also produce greenhouse gases.

Carbon dioxide is a greenhouse gas, along with methane and nitrous oxides (produced by factories and vehicles). Greenhouse gases act rather like the glass in a greenhouse. They let the Sun's heat pass through the atmosphere but prevent it all escaping back into space. As the volume of greenhouse gases in the atmosphere increases, so the temperature of the atmosphere will rise.

Global warming will affect everyone on Earth. Climates will change and sea levels will start to rise. Global warming will also have a great impact on our water, soils, plants, and animals.

Global warming will melt polar ice and raise sea levels. Some islands will then vanish.

Weather Records

Sun and rain

The driest place on Earth is the Atacama Desert in northern Chile. Years often go by with no rain, until a small freak storm occurs. By contrast, Cherrapunji, a village in northeastern India, had a record total rainfall of 1,041.77 inches (26,461 mm) in just one year. The sunniest place in the world is claimed to be southwestern Arizona in the United States.

Left A scientist measures extremely low temperatures in Antarctica.

Left The coldest place on earth is the Antarctic. The sea ice never melts completely, even in the brief summer months.

Cold and hot

The coldest continent is Antarctica. The world's lowest temperature was recorded at Vostok, a Russian research station there. In 1983, a temperature of -89.2°F (-128.6°C) was measured. The highest temperature, 136°F (58°C), was recorded at Al-Aziziyah, near Tripoli in Libya, North Africa.

Even camels feel the heat.

Above The driest place on Earth is the Atacama Desert, Chile, South America.

Above In California's Death Valley, the heat of the Sun evaporates any water, leaving salt behind.

Disasters

Floods often cause great damage.

Floods can occur anywhere—even in some desert areas where flash floods briefly fill dry river beds. The world's worst flood took place in 1887, when the Huang He (Yellow River) burst its banks in China. Nearly a million people died. Bangladesh has regular floods. Some occur when winds drive the sea inland, others when the Brahmaputra, Ganges, and Meghna rivers are swollen by rainwater.

Right In Bangladesh, people are used to dealing with monsoon conditions.

Winds

Right Mount Washington claims the honor of "the world's fastest gust."

The fastest-ever wind speed across the Earth's surface was recorded on the slopes of Mount Washington, in the United States. One gust of wind in April 1934 reached a speed of 231 mph (371 km/h). Gusts of wind that reach 220mph (354 km/h) often occur on Mount Washington. Strong winds can cause great damage, alone or in combination with other types of bad weather.

Left Hanging on for dear life!

Storms

Right Storms are a great hazard to shipping.

In 1988, a hurricane killed more than 350 people in the Caribbean, Mexico, and Texas. It made 750,000 people homeless and caused a massive amount of damage. In 1989, a tornado killed about 1,300 people in Bangladesh. In 1970, a million Bangladeshi people were killed by a tropical cyclone.

Left Global warming poses an increasing threat of flooding in coastal regions.

Above A hailstorm with stones the size of golf balls hit this main street in southern USA, where people know all about violent weather (**right**).

Lightning

Left A lightning strike can be deadly.

Lightning kills about 100 people a year in the United States alone. Lightning struck a former American park ranger named Roy C. Sullivan seven times between 1942 and 1977. He suffered a variety of injuries and his hair was set alight— twice. But he was not killed by any of the strikes.

Right Soccer ball-sized hailstones have fallen in Asia.

Snow and hail

Between February 19, 1971 and February 18, 1972, 1,224.5 inches (31,102 mm) of snow fell at Paradise Ranger Station, Mount Rainier, in the US state of Washington. The largest known hailstones weighed up to 2 lb 3 oz (1 kg). They fell during a storm in Bangladesh in 1986. Reports stated that 92 people were killed.

Chapter 3:
The Angry Earth

Nature can be cruel as well as beneficial to all living things on Planet Earth. Earthquakes and volcanic eruptions reveal the changing nature of our Earth, but they can also kill people and destroy their homes. Extreme weather conditions can also cause havoc in every part of our world.

North America

North America sits on the North American plate. In the west, this plate presses up against three other plates, including the huge Pacific plate. Their collision, from Alaska to Mexico, causes a crumple zone all along the western edge of the continent. The Pacific plate slides underneath this region, scraping and rumbling, causing earthquakes and giant waves (tsunamis).

Icy Arctic winds blow as far south as New York, while the wide open spaces of the Atlantic and the Great Plains give rise to spectacular storms.

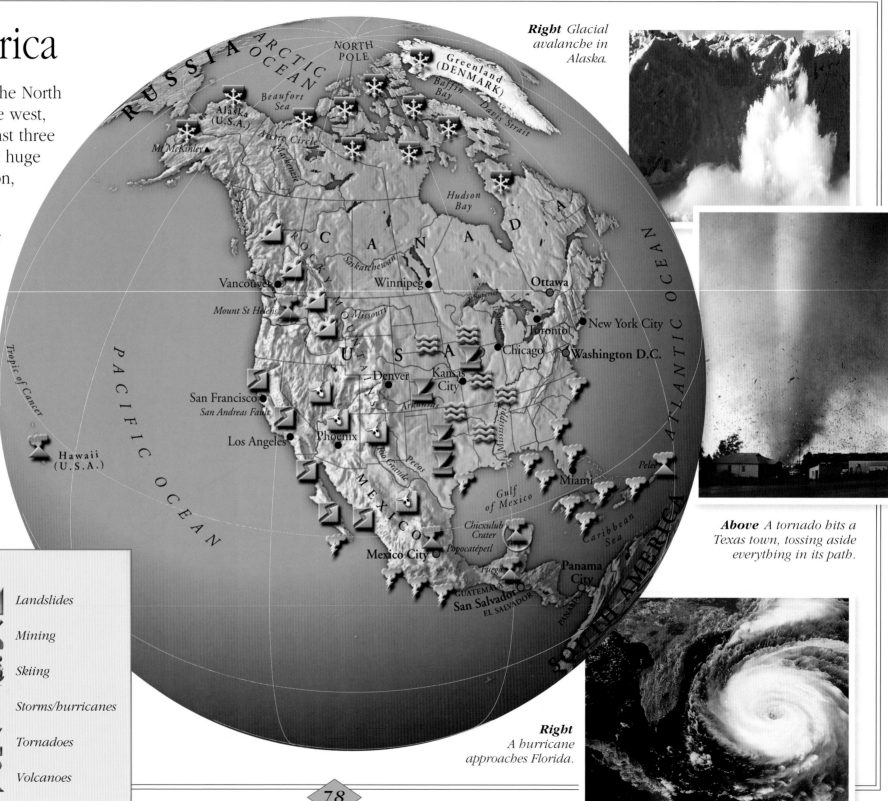

Right *Glacial avalanche in Alaska.*

Above *A tornado hits a Texas town, tossing aside everything in its path.*

Right *A hurricane approaches Florida.*

Key to maps

	Avalanches		*Landslides*
	Blizzards/Ice Storms		*Mining*
	Droughts		*Skiing*
	Earthquakes		*Storms/hurricanes*
	Floods		*Tornadoes*
	Forest Fires		*Volcanoes*

Below *Yellowstone Park is North America's most powerful hotspot. Its eruption, two million years ago, was 3,000 times bigger than Mount St. Helens.*

Volcanoes And Earthquakes

North America has some spectacular volcanic activity, none more so than the eruption of Mount St. Helens in Washington State in 1980. In the spring of that year the volcano began to rumble, a bulge appearing on the side of the volcano. On May 18, an earthquake with a Richter scale rating of 5.1 shook the bulge loose, sending a quarter of the mountain tumbling to the valley. The landslide opened up the volcano, and a huge explosion followed.

Trees were knocked over up to 20 miles (32 km) from the blast, while an ash plume rose 15 miles (24 km) into the sky over a period of nine hours. Within three days, the ash was falling as far away as New York. Fifty-seven people are known to have been killed.

Above *When this massive volcanic peak, 5.5 miles (9 km) across, collapsed, it formed a snowmelt lake (Crater Lake, Oregon) 4,000 feet (1,220 m) deep.*

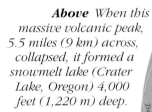

Below ❶ *In May 1980, an earthquake of magnitude 5.1 hit Mount St. Helens, blowing the dome away.* **❷** *The release of trapped magma caused a huge rockslide and avalanche.* **❸** *Over 1,300 feet of the peak was thrown into the air, forming a deep crater.*

(Map labels: RUSSIA, ARCTIC OCEAN, BROOKS RANGE, Mt. McKinley, Arctic Circle, MACKENZIE MTS, NORTH AMERICA, Hudson Bay, ROCKY MOUNTAINS, L. Superior, L. Huron, L. Michigan, APPALACHIAN MTS, ATLANTIC OCEAN, Mount St. Helens, Crater Lake, Yellowstone, GREAT PLAINS, Mt. Elbert, SIERRA MADRE OCCIDENTAL, Tropic of Cancer, PACIFIC OCEAN, Hawaii (U.S.A.), Gulf of Mexico, Pelee, Chicxulub Crater, Caribbean Sea, Popocatepetl, Pico de Orizaba, Fuego, CENTRAL AMERICA, SOUTH AMERICA, Equator)

❶

❷

❸

Earthquakes

Earthquakes are frequent occurrences in North America, and some have caused serious disasters, especially in heavily-populated parts of Central America. The west coast is most vulnerable to earthquakes. The San Andreas Fault is just one of several huge cracks that run deep into the Earth, all along the join between the continental and Pacific plates. Los Angeles and San Francisco are both at risk when these faults slip. In 1906, San Francisco was devastated by an earthquake, followed by a huge fire that burned for several days.

When earthquakes occur further east, shock waves travel hundreds of miles over the more solid rock.

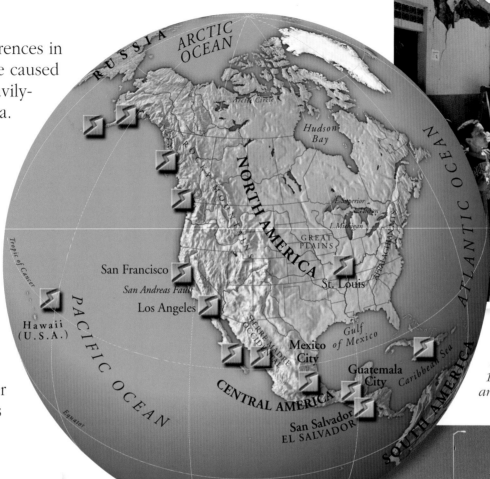

Above *A major quake near El Salvador on January 13, 2001, triggered off around 500 landslides.*

Below *In San Francisco, the 1989 earthquake caused damage to reinforced roadways. Sixty-two people were killed.*

Left *In 1985, an 8.1 Richter tremor, some distance from Mexico City, caused loose earth to liquify (turn to jelly) beneath the city. Even modern buildings collapsed.*

Floods And Storms

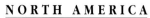

Left
Only complete evacuation of an area will save lives from the devastation a storm surge can cause.

Two main kinds of floods afflict North America. In the gullies and gorges of mountain ranges, flash floods from a single storm can add 20 ft (6 m) to a mountain stream in minutes, turning it into a raging torrent. On the plains, the slow-moving Mississippi can burst its banks and submerge thousands of square miles of farmland.

North America is also battered by hurricanes from the Atlantic that collect huge storm surges—bulges of sea water up to 30 ft (9 m) higher than normal sea level—which lash the eastern and southern coasts. Hurricanes are rotating storm systems, often hundreds of miles across, with a low pressure "eye" in the center. Strong winds pile waves on top of each other. Storm surges account for about half of all hurricane deaths in North America.

The west coast doesn't escape either. The Pacific coast has been swamped by tidal waves (tsunamis) in the recent past.

Above *In 2005, floods caused by Hurricane Katrina in New Orleans killed 1,383 people. It was the most costly natural disaster in the history of the United States.*

Left *In 1992, Hurricane Andrew left a trail of devastation as it moved through Florida.*

Right *A boat is deposited in a field in Florida, showing the awesome power of a hurricane.*

Tornado Alley

The Great Plains of midwestern America are plagued by whirling, twisting vortexes of 200-mph (320-kph) winds called tornadoes. Sweeping across the country like huge vacuum cleaners, they suck up and scatter houses, cars, trains, and people. About 1,000 of these storms hit America's "Tornado Alley" every year. In March 1925, the most destructive tornado ever recorded plowed 219 miles (352 km) from Missouri to Indiana. It killed 689 people, plucked chickens bare, and destroyed a restaurant with a flying cow.

When rains fail, the soil of the Great Plains is swept up into giant dust storms by strong winds, suffocating birds in mid-flight, and causing thousands of deaths as a result of breathing the choking dust.

Above *A tornado heads towards a cornfield. The rising air creates a bulge, or dome, in the top of the cloud.*

Right *Houses in north-central Kentucky are devastated by a tornado. The debris spreads over the surrounding area.*

Right *A tornado begins to form in Pampa, Texas.*

Left *During the great Dust Bowl storms of the 1930s, the inhabitants of the Great Plains sometimes thought it was the end of the world. The sun could be blotted out as far away as New York.*

Left An adjustable avalanche warning sign on display at the Waterton-Glacier International Peace Park in the Rocky Mountains, an area prone to avalanches. The Park spills over into Canada from Montana.

Fire And Ice

North America stretches from the hot tropics of Mexico to the freezing Arctic Circle of northern Canada. The extremes between these temperatures are increased by special features, such as the mountain ranges along the west coast.

The snow-capped Rockies are prone to blizzards and avalanches—up to 100,000 every year. Blizzards are also caused by icy blasts from the Arctic. One weather pattern over the Great Lakes produces powerful blizzards that sweep southward, burying New York City and other cities.

To the south and west, prolonged droughts and blazing sunshine can combine to turn plant life into dry kindling—just waiting for a lightning strike to spark a raging forest fire. In Yellowstone Park in 1988, a drought was followed by a fire that obliterated 2,200 square miles (5,670 sq km) of forest, leaving just ash and cinders.

Above Power lines are downed by an ice storm in North Dakota. In some areas, people can be left without power for weeks.

Right New York City is frequently hit by severe blizzards. The notorious blizzard of 1888 brought the city to a standstill. Here, a team of snowplows clears Manhattan's Times Square after a blizzard.

Right A forest fire rages through Boise National Forest in Idaho, destroying everything in its path. Both plant and animal life are threatened. Forest fires can reduce large areas to ash and cinders.

South America

The 5,500-mile (8,850-km) long Andes mountain range follows South America's west coast, rising to heights of more than 20,000 feet (6,100 m). Tucked among its peaks are hundreds of volcanoes. This area is also a major earthquake zone.

One of the world's driest spots, the Atacama Desert, is also to the west. It is a cool desert; temperatures rarely reach 68 °F (20 °C). When rains do occur, they cause flash floods because the water cannot sink into the baked, salty land.

In the east, floods are more common as the mighty Amazon meanders through the world's largest tropical rainforest.

ATLANTIC OCEAN

Tropic of Cancer

Caribbean Sea

Caracas

VENEZUELA

GUYANA

SURINAM

French Guiana

GUIANA HIGHLANDS

Nevado del Ruiz

Bogotá

COLOMBIA

Quito

Chimborazo

Putumayo

Negro

Amazon

Amazon

AMAZON BASIN

Madeira

ECUADOR

Equator

PERU

BRAZIL

MATO GROSSO PLATEAU

BRAZILIAN HIGHLANDS

Nevado Huascarán

Lima

ANDES

BOLIVIA

La Paz

Nevado Sajama

Paraná

PARAGUAY

Rio de Janeiro

São Paulo

PACIFIC OCEAN

Tropic of Capricorn

ATACAMA DESERT

CHILE

Cerro Ojos del Salado

URUGUAY

Cerro Aconcagua

PAMPAS

Santiago

ARGENTINA

Buenos Aires

PATAGONIA

TIERRA DEL FUEGO

ATLANTIC OCEAN

Antarctic Circle

Above In the mountainous Altiplano region of Chile, high in the Andes, llamas graze on the sandy grasslands.

Below The growing population of Rio de Janeiro is crammed into shanty towns, making them more vulnerable to earthquakes.

Left The Atacama Desert is protected from rain-bearing clouds by mountains.

Volcanoes And Earthquakes

The western part of South America lies along an area of intense volcanic activity—the Pacific Ring of Fire. Its volcanoes have formed along the plate boundary where the Nazca oceanic plate is disappearing under the South American continental plate. The continent's major volcanoes are concentrated in Colombia, Ecuador, Peru, and Chile. They include Cotopaxi in Ecuador (the world's highest active volcano) and the Nevado del Ruiz in Colombia. These remote volcanoes do not cause great loss of life, but they can still cause disasters, by killing grazing cattle and poisoning water. Earthquake activity is also centered on the Andes. South America's most serious quake was the Callejon de Huaylas quake that struck Peru in May 1970. Around 66,800 people were killed, with many more missing.

Above Vapor rising from the Guagua Pichincha volcano, located just 7.5 miles (12 km) from Ecuador's capital city. In September 1999, the government closed off access to the volcano, declaring an "orange" alert, as the volcano was expected to erupt in a matter of days or weeks.

Below Easter 1982: a nun surveys the damage caused to the interior of a church by an earthquake in Popayán, Columbia.

Right The crater formed by the eruption of Guagua Pichincha in Ecuador.

Map labels:
Tropic of Cancer
VENEZUELA
GUYANA
SURINAM
French Guiana
Nevado del Ruiz
Armenia
Tolima
COLOMBIA
Guagua Pichincha
Cotopaxi
Purace
GUIANA HIGHLANDS
Tungurahua
El Misti
AMAZON BASIN
Amazon
ECUADOR
Sangay
PERU
Equator
Callejon de Huaylas
BRAZIL
PACIFIC OCEAN
Guallatiri
BOLIVIA
PARAGUAY
Parana
Tropic of Capricorn
Lascar
CHILE
ANDES
ATACAMA DESERT
ARGENTINA
URUGUAY
Tupungatito
Llaima
Villarrica
Copahue
ATLANTIC OCEAN
Hudson
TIERRA DEL FUEGO
Antarctic Circle

Sliding Lands

The landslides and avalanches that occur frequently in South America turn into major disasters when they hit over-populated shanty towns. Another problem is deforestation (chopping down trees). When no roots bind the soil, a mountainside may slip in heavy rains, or after an earthquake. This happened in the Peruvian region of Yungay in 1970, and 17,500 people died.

The world's worst mudslide happened when Nevado del Ruiz erupted in 1985. The town of Armero had been built in the likely path of volcanic mudflows and 23,000 people were killed.

Peru has suffered some of the Andes' worst avalanches. One at Huarás in 1941 killed 5,000 people, while 3,500 died in 1971 at Nevado de Huascarán.

Right In 1970, the Yungay landslide in Peru followed in the wake of the Callejón de Huaylas quake and widespread flooding. In total 70,000 people were killed.

Above Mudslides engulf homes and buildings along the Caribbean coast of Venezuela in December 1999. There were between 200–300 dead and 7,000 missing.

Left The Andes have rich reserves of gold, copper, and tin, but mining makes mountains prone to landslides. A landslide in Bolivia in 1992 killed nearly 1,000 miners.

Right Torrential rains, in Venezuela caused mudslides which swept away homes and property. Over 30,000 people were killed.

Wild Waters

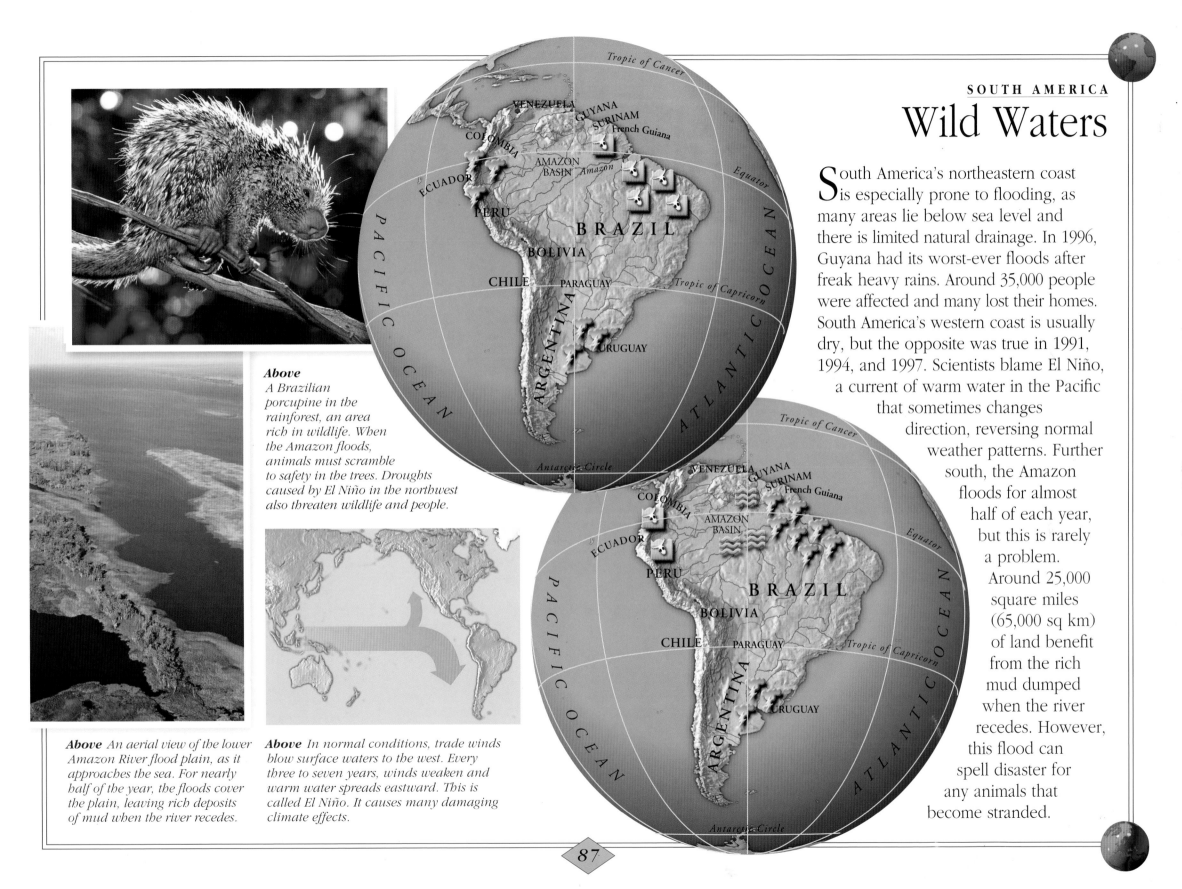

Above
*A Brazilian
porcupine in the
rainforest, an area
rich in wildlife. When
the Amazon floods,
animals must scramble
to safety in the trees. Droughts
caused by El Niño in the northwest
also threaten wildlife and people.*

Above *An aerial view of the lower
Amazon River flood plain, as it
approaches the sea. For nearly
half of the year, the floods cover
the plain, leaving rich deposits
of mud when the river recedes.*

Above *In normal conditions, trade winds
blow surface waters to the west. Every
three to seven years, winds weaken and
warm water spreads eastward. This is
called El Niño. It causes many damaging
climate effects.*

South America's northeastern coast
is especially prone to flooding, as
many areas lie below sea level and
there is limited natural drainage. In 1996,
Guyana had its worst-ever floods after
freak heavy rains. Around 35,000 people
were affected and many lost their homes.
South America's western coast is usually
dry, but the opposite was true in 1991,
1994, and 1997. Scientists blame El Niño,
a current of warm water in the Pacific
that sometimes changes
direction, reversing normal
weather patterns. Further
south, the Amazon
floods for almost
half of each year,
but this is rarely
a problem.
Around 25,000
square miles
(65,000 sq km)
of land benefit
from the rich
mud dumped
when the river
recedes. However,
this flood can
spell disaster for
any animals that
become stranded.

Europe

Despite the potential dangers of the snow-covered peaks of the Alps and the Pyrenees, and the bubbling geysers of Iceland, Europe's biggest calamities are usually caused by people: the nuclear reactor melt-down in Chernobyl in 1986, or the oil spill of the Amoco Cadiz. In the west of Europe, damp air blows in from the Atlantic Ocean, and may dump several inches of rain in a few hours, causing floods and even dam bursts.

In the south, problems more often come from the heat, and from the slow collision between the African and European plates, causing earthquakes and volcanic activity.

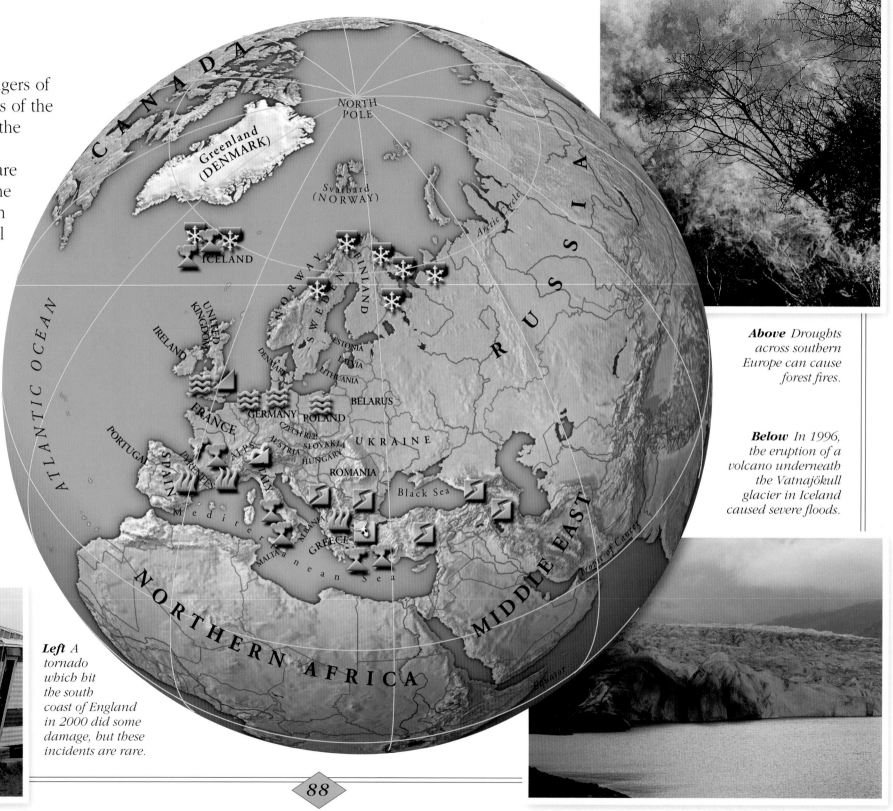

Left A tornado which hit the south coast of England in 2000 did some damage, but these incidents are rare.

Above Droughts across southern Europe can cause forest fires.

Below In 1996, the eruption of a volcano underneath the Vatnajökull glacier in Iceland caused severe floods.

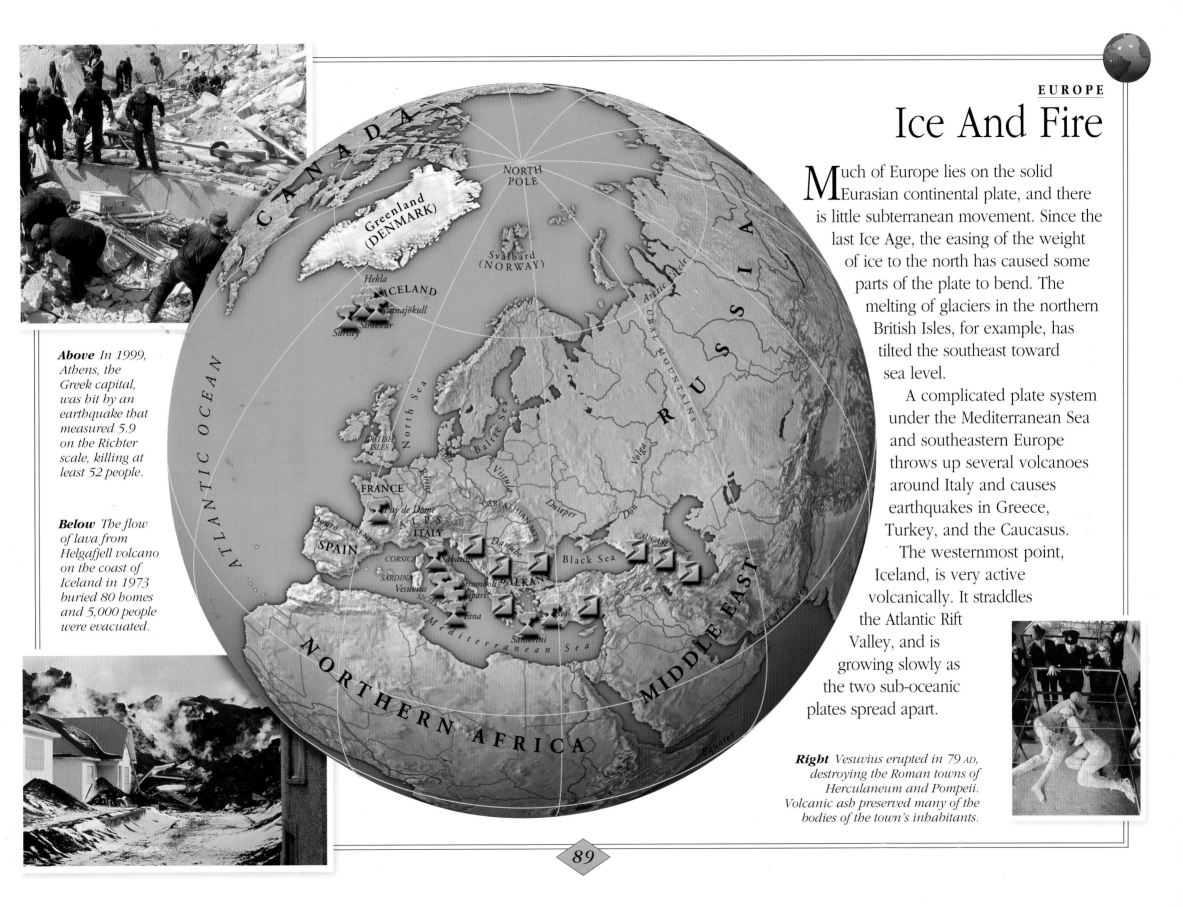

Ice And Fire

Much of Europe lies on the solid Eurasian continental plate, and there is little subterranean movement. Since the last Ice Age, the easing of the weight of ice to the north has caused some parts of the plate to bend. The melting of glaciers in the northern British Isles, for example, has tilted the southeast toward sea level.

A complicated plate system under the Mediterranean Sea and southeastern Europe throws up several volcanoes around Italy and causes earthquakes in Greece, Turkey, and the Caucasus.

The westernmost point, Iceland, is very active volcanically. It straddles the Atlantic Rift Valley, and is growing slowly as the two sub-oceanic plates spread apart.

Above *In 1999, Athens, the Greek capital, was hit by an earthquake that measured 5.9 on the Richter scale, killing at least 52 people.*

Below *The flow of lava from Helgafjell volcano on the coast of Iceland in 1973 buried 80 homes and 5,000 people were evacuated.*

Right *Vesuvius erupted in 79 AD, destroying the Roman towns of Herculaneum and Pompeii. Volcanic ash preserved many of the bodies of the town's inhabitants.*

CANADA
Greenland (DENMARK)
NORTH POLE
Svalbard (NORWAY)
Hekla
ICELAND
Vatnajökull
Strokkur
Surtsey
RUSSIA
Arctic Circle
URAL MOUNTAINS
ATLANTIC OCEAN
North Sea
Baltic Sea
BRITISH ISLES
Volga
FRANCE
Elbe
Rhine
Vistula
Puy de Dôme
PYRENEES
ALPS
Douro
SPAIN
ITALY
CARPATHIAN MTS
Danube
Dnieper
Don
CAUCASUS
CORSICA
Sabatini
Black Sea
SARDINIA
Vesuvius
Stromboli
Lipari
BALKANS
SICILY
Etna
Kos
MIDDLE EAST
Mediterranean Sea
Santorini
Tropic of Cancer
NORTHERN AFRICA
Equator

Floods

Europe has faced severe flooding in the past. As well as flash floods in mountainous regions, there have been many estuary-type floods around large rivers.

Although floods seemed to be more frequent than ever before in France, Germany, and the UK in the 2000s, reliable records are not available for previous centuries. A study of stalagtites in caves in western England suggests that floods in the past were more severe.

In the south, snowmelt and flash floods are the biggest danger. Deep snow on mountains may melt for some time before breaking through ice and racing down narrow gorges.

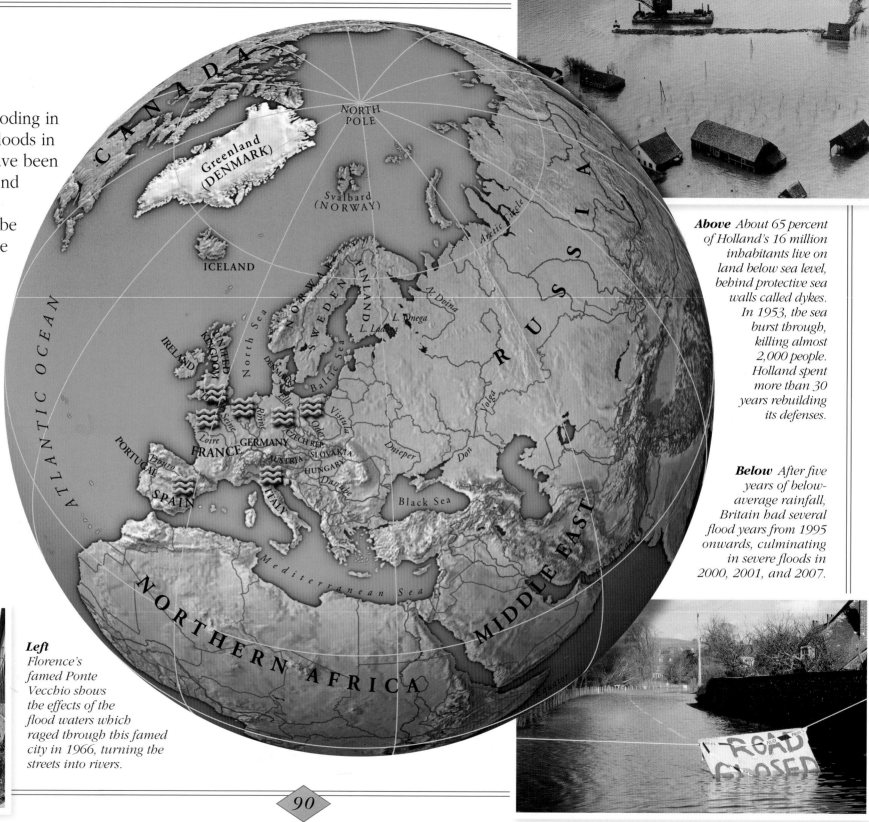

Above *About 65 percent of Holland's 16 million inhabitants live on land below sea level, behind protective sea walls called dykes. In 1953, the sea burst through, killing almost 2,000 people. Holland spent more than 30 years rebuilding its defenses.*

Below *After five years of below-average rainfall, Britain had several flood years from 1995 onwards, culminating in severe floods in 2000, 2001, and 2007.*

Left
Florence's famed Ponte Vecchio shows the effects of the flood waters which raged through this famed city in 1966, turning the streets into rivers.

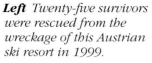

Left *Twenty-five survivors were rescued from the wreckage of this Austrian ski resort in 1999.*

Below *The eastern coast of England is very susceptible to erosion, as it is battered by violent seas for much of the year. In June 1993, a cliffside hotel near Scarborough in the northeast slid into the sea when erosion caused a landslide.*

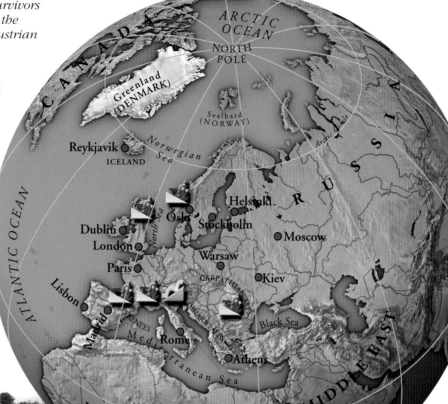

Deadly Slopes

Alpine slopes attract millions of visitors in midwinter to ski, snowboard, and take in the clear, sunny skies. But the Alps also have quite a record for avalanche disasters—up to 150 tourists die in avalanches each year.

In 1999, there were deadly avalanches in the Austrian villages of Galtür and Valzur, and the Swiss village of Wengen. Rain fell on the mountains and loosened the thick sheets of snow. The two Austrian resorts were completely cut off by the avalanches. As they happened during a blizzard, not even helicopters could reach the survivors. It took days to dig the buildings out from underneath 16.4 ft (5 m) of snow. While avalanches are confined to a few snowy peaks dotted around Europe, slopes can bring other problems: from dramatic rock-plunges from the cliffs of eastern England, to suffocating mudflows from volcanic hillsides in southern Italy.

Asia

Asia, the biggest continent, has a wide range of climates and conditions. The far north has sub-zero temperatures for much of the year. Dry, desert regions contrast with stretches of wet, tropical forests in the south. Across southern Asia, the rainy season produces widespread flooding, but millions of people continue to live on low-lying flood plains. Asia sits mostly on the Eurasian, Arabian, and Indian plates. To the east, it forms part of the Pacific Ring of Fire, while numerous small fault lines dotted across the continent cause earthquakes. Seismic activity causes tsunamis, like the one that devasated coastal areas in southern Asia in 2004.

Above *Traffic keeps moving in Tamil Nadu, India, despite the monsoon floods, which affect large areas of southern Asia.*

Below *On Boxing day in 2004, a tsunami caused by an earthquake, in the Indian Ocean killed over 230,000 people.*

Left *An asteroid or comet impact at Tunguska in Siberia in 1908 had the force of 2,000 Hiroshima bombs.*

Map labels

ARCTIC OCEAN

EUROPE

RUSSIA

Arctic Circle

URAL MTS.

Ob
Irtysh
Yenisey
Lena
Kolyma

S I B E R I A

Yakutsk

Sea of Okhotsk

KAZAKHSTAN

Novosibirsk

Site of asteroid impact, 1908

Irkutsk
Lake Baykal

Tbilisi
Caspian Sea
Aral Sea
Lake Balkhash

Baghdad
Tehran
Tashkent

IRANIAN PLATEAU
ZAGROS MTS.
Communism Peak
PAMIRS
TIAN SHAN
HINDU KUSH
TAKLIMAKAN DESERT

MONGOLIA
PLATEAU OF MONGOLIA
GOBI DESERT

Vladivostok

NORTH KOREA

Sea of Japan

SOUTH KOREA

JAPAN

Tokyo
HONSHU

Beijing

Huang He

PACIFIC OCEAN

East China Sea

Tropic of Cancer
AR RUB' AL KHALI

PAKISTAN
THAR DESERT
Indus

C H I N A

PLATEAU OF TIBET
Mt. Everest
HIMALAYAS

Chang Jiang (Yangtze)

RYUKYU ISLANDS (JAPAN)

Karachi
Delhi

Arabian Sea
Gujarat

I N D I A

Ganges

MYANMAR (BURMA)
Mekong

Hong Kong

HAINAN

Philippine Sea

Mumbai (Bombay)

Kolkata (Calcutta)
Bay of Bengal
Irrawaddy

THAILAND
Bangkok

PHILIPPINES

SRI LANKA
Colombo

South China Sea

INDIAN OCEAN

Equator

SUMATRA

BORNEO

JAVA

New Guinea

Jakarta

Mountains Of Fire

Left *Fuji, on the main Japanese island of Honshu, has erupted 16 times. The last time was in 1707.*

The eastern edge of the Eurasian plate is part of the Pacific Ring of Fire and there are hundreds of volcanoes along this boundary. In the north, the Kamchatka peninsula has 22 active volcanoes. When Bezymianny erupted here in 1956, its mudflows extended for 40 miles (80 km). The islands of Japan are home to Sakurajima, one of the most active volcanoes on Earth. More volcanoes are to be found in the Philippines, while Indonesia has over 50. When Krakatoa erupted in Indonesia in 1883, it threw out more than 1,300 cubic yards (10 cubic km) of magma, and the explosions were heard 2,800 miles (4,500 km) away. The eruption caused a giant tidal wave and 36,000 people on Java and Sumatra died.

Above *When Tambora, Indonesia, erupted in 1815, it caused the deaths of 92,000 people.*

Below *A village house on Java sits between the active Merapi and another active volcano on Java.*

Below *The volcano of Sakurajima in Japan erupts about 150 times a year.*

Earthquakes

Many destructive earthquakes happen in Japan, where there are about 5,000 tremors a year. Other hotspots include northern India, where the Indian plate meets the Eurasian plate, and Iran and Turkey, on the boundary with the Arabian plate. In December 2003, 26,000 people died after an earthquake measuring 6.9 on the Richter scale hit Bam in southern Iran. In May 2006, a quake killed over 6,000 people on the island of Java, Indonesia. The worst earthquake disaster, at Tangshan in China in 1976, was caused by stress in the middle of the Eurasian plate. At least 655,000 people died.

Right Long sections of the expressway were twisted by an earthquake that shook Kobe, Japan, in 1995, causing millions of dollars of damage and killing 6,430 people.

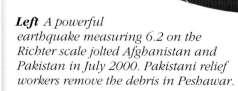

Left A powerful earthquake measuring 6.2 on the Richter scale jolted Afghanistan and Pakistan in July 2000. Pakistani relief workers remove the debris in Peshawar.

Right An office building shows cracks after the Kobe earthquake in 1995. Many parts of the city were razed to the ground.

Storms And Floods

Left Flood victims in Bangladesh's western Kushtia district wade through waist-high water in September 2000. The floods killed at least 70 people and left more than a million homeless.

In much of southern Asia, people depend on the summer monsoons; winds that bring rains that water the crops. But in 2000, monsoon winds bought the worst floods in a century to India and Bangladesh. In flood conditions, water-borne diseases, from upset stomachs to cholera, are the main danger. In the first two weeks of the 2000 floods, 30,000 people in West Bengal suffered from diarrhea. This region is also lashed by tropical storms. The worst typhoon hit Bangladesh in 1970. Winds of 140 mph (240 kph) whipped up a tidal wave 49 feet (15 m) high and nearly half a million people died. Asia has its share of freak storms, too, like the 1989 tornado in Shaturia, Bangladesh that killed 1,300 people.

Below This is the Huang He (Yellow River), China's second-longest river. When it burst its banks in 1887, around 900,000 people lost their lives. Melting snow from Tibet, and monsoon rains, still flood the Huang He regularly.

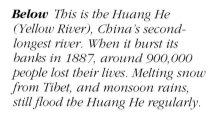

Right According to the Bible, there was a Great Flood in ancient times. Many people believe that Noah's ark ended up here, on Mount Ararat in Turkey.

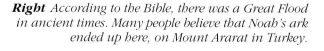

When The Rains Fail

The world's worst-ever drought happened in Asia in the 1870s, when northern China went without rain for three years and over 10 million people died. China still suffers droughts today. The Huang He River, famous for its floods, often dries up, threatening the livelihoods of the 52 million Chinese who depend on it. In summer 1997, the Huang He's lower reaches stayed dry for nearly five months.

Many parts of Asia are desert, but even the parts that expect a rainy season sometimes have droughts when the monsoons fail to bring rains—as happened in 1997 and 1998, when El Niño caused droughts in many parts of Asia, Africa, and South America. In Indonesia and Malaysia, tinder-dry forests caught fire and blazed for months. A thick, suffocating smog hospitalized more than 40,000 people with breathing problems.

Above Droughts in the Thar Desert in Pakistan since 1996 have killed over a third of the cattle, wiping out the livelihoods of nomadic herders.

Left and below Over 500,000 people from the state of Orissa in India were forced from their homes by the 1998 drought.

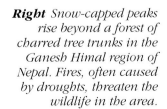

Right Snow-capped peaks rise beyond a forest of charred tree trunks in the Ganesh Himal region of Nepal. Fires, often caused by droughts, threaten the wildlife in the area.

Snow, Avalanches, And Landslides

Northern Asia is dominated by the bleak region of Siberia, which is one of the coldest places on Earth. Temperatures may drop as low as −90 °F (−68 °C), but the climate is mostly too dry for snow. Northern China, on the other hand, suffers from sub-zero temperatures and snow. In January 2001, temperatures of −40 °F (−40 °C) were recorded in Inner Mongolia. At least 180,000 people were affected, many losing their precious sheep, cattle, or horses. Avalanches in the Himalayas are common, but in such remote areas they rarely affect people's lives. In 1978, in the Pin Valley of Spiti, India, an avalanche dammed a river, causing flash flooding.

Above *This mudslide was one of many that happened on the islands of Leyte and Negros in the Philippines in 1991. Typhoon rain soaked the soil on the mountain slopes, causing it to slip away.*

Above *Rockslides on bare, rocky mountains, like this one on the Karakoram Highway in 1980, block roads and railways.*

Left *Wranglers round up yaks on a cold winter day. Winter blizzards in northern China were so extreme in 2001 that horses froze to death where they stood.*

97

Africa

The African continent is dry and dusty in the north, with a steamy tropical rainforest belt across the middle, and open, fertile land to the south. It was once attached to South America, but 225 million years ago, a great split occurred, caused by the mid-Atlantic Rift, which is still forcing the continents apart. Africa itself has suffered only a few volcanic upheavals. Natural disasters in Africa are more often brought about by severe weather.

Drought is Africa's most serious problem, because the people rely closely on their crops, and crop failures cause famine. Too much water can also bring trouble. Floods spoil crops, threaten livestock, devastate homes, and destroy infrastructure, such as bridges. They can also spread water-borne disease.

Right Hot spring at Lake Bogoria, Kenya.

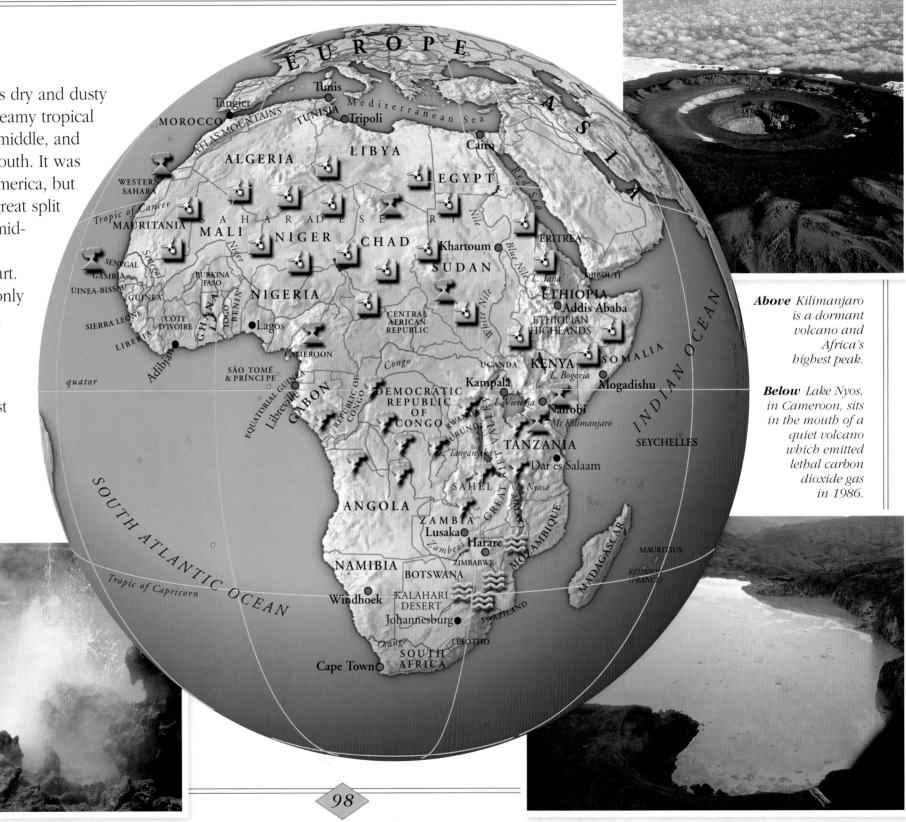

Above Kilimanjaro is a dormant volcano and Africa's highest peak.

Below Lake Nyos, in Cameroon, sits in the mouth of a quiet volcano which emitted lethal carbon dioxide gas in 1986.

Extreme Weather

Right Humans hug the ground to avoid the choking and blinding sand whipped up by Saharan winds.

Below The desert is spreading south as a result of deforestation and the over-exploitation of the land.

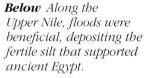

Left A hippo bathes in water and finds relief from the baking sun in Africa.

Below Along the Upper Nile, floods were beneficial, depositing the fertile silt that supported ancient Egypt.

Although most of Africa is warm, only a central belt running below the western bulge and across central Africa enjoys lush, tropical rainforest conditions. In northern Africa, the Sahara Desert bakes under the hot sun, reaching temperatures of 122 °F (50 °C) by day, and freezing at night. Rain may not fall here for years at a time.

Increasing rainfall attracted farmers to the southern fringe of the Sahara, called the "Sahel" (shoreline). But in 1967, a drought turned the land back to desert, and an estimated 400,000 people died from starvation. The desert is gradually spreading south—a result of drought, deforestation, and over-exploitation of the land. While the Sahara bakes, other parts of Africa drown. In Mozambique, massive floods in 2000 and 2001 killed thousands of livestock and swept away precious roads, farms, and bridges, requiring a large-scale, international rescue effort.

Australasia

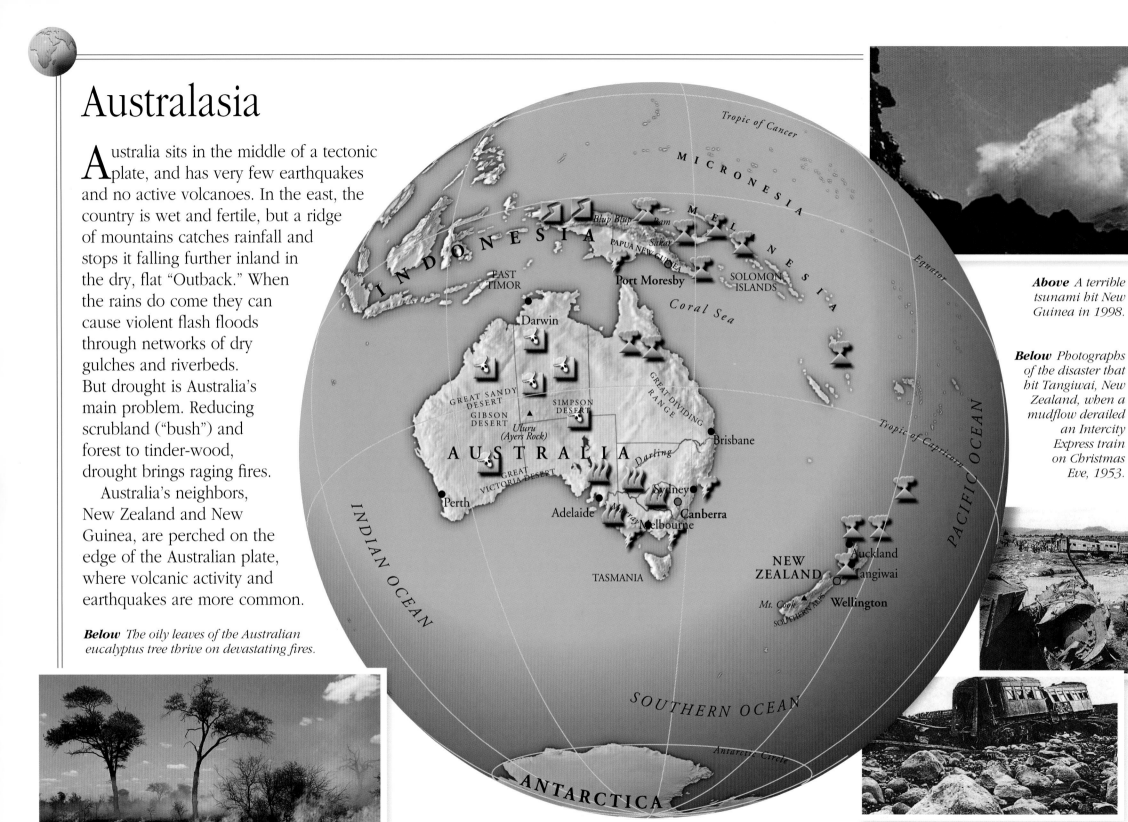

Australia sits in the middle of a tectonic plate, and has very few earthquakes and no active volcanoes. In the east, the country is wet and fertile, but a ridge of mountains catches rainfall and stops it falling further inland in the dry, flat "Outback." When the rains do come they can cause violent flash floods through networks of dry gulches and riverbeds. But drought is Australia's main problem. Reducing scrubland ("bush") and forest to tinder-wood, drought brings raging fires.

Australia's neighbors, New Zealand and New Guinea, are perched on the edge of the Australian plate, where volcanic activity and earthquakes are more common.

Below *The oily leaves of the Australian eucalyptus tree thrive on devastating fires.*

Above *A terrible tsunami hit New Guinea in 1998.*

Below *Photographs of the disaster that hit Tangiwai, New Zealand, when a mudflow derailed an Intercity Express train on Christmas Eve, 1953.*

Map labels

Tropic of Cancer

MICRONESIA

MELANESIA

INDONESIA

Equator

Blup Blup · Bam

Sakar

PAPUA NEW GUINEA

EAST TIMOR

Port Moresby

SOLOMON ISLANDS

Coral Sea

Darwin

GREAT DIVIDING RANGE

GREAT SANDY DESERT

GIBSON DESERT

SIMPSON DESERT

Uluru (Ayers Rock)

AUSTRALIA

GREAT VICTORIA DESERT

Darling

Brisbane

Perth

Murray

Adelaide

Sydney

Canberra

Melbourne

PACIFIC OCEAN

Tropic of Capricorn

Auckland

NEW ZEALAND

Tangiwai

TASMANIA

INDIAN OCEAN

Mt. Cook **Wellington**

SOUTHERN ALPS

SOUTHERN OCEAN

Antarctic Circle

ANTARCTICA

Antarctica

ATLANTIC OCEAN

Scotia Sea

Antarctic Circle

Limit of summer pack ice

SOUTH AMERICA

Weddell Sea

LARSEN ICE SHELF

FILCHNER ICE SHELF

RONNE ICE SHELF

PENSACOLA MTS.

Vinson Massif

ELLSWORTH MTS.

Bellingshausen Sea

Limit of summer pack ice

SOUTH POLE

Vostok Station (Russia)

TRANSANTARCTIC MOUNTAINS

GETZ ICE SHELF

Amundsen Sea

QUEEN MAUD MTS.

Mt. Kirkpatrick

ROSS ICE SHELF

Mt. Erebus

Ross Sea

PACIFIC OCEAN

Limit of summer pack ice

NEW ZEALAND

PRINCE CHARLES MTS.

LAMBERT GLACIER

AMERY ICE SHELF

WEST ICE SHELF

SHACKLETON ICE SHELF

INDIAN OCEAN

KERGUELEN IS. (FRANCE)

Limit of summer pack ice

Above *Icebergs are floating lumps of freshwater ice that have broken off a glacier. When they float out to sea, they pose a real danger to shipping.*

Left *Mount Erebus, 12,500 feet (3,810 m) above sea level, on Ross Island, Antarctica, is the southernmost active volcano.*

Antarctica is the coldest and most dangerous continent of all. In the skies overhead, a layer of ozone gases in the atmosphere has disappeared over recent years, flooding the area with harmful ultraviolet rays.

Most of the continent is frozen solid. At the edges, large glacial slabs break apart and crash into the sea, causing waves that could sink a small ship. About 70 percent of the world's fresh water is locked in the ice floes.

The biggest disasters are caused by freezing temperatures, ice storms, and fierce blizzards. In 1983, the Russian research base, Vostok, recorded the lowest temperature ever encountered on Earth: –128 °F (–89.2 °C).

Below *Research scientists are the only permanent population of Antarctica.*

Chapter 4:
Discovery And Exploration

Just over 500 years ago, the voyages of Christopher Columbus opened up a New World to the people of Europe. Human beings have an urge to find out what is beyond the horizon. Our curiosity has given us a deep knowledge of our Planet Earth, we have now begun the exploration of space.

Great General And Explorer

Alexander the Great was only 20 years old when he became King of the Greek kingdom of Macedonia in 336 BC. After suppressing rebellions at home, he turned to the huge Persian Empire of Darius III, which had dominated the ancient world for over two centuries.

In 334 BC he invaded the Persian Empire. Although he had far fewer men, Alexander used his superior tactical skills in a succession of battles, finally defeating Darius at Gaugamela in 331 BC. Alexander continued ever further eastward, battling nomadic warriors on the northeastern fringes of the known world. In 327 BC he began his assault on India, but within two years his weary troops had forced him to turn back. By the time he reached

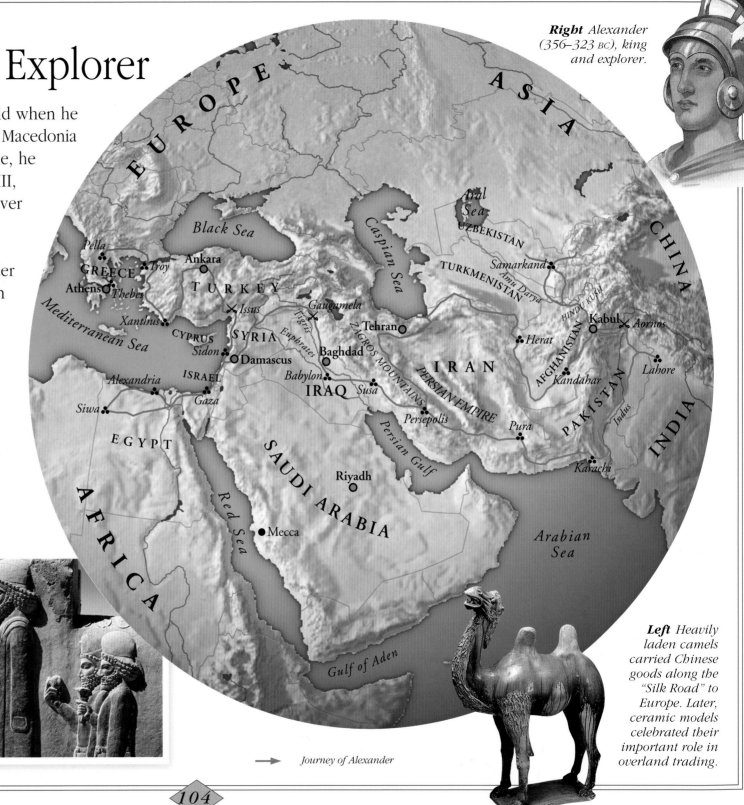

Right Alexander (356–323 BC), king and explorer.

→ Journey of Alexander

Left Heavily laden camels carried Chinese goods along the "Silk Road" to Europe. Later, ceramic models celebrated their important role in overland trading.

EASTERN ADVENTURER

Chang Ch'ien was an ambassador of the Chinese emperor who was sent to Bactria (Afghanistan) in 138 BC to seek allies against the fierce, nomadic Huns. Captured by the enemy, he was held prisoner for ten years before he escaped and returned to China through Tibet. His mission brought China into contact with Central Asia and the Middle East, and opened new trade routes, such as the "Silk Road" to Persia.

Right Persepolis, the symbolic center of Persia, has carved reliefs showing subjects bringing tribute to the emperor. In 330 BC Alexander's troops put the city to the torch.

Pioneering Seafarer

Around 300 BC, the geographer Pytheas of Massalia (modern-day Marseilles) was the first Greek to visit the British Isles and Europe's Atlantic coast. His account of his voyages has been lost, but is referred to by later writers.

Pytheas was curious to find the reputed source of tin. He eventually reached Cornwall and visited the tin mines there, as well as an island called Ictis (probably St. Michael's Mount). He sailed on along the west coast of Britain and accurately estimated the length of its coastline at 4,000 miles (6,437 km). Sailing across the North Sea, possibly as far as the Baltic, he discovered a source of amber, in either the Elbe estuary, or Denmark.

WORLD'S FIRST GAZETTEER

The greatest ancient geographer, Ptolemy of Alexandria, lived around AD 140. His *Guide to Geography* contained maps and the world's first geographical gazetteer, but his map grid was based mainly on guesswork and was inaccurate. Despite this, up until the mid-1570s, explorers continued to use his calculations, causing Columbus, for example, to hugely underestimate the distance from Asia to Europe.

→ Route of Pytheas

⋯⋯► Conjectural route

Above *The island Pytheas called "Thule" was six days' journey from Scotland.*

This land of the midnight sun was probably Iceland or one of the Shetland Islands.

Right *Ptolemy (c. 90–168 AD) astronomer and geographer.*

Below *Greek ships were powered by oar and sail. Navigational knowledge was very limited. Pytheas was an experienced seafarer, but his journey took him along coasts where he had no knowledge of the prevailing winds. He probably used a lead line to determine the depth of water in shallow areas, and navigated by observing the position of his ship in relation to the sun and the Pole Star.*

Right *Ptolemy laid out the geography of the known world by 150 AD. His map of classical Eurasia was copied many times in the Middle Ages.*

Passage To India

On November 22, 1497, a small Portuguese fleet, commanded by Vasco da Gama, rounded Africa's southern tip in search of a route to the spices of Asia.

Aided by a friendly east African navigator, the fleet arrived in Calicut on India's southwestern coast on May 20, 1498. Da Gama insulted Zamorin, the powerful local king, with worthless trinkets and made a hasty departure in August, but had succeeded in opening a trade route to India.

Da Gama finally reached Lisbon in September 1499.

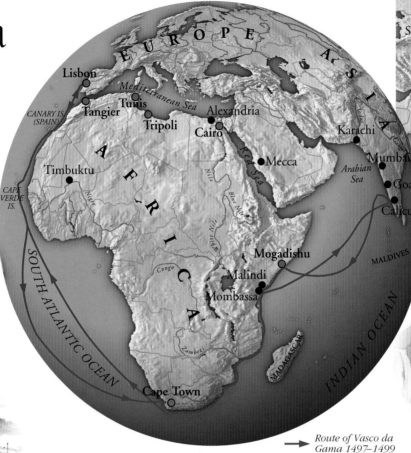

→ *Route of Vasco da Gama 1497–1499*

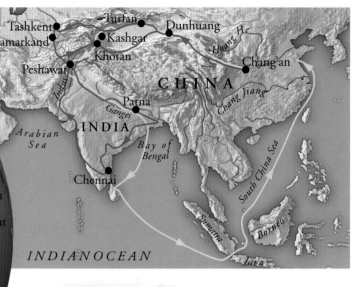

Left Early Chinese explorers of Central Asia and India returned to China with pack-horse trains that were heavily laden with Buddhist manuscripts.

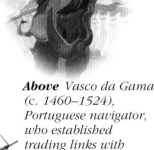

Above *Vasco da Gama (c. 1460–1524), Portuguese navigator, who established trading links with the East.*

Left *Vasco da Gama set out for India with three ships carrying a combined crew of about 150.*

Above *The Cape of Good Hope, the southern tip of Africa, was first rounded in 1488 by Bartholomeu Dias who named it "Cabo Tormentoso" (Cape of Storms).*

IN THE NAME OF GOD

Religion was a powerful motive for early travelers in Asia, whether the travelers were themselves Buddhists, Hindus, Muslims, or Christians. In 399 AD, for instance, the Chinese Buddhist monk Fa Hsien skirted the southern edge of the Takla Makan desert and crossed into India through the snows of the northern Himalayas. In 629 AD Hsüan Tsang, another pioneering Buddhist, first traveled extensively in central Asia and then followed Fa Hsien's footsteps into India, returning to China in 645 AD with hundreds of relics, manuscripts, and prayer wheels.

More than a thousand years later, in 1661, two Catholic Roman priests sought an overland route from China to India. Austrian-born Johann Gruebner left Beijing in October with Frenchman Albert d'Orville. They became the first Europeans to visit the forbidden Tibetan city of Lhasa, which no European would do again for another 200 years.

The Travels Of Marco Polo

Journeys of Marco Polo
1271–1295

Journeys of Ibn Battuta
1325–1354

Ibn Battuta return journey
1346–1349

Ibn Battuta possible journey
(to Beijing)

In 1271, the 17-year-old Venetian Marco Polo accompanied his father and uncle to the court of Kublai Khan, the Mongol Emperor of China, at Shang-tu, China. The Khan was impressed by the young man and accepted his offer of service.

Marco stayed for 17 years, acting as the Khan's personal messenger and reporter, receiving a golden safe-conduct pass that required people across the Khan's empire to help him on his way.

The journey home took three years via Sumatra, Sri Lanka, and India.

On his return, Marco Polo served briefly in the Venetian fleet in its war with Genoa, and was captured and imprisoned. During this time he compiled an account of his journey that was to influence generations of travelers.

Above In 1271, when Niccolo, Maffeo, and Marco Polo arrived at the court of Kublai Khan they brought oil from the lamp of the holy sepulcher in Jerusalem.

Left The Mongols, mounted on stocky ponies, were fine horsemen. They could accurately fire arrows at a fast gallop.

THIRTY YEARS ON THE ROAD

Ibn Battuta was an Islamic scholar who set out from Tangier in 1325 on his first pilgrimage to Mecca. Thirty years later he had traveled over 75,000 miles (120,700 km) through Africa, Europe, and Asia. Traveling as far east as China, where he had been sent as an ambassador by an Indian sultan, Battuta eventually returned home to describe his journeys in a *ribla*, a type of scholarly handbook.

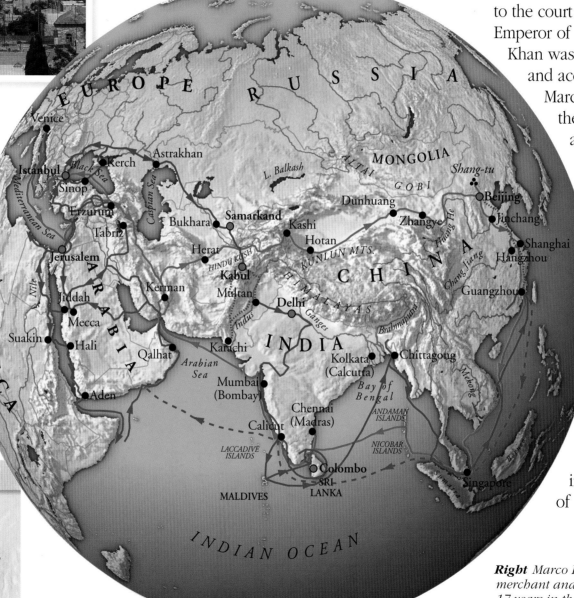

Right Marco Polo (1254–1324), merchant and traveler, spent 17 years in the service of Kublai Khan, the Mongol ruler of China.

A Buccaneer's Life

The English pirate William Dampier began his first circumnavigation of the globe in 1679. He was involved in a huge privateering expedition with 500 men and nine ships traveling to the Americas and Australia. He made a perilous journey by canoe from the Nicobar Islands to Sumatra, continuing alone to India and Indochina. In 1691, he returned to England.

In 1699, he led a naval expedition to Australia and New Guinea, but it was beset by illness and near-mutiny. His third voyage, in 1703, also ended unhappily, limping back to England with the remnants of his crew in 1707. He set sail a year later, capturing the *Encarnacion*, a galley laden with silks, porcelain, and spices.

At the end of a dramatic and often lawless career at sea that included three circumnavigations of the world, Dampier eventually retired to London, where he died in 1715.

Right
*William Dampier
(c. 1651–1715),
English buccaneer
and explorer*

Right *Dampier
discovered a rich
tribal culture on
his 1699 journey
to New Guinea.*

→ *Southeast Asian explorations
of William Dampier, 1699*

Right *Isabella Bird, who began
her extensive journeys in eastern
Asia at the age of 40 in 1872.*

A VICTORIAN LADY IN THE EAST

Isabella Bird started traveling in 1872 at the age of 40. Her life as a clergyman's daughter had been stifling and dull and, after years of back trouble, she came to the conclusion that only a complete change would improve her health and her life.

Bird's life was transformed first by a grueling sea voyage and then a prolonged stay in Honolulu. She later visited Japan, traveled in America's Rocky Mountains, and ventured as far as China, Korea, and Tibet.

Right and below *On her trip to the East,
Isabella Bird saw much of traditional
Japanese culture—such as geisha girls
and Shinto temples.*

On Top Of The World

The Himalayan peak of Mount Everest, at 29,035 ft (8,850 m), is the highest mountain in the world. In the early 1950s, the summit had not yet been reached.

In March, New Zealander Sir Edmund Hillary and the Sherpa, Norgay Tenzing, set off from their base camp on the Khumbu Glacier, at 17,572 ft (5,356 m), reaching the Southeast Ridge at the end of May. On May 29, 1953, they struck out for the summit, cutting steps in the snow above an alarming precipice and scaling a 40-ft (12-m) rock wall with crampons and ice axes. By 11:30 a.m., Tenzing and Hillary were standing on the highest spot on Earth.

Above *Sir Edmund Hillary and Norgay Tenzing, who climbed Everest in 1953.*

Left *To the Tibetans, Everest is the "goddess mother of the world." To Sherpa tribespeople it is "the mountain so high that no bird can fly over it."*

→ *Journey of Ippolito Desideri, 1714–16*

INTO THE UNKNOWN

Jesuit priest Antonio de Andrade was the first European to cross the Himalayas. Disguised as Hindus, he and two Indian Christians set out in 1624 to investigate unconfirmed rumors of Christian communities in Tibet. After joining a Hindu pilgrimage to the shrine at Badrinath, de Andrade entered Tibet. At Tsaparang he founded a mission.

In 1714, meanwhile, the Italian Ippolito Desideri traveled with his Portuguese companion Manuel Freyre from Lahore to Kashmir. After recovering from snow blindness and other ailments, they reached Leh, on the Tibetan plateau, the following year. The pair went on to Lhasa—the home of the Dalai Lama, the leader of Tibetan Buddhism—where Desideri stayed until 1721. Having learned to speak Tibetan, Desideri revisited Tibet several times before he returned to Europe in 1727.

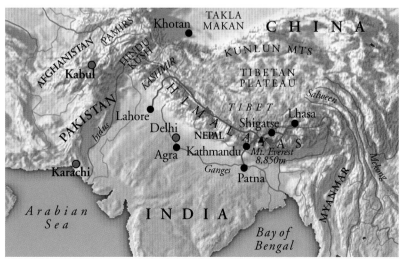

Above *Lhasa's Potala Palace, home of the Dalai Lama, was built in the 17th century.*

The New World

On September 6, 1492, three small ships with a crew of 90 men sailed from the Canary Islands into unknown waters under the command of Christopher Columbus, who was intent on proving that it was possible to reach the Indies by sailing west from Europe.

Land was sighted on October 12, about 33 days after leaving the Canaries, and Columbus claimed the new territory—the Bahamas—for Spain. Thinking he had found the Indies, he named the inhabitants "Indians."

He crossed the Atlantic three more times but it was not until his fourth voyage, in 1502, that he touched on the mainland of America. He finally returned home, rich but disillusioned, in November 1504.

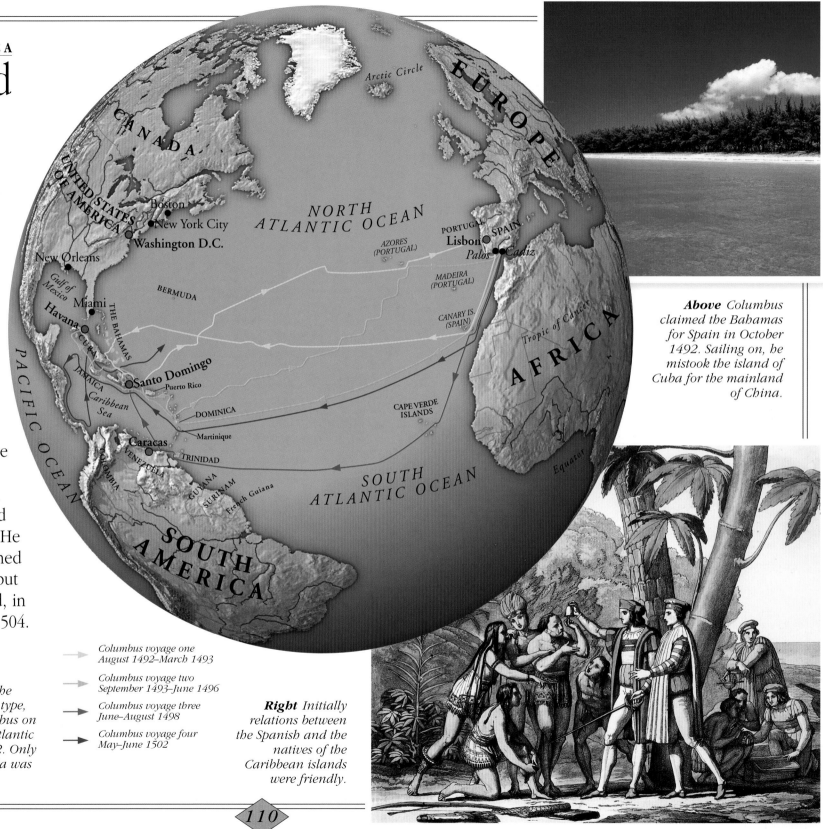

Above Columbus claimed the Bahamas for Spain in October 1492. Sailing on, he mistook the island of Cuba for the mainland of China.

Left *A ship of the "Santa Maria" type, used by Columbus on his epic transatlantic voyage in 1492. Only the Santa Maria was fully decked.*

→ Columbus voyage one
August 1492–March 1493

→ Columbus voyage two
September 1493–June 1496

→ Columbus voyage three
June–August 1498

→ Columbus voyage four
May–June 1502

Right *Initially relations between the Spanish and the natives of the Caribbean islands were friendly.*

110

Right Lewis and Clark's overland route to the Pacific was arduous and dangerous. Harsh winter weather made mountains impassable.

Below La Salle taking possession of "Louisiana."

Crossing The New Continent

In the winter of 1803–1804, Captain Meriwether Lewis and his deputy, Lieutenant William Clark, prepared for an epic journey that was to cover 8,000 miles (12,875 km). Their mission was to find an overland route to the Pacific.

The expedition overwintered at the Mandan villages in North Dakota, setting off again on April 7, 1805 with a Shoshoni guide, Sacajawea, carrying her two-month-old baby on her back. They reached the Great Falls of the Missouri in June and hauled their boats and equipment overland.

The group eventually crossed the Rocky Mountains, and accompanied by friendly Nez Percé Indians, they took to the water again, first on the Clearwater River, then on the Snake, and finally on the mighty Columbia. The fast-flowing waters bore them past the site of modern Portland and on to the Pacific coast on November 15, 1805.

Right Meriwether Lewis (1774–1809) and William Clark (1770–1838) whose expedition to the Pacific was sponsored by President Thomas Jefferson.

Map labels

Hudson Bay

CANADA

Vancouver
Seattle Spokane
Great Falls
Winnipeg
L. Superior
L. Huron
Boston
New York
Lewiston
Fort Mandan
St. Paul
Fort Clatsop Portland Butte
Yellowstone
Missouri
Minneapolis
Chicago
Philadelphia
Snake
N. Platte
St. Louis
Washington D.C.
Salt Lake City
Denver
Kansas City
Wabash
San Francisco
Colorado
Arkansas
Nashville
ATLANTIC OCEAN
Los Angeles
San Diego Phoenix
Santa Fe
Rio Grande
Pecos
Mississippi
New Orleans
Gulf of Mexico
PACIFIC OCEAN

Journey of La Salle, 1681–1682

Journeys of Lewis & Clark, 1804–1807

Clark's return, 1807

FROM THE GREAT LAKES TO THE GULF OF MEXICO

In January 1682, the French explorer Sieur de la Salle traveled from Fort Crevecoeur ("Fort Heartbreak") on the Illinois River to the confluence of the Illinois and the Mississippi. His expedition included 23 fellow Frenchmen, 18 American Indians, and his second-in-command, Henri de Tonti. Their objective was to navigate the entire length of North America's mightiest river. Once the winter ice had broken up in mid-February, the group progressed in canoes meeting friendly Arkansas, Taensa, and Coroa Indians. The successful journey was completed in early April when the travelers reached the Gulf of Mexico and la Salle formally claimed Louisiana (so named in honor of Louis XIV) for France in a ceremony on April 9, 1683.

Right The West was wilderness, rich in wildlife, some of it very dangerous. On April 7, 1805, Lewis and Clark survived their first encounter with a grizzly bear.

Northern Territory

Canada is a vast country, and its exploration involved many intrepid travelers and took several centuries. In May 1497, John Cabot was the first documented transatlantic voyager to reach Canada's eastern coast, followed in 1534 by Jacques Cartier who explored the Gulf of St. Lawrence and the St. Lawrence River. In 1535, Cartier reached 1,000 miles (1,600 km) inland, to the site of today's Montreal. In 1698, Samuel de Champlain founded the first permanent French colony in the New World.

In the west, James Cook surveyed the coast in 1778 while searching for the Northwest Passage, and in 1792, George Vancouver sailed around the island now called Vancouver. In 1789, Alexander Mackenzie followed the river that now bears his name to the Arctic. In 1793, he was the first European to cross North America by land.

Left The distinctive totem poles of the Kwakiutl.

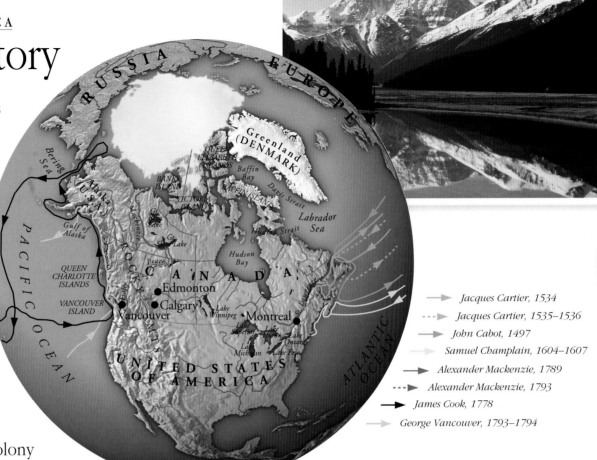

→ Jacques Cartier, 1534
--→ Jacques Cartier, 1535–1536
→ John Cabot, 1497
→ Samuel Champlain, 1604–1607
→ Alexander Mackenzie, 1789
--→ Alexander Mackenzie, 1793
→ James Cook, 1778
→ George Vancouver, 1793–1794

Left In 1793, Scotsman Alexander Mackenzie was the first explorer to prove that the Rockies could be crossed.

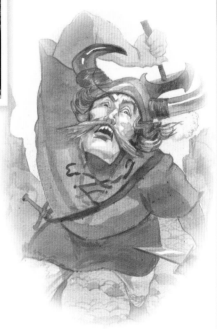

Above Vikings were notorious warriors who regularly descended on the coasts of Britain, Ireland, and France to raid and trade.

"VINLAND"

Leif Eriksson was the son of the Viking, Erik the Red, who had established a settlement at Brattahild in southern Greenland. Around 1000 AD, Leif Eriksson sailed with a crew of 35 in search of the mysterious land to the west. After sailing for 200 miles (320 km) he reached a place he called Helluland ("land of stone slabs"), probably the southern part of Baffin Island. Then he traveled south to Markland ("land of woods"), now identified as southern Labrador.

Eriksson reached a bountiful country, with rivers full of salmon. One member of the group became tipsy on wild grapes so Leif Eriksson called the land Vinland ("land of wine"). The party spent the winter in Vinland, and were the first Europeans to set foot in North America.

→ Voyage of Leif Eriksson

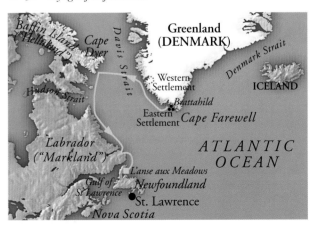

Hernán Cortés, Conqueror Of Mexico

On February 18, 1519, the Spanish governor of Cuba sent 11 ships commanded by Hernán Cortés to explore the rich mainland empire of the Aztecs, ruled over by the mighty Moctezuma II.

The expedition was welcomed by a local Indian chief who complained bitterly about the brutal Aztecs. Cortés marched on the Aztec capital, Tenochtitlán, with thousands of Indian allies. He seized and imprisoned Moctezuma, turning him into a Spanish puppet-ruler. But Cortés was forced to return to Veracruz to confront Spanish troops sent to arrest him and the Aztecs rebelled. On his return Cortés was captured but escaped to Tlaxcala. Cortés laid siege to Tenochtitlán and the starving city finally yielded in 1521. Cortés had conquered the Aztecs.

Invasion route to Tenochtitlán, Aug–Nov 1519

Conjectural route of forced march to Veracruz, 1520

Cortés route to Mexico, 1519–1520

Cortés expedition to Honduras, 1524

Above Although Cortés defeated Moctezuma and won Mexico for Spain, he was never made governor of Mexico.

Left The Aztecs sacrificed 50,000 captives a year to the sun and the earth.

Above An Aztec mask of turquoise, shell, and wood, representing the much-feared feathered serpent god, Tzalcoatl.

Right The Aztecs ruled their empire from the island city of Tenochtitlán on Lake Texcoco.

Uncharted Waters

In 1519, Ferdinand Magellan embarked on a momentous journey to find a western route to Asia.

Magellan's fleet of five ships set off down the coast of South America in October 1520. The fleet soon sighted the straits they had been searching for and for 38 days they headed into strong winds. On November 28, 1520, they entered the unknown waters of the Pacific Ocean.

At least 19 men died during the crossing. Magellan himself was killed in a battle on the island of Mactan. His surviving ships limped on and one eventually reached Spain in September 1522.

Left The Spaniards must have been fascinated by the Patagonian penguins. Unique to the southern hemisphere, they were first seen when Magellan's fleet rounded Cape Horn on the southern tip of South America in November 1520.

Below Magellan's men marveled at Brazil's multicolored parrots.

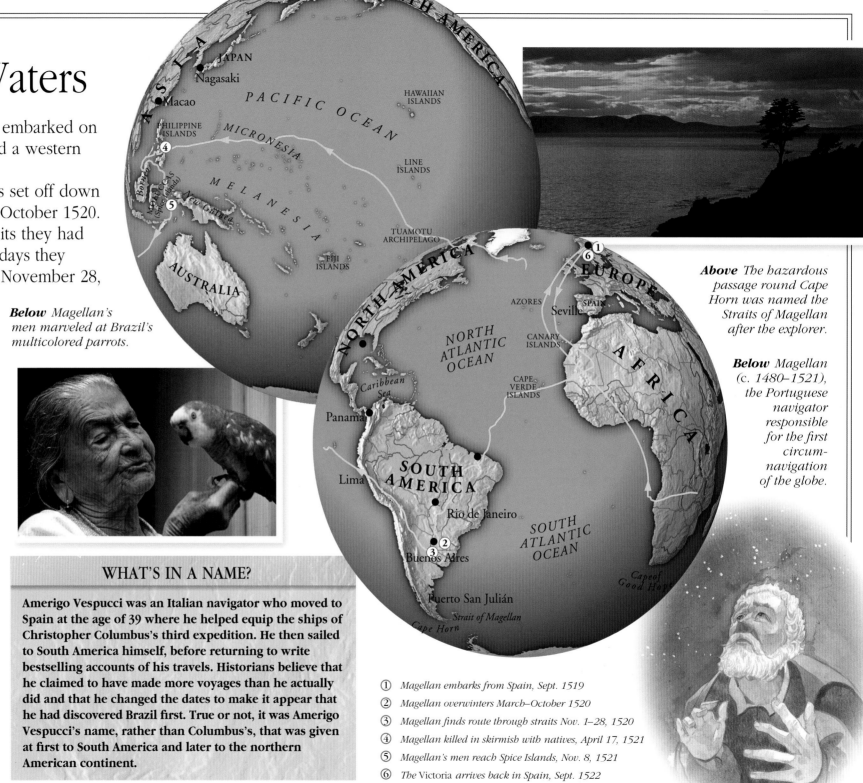

Above The hazardous passage round Cape Horn was named the Straits of Magellan after the explorer.

Below Magellan (c. 1480–1521), the Portuguese navigator responsible for the first circumnavigation of the globe.

WHAT'S IN A NAME?

Amerigo Vespucci was an Italian navigator who moved to Spain at the age of 39 where he helped equip the ships of Christopher Columbus's third expedition. He then sailed to South America himself, before returning to write bestselling accounts of his travels. Historians believe that he claimed to have made more voyages than he actually did and that he changed the dates to make it appear that he had discovered Brazil first. True or not, it was Amerigo Vespucci's name, rather than Columbus's, that was given at first to South America and later to the northern American continent.

① Magellan embarks from Spain, Sept. 1519

② Magellan overwinters March–October 1520

③ Magellan finds route through straits Nov. 1–28, 1520

④ Magellan killed in skirmish with natives, April 17, 1521

⑤ Magellan's men reach Spice Islands, Nov. 8, 1521

⑥ The Victoria arrives back in Spain, Sept. 1522

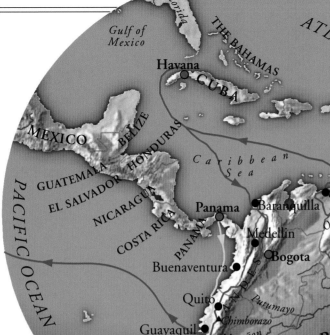

Above *Francisco Pizarro (c. 1475–1541), who defeated the Inca empire with only 185 men.*

Below *Von Humboldt climbed Chimborazo in Ecuador (19,000 ft/5790 m), a record at that time.*

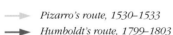
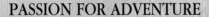

→ *Pizarro's route, 1530–1533*
→ *Humboldt's route, 1799–1803*

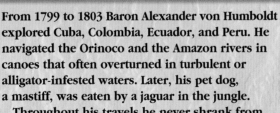

PASSION FOR ADVENTURE

From 1799 to 1803 Baron Alexander von Humboldt explored Cuba, Colombia, Ecuador, and Peru. He navigated the Orinoco and the Amazon rivers in canoes that often overturned in turbulent or alligator-infested waters. Later, his pet dog, a mastiff, was eaten by a jaguar in the jungle.

   Throughout his travels he never shrank from danger, even drinking Indian arrow-poison to show it was only lethal when injected in the bloodstream. He also measured earthquakes, climbed volcanoes, and braved altitude sickness and storms to climb Mount Chimborazo in Ecuador, reaching a record-breaking height of 19,000 ft (5,790 m).

Conqueror Of The Incas

Lured by stories of Inca gold, Spanish conquistador Francisco Pizarro and a small force of soldiers of fortune arrived at Tumbes in northern Peru in 1532.

Pizarro set off to meet the Inca ruler, Atahuallpa. On November 16, they reached Cajamarca where Atahuallpa and his army of 30,000 awaited them. Pizarro trapped Atahuallpa in the main square and surrounded it with hidden cavalry. The Spaniards attacked with muskets and cannons, massacring at least 2,000 Incas. Atahuallpa was captured and produced a massive ransom. When he had served his purpose, however, he was garrotted.

The conquistadors finally took the Inca capital, Cuzco, in November 1533. A tiny but ruthless force had conquered the mightiest empire in South America.

Above *The Inca ruler Atahuallpa was brutally murdered by the Spanish.*

Left *Alexander von Humboldt (1769–1859), the Prussian natural scientist who traveled to South America.*

Descending The Amazon

In 1540, Gonzalo Pizarro (brother of Francisco) set off to survey the densely forested area to the east of Quito. When supplies became short, a small party of 60 men, led by Francisco de Orellana, was sent down the Napo River in a two-masted sailing ship in search of food.

They soon reached the Amazon. Orellana decided to drift with the river, hoping to reach the Atlantic Ocean. Over the next nine months, the group fought off countless Indian war parties in canoes. Despite these dangers, after a journey of 3,000 miles (4,825 km), the ship eventually reached the ocean.

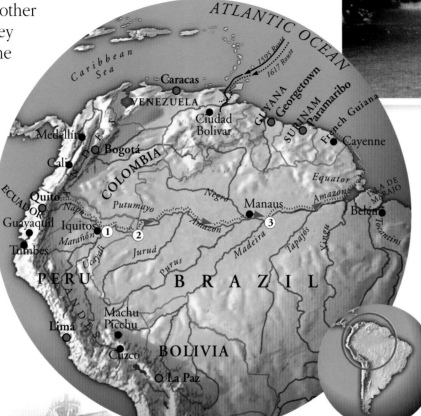

Above On his journey down the mighty Amazon, de Orellana was attacked by fierce female warriors and so he named the river "Amazon" after the mythical women warriors of Ancient Greece.

┄┄┄▶ Route of Francisco de Orellana

① Orellana sails into the Amazon, February 12, 1542

② Orellana encounters warlike Indians, May 12, 1542

③ Orellana claims to have fought women warriors, or Amazons, June 24, 1542

──▶ 1595 Route of Sir Walter Raleigh

┄┄┄▶ 1617 Route of Sir Walter Raleigh

Right South American gold lured European explorers.

EL DORADO

Some explorers are driven by the lure of fabulous riches. Sir Walter Raleigh was such a man. Motivated by the myth of El Dorado ("the gilded man"), Raleigh sailed from England to South America in 1595 to find the fabled inland city of the same name. After losing two of his expedition's ships in Atlantic storms, he and his remaining crew landed in Trinidad before canoeing more than 500 miles (800 km) up the Orinoco. During their arduous journey they were often lost in a maze of streams and tributaries and were finally forced back by the seasonal rains, which turned the river into a raging torrent. In 1617, Raleigh returned to search for El Dorado but was ambushed by the Spanish. His son Wat was killed and Raleigh returned home in disgrace. He never found the mythical golden city.

Right Sir Walter Raleigh (c. 1554–1618). English adventurer, who founded a colony in Virginia, and explored the Orinoco river in search of El Dorado ("the gilded man"). His search ended in tragedy and the mythical city was never found.

Right Amazonian piranhas can strip a man to his bones in minutes.

High Peaks Of The Andes

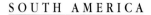

Above *A 19th-century engraving, based on Whymper's popular account of his Ecuadorean adventures, showing an attempt to pitch camp against driving snow.*

..... *Route taken by Whymper*

△ *Peak climbed by Whymper*

PACIFIC OCEAN

Cotocachi △   Ibarra
Otavalo ● ● Cayambe
  △ *Cayambe*
Quito ●   △ *Sara-Urcu*
Corazon △ △ *Antisana*
Illiniza △ △ △ *Sincholagua*
  Cotopaxi
ECUADOR ● Latacunga
Carihuairazo △ ●Ambata *Napo*
Chimborazo △
Guaranda ● ● Riobamba
  Babahoyo
Guayaquil ●

Daule   *Vinces*

Gulf of Guayaquil   Cuenca ●

Left *The spectacular Inca town of Machu Picchu perches on top of a rugged mountain. Workers smoothed the rock to form flat surfaces on which to build major temples. The steep flanking slopes were terraced to support small thatched houses, as well as for cultivation. Machu Picchu has become one of Peru's main tourist attractions.*

THE INCAS' HIDDEN CITY

When Hiram Bingham, a lecturer in Latin American history at Yale University, set off in 1911 in search of the lost Inca cities of Vilcabamba and Vitcos little did he know what he would soon discover. Local guides led him to a site high above the Urubamba Valley where he saw, "a great flight of beautifully constructed stone-faced terraces, perhaps a hundred of them, each hundreds of feet long and ten feet high." Bingham had found Machu Picchu. Although it has since been shown not to be Vilcabamba or Vitcos, as Bingham believed, Machu Picchu is a breathtaking place that is recognized as one of the architectural wonders of the world.

In 1879, the European mountaineer, Edward Whymper, arrived in Ecuador to pioneer exploration of the Andes.

Whymper headed straight for the mountain of Chimborazo, northeast of Guayaquil. Despite a desperate struggle against altitude sickness he scaled both Chimborazo's western and eastern peaks.

Whymper's party began the ascent of Cotopaxi, the active volcano to the north. The closer they got to the crater's rim the more the volcanic ash penetrated their ears, eyes, and nostrils. Whymper crawled over to peer down into the volcano at the red, molten lava below.

Whymper conquered many other high peaks, surveying the land and collecting samples of local plants and insects. He also established that altitude sickness is directly related to atmospheric pressure.

Left *Hiram Bingham (1875–1956), US archeologist and explorer of Inca Peru.*

Right *Edward Whymper (1840–1911), English writer and mountaineer.*

AFRICA
Ibn Battuta

In 1325, Ibn Battuta, an Arab from Tangier, in present-day Morocco, decided to embark on a journey to all the holy places of the Muslim world. His travels were to take 30 years.

First, Ibn Battuta explored the ancient cities of the Nile valley. He made the Muslim holy city of Mecca into his second home, using it as a base from which to explore much of the Middle East, Central Asia, and the Muslim states of East Africa.

In 1351, he journeyed south through the Sahara to Mali. Battuta explored the River Niger by canoe and visited the fabled desert city of Timbuktu.

In 1354, he returned home to write *Rihla*, an account of his travels, a fascinating insight into one of the medieval world's greatest explorers.

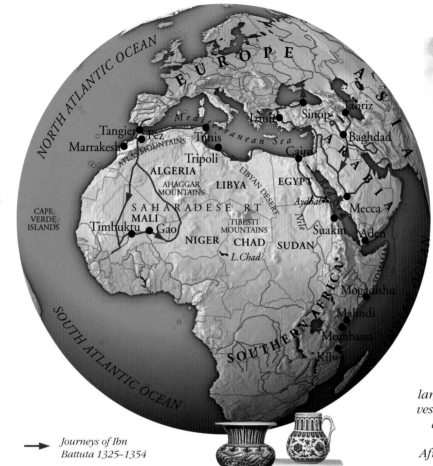

→ *Journeys of Ibn Battuta 1325–1354*

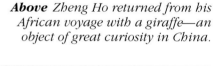

Above *Zheng Ho returned from his African voyage with a giraffe—an object of great curiosity in China.*

Right *The construction of larger ocean-going vessels was banned after Zheng Ho's voyages to east Africa, when Ming China became isolationist and inward-looking.*

Left *Muslim Arab traders have been making the arduous trans-Saharan crossing by camel caravan in search of salt, gold, and slaves since the 10th century.*

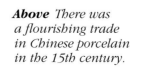

Above *There was a flourishing trade in Chinese porcelain in the 15th century.*

ADMIRAL ZHENG HO

In the early 15th century, Africa was visited by a bold Chinese seafarer, Admiral Zheng Ho. Between 1405 and 1433 he made seven trading missions across the Indian Ocean, visiting Mogadishu in present-day Somalia and traveling as far south as Malindi. But Zheng Ho relied on the backing of the emperors of China's Ming dynasty, and when they became suspicious of foreign influences, the admiral's expeditions were stopped.

The Source Of The Nile

Left John Hanning Speke (1827–94), English soldier and explorer who discovered the headwaters of the River Nile.

Right Sir Richard Francis Burton (1821–90), English linguist, writer, and explorer of Saudi Arabia and Lake Tanganyika.

Above *Lake Victoria, source of the River Nile, is the second-largest freshwater body in the world. It is approximately 250 miles (400 km) long. It was explored by J.H. Speke in 1858, and again, with J.A. Grant, in 1862.*

Right *Dinka dancer in southern Sudan playing a horn.*

The Nile, the world's longest river, flows for 3,500 miles (5,630 km) through Sudan and Egypt. But in the mid-19th century its origin was a mystery.

In 1856, celebrated explorer Richard Burton, accompanied by John Hanning Speke, an ex-soldier and big game hunter, set off from Zanzibar to find the source of the Nile. Having overcome desperate fevers and rebellious porters they discovered Lake Tanganyika, but realized it could not be the source of the Nile.

Speke headed on alone in search of a lake known by locals as Lake Ukerewe. After 25 days of hard trekking, he reached it and named it Lake Victoria. This, he believed, was the source of the Nile.

Burton was skeptical, but Speke returned to England a hero. Two years later, he reached Lake Victoria again. He traced the Nile to the lake's northern end, and sent a triumphant telegram: "The Nile is settled."

→ Route of Richard Burton and John Speke, 1856–59

→ Route of John Speke, 1858

→ Route of John Speke and James Grant, 1860–63

SUDAN

Speke and Grant rendezvous with porters and proceed to Khartoum

Juba Gondokoro

UGANDA KENYA

ZAIRE *Lake Albert* Urondogani

Lake Edward Kampala

Lake Kivu RWANDA *Lake Victoria* Nairobi

Bujumbura Mwanza

BURUNDI SERENGETI PLAIN

Ujiji Tabora GREAT RIFT VALLEY

Lake Tanganyika Dodoma Zanzibar

Lake Rukwa Dar es Salaam

Mombasa

TANZANIA INDIAN OCEAN

Right *James Bruce (1730–94), who reached the headstream of the Blue Nile in 1722.*

Africa, From Coast To Coast

Scottish explorer David Livingstone was a medical doctor and missionary who arrived in Karuma (Botswana) in 1841. Frustrated by his missionary activities, he turned to exploration. Crossing the Kalahari Desert in 1849, he visited Lake Ngami. He eventually reached the Zambezi River in 1851, and in 1856, after an epic 21-month journey, became the first European to cross Africa.

Above David Livingstone (1813–73), Scottish explorer of Africa.

In 1866, he set out to find the sources of the Nile and the Congo. For five years he lost contact with Europeans. When reporter Henry Stanley found him on Lake Tanganyika, he met him with the famous words, "Doctor Livingstone, I presume."

Right David Livingstone was mauled by a lion at Mabotsa in southern Africa, but this did not deter him from his travels.

Map labels

EUROPE
ASIA
Mediterranean Sea
Tangier
Algiers
Tripoli
Cairo
AHAGGAR MOUNTAINS
TIBESTI MOUNTAINS
Red Sea
Nile
SAHARA DESERT
Timbuktu
Agadez
Khartoum
Asmara
Blue Nile
Nouakchott
L. Chad
Bamako
Niger
Kano
N'Djamena
Djibouti
Abuja
Benue
Addis Ababa
White Nile
Bangui
Uele
Yaoundé
Congo
INDIAN OCEAN
L. Victoria
Nairobi
Kasai
Nyangwe
Ujiji
SOUTH ATLANTIC OCEAN
Kinshasa
Tabora
Zanzibar
L. Tanganyika
Cabango
Luanda
Mtwara
L. Nyasa
COMOROS
Lusaka
Mozambique
Zambezi
Quelimane
Livingstone
KALAHARI DESERT
Windhoek
Gabarone
Kuruman
Mabotsa
Orange
Cape Town

ACROSS THE SAHARA

In 1849, the British government sent an expedition across the Sahara desert from Tripoli. Many of the explorers died early on, but the German-born geographer Heinrich Barth pressed on, traveling over 10,000 miles (16,000 km), with only his porters, in five years. Having crossed the fearsome Sahara, he explored Lake Chad, the Benue River, and later traveled west to Timbuktu.

On his return to England in 1855, however, his long, scholarly books were largely ignored by a public that wanted tales of adventure. In his lifetime, Barth never received the recognition his bravery and endurance deserved.

Left Heinrich Barth (1821–65), German explorer and geographer, who traveled in the Mediterranean and Saharan regions.

Legend

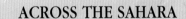

→ Journeys of David Livingstone, 1849–1856

--→ The Great Zambezi expedition, 1858–1864

····→ Journeys of David Livingstone, 1866–1873

→ Journeys of Heinrich Barth, 1850–1855

A Woman In West Africa

Left *The stone tablet and cross in honor of Diogo Cão, the first European to arrive in Namibia in 1482.*

Left *The brass sculptures of the West African civilization of Benin are famous. This armed Portuguese soldier dates from the 17th century.*

EUROPE ASIA

Lisbon
Tangier
Marrakesh
Tripoli
Cairo
AHAGGAR MOUNTAINS
ARABIA
Mediterranean Sea
Red Sea
TIBESTI MOUNTAINS
Timbuktu
SAHARA DESERT
Nile
Niger
L. Chad
CAPE VERDE ISLANDS
Blue Nile
White Nile
Elmina
Mt Cameroon
Congo
Ogooué
Kisangani
Kampala
GABON
L. Victoria
Brazzaville
Kinshasa
Boma Matadi
Zanzibar
Luanda
ATLANTIC OCEAN
Zambezi
INDIAN OCEAN
Quelimane
NAMIBIA
Walvis Bay
Orange
Cape Town

Although the first coastal map of West Africa was made by Diogo Cão in 1482, early explorers made few journeys inland until 1874, when Henry Stanley descended the great Congo River as far as Boma on the Atlantic Ocean. Englishwoman Mary Kingsley left for Africa in 1893 with little more than a bag of books and blankets. She sailed up the Congo River and traveled in the interior, trading tobacco and collecting specimens of insects and fish. In 1894, she made a second journey to Gabon. She canoed up the crocodile-infested Ogooué River and spent a terrifying night with the Fang cannibals. She became the first woman to climb Mount Cameroon.

→ *Explorations of Diogo Cão, 1482*
⋯⋯▷ *Explorations of Diogo Cão, 1485*
━━▶ *Journey of Henry Stanley, 1874–1879*
━▶ *Journey of Mary Kingsley, 1893*
⋯⋯▶ *Journey of Mary Kingsley, 1894*

Left *Henry Morton Stanley (1841–1904), British-American explorer of central Africa, especially the Congo region.*

Right *Mary Kingsley (1862–1900), the English traveler who journeyed through western Africa and became the first European to visit Gabon.*

Continent In The South

In 1769, Captain James Cook embarked on his first voyage to the South Seas when he sailed to Tahiti. He then turned south and sighted New Zealand. At a place he named Poverty Bay he was attacked by Maoris. In April 1770, he became the first European to see the eastern coast of Australia and, on August 21, 1770, he took possession of the eastern half for the British Crown.

On his later voyages, Cook journeyed from the Gulf of Alaska to Antarctica gathering detailed information on natural history, cartography, and meteorology.

On St. Valentine's Day 1779, Cook and his crew fell into an argument with some native people in Hawaii. Cook was surprised and stabbed to death by a local chieftain.

THE REAL ROBINSON CRUSOE

William Dampier was a British navigator and buccaneer who specialized in looting Spanish galleons, and mapped Australia and New Guinea in three voyages between 1679 and 1711. The real-life story of one of his crew members, Alexander Selkirk, was the inspiration for Daniel Defoe's *Robinson Crusoe*. Selkirk apparently disliked Dampier so much that he insisted on being put ashore on the uninhabited island of Juan Fernandez, about 400 miles (643 km) west of Chile, during Dampier's fourth voyage. He then began to scrape an existence on the barren island. But when rescued four years and four months later by Dampier's ship, Selkirk is said to have been difficult to persuade aboard, such were his continued feelings of resentment!

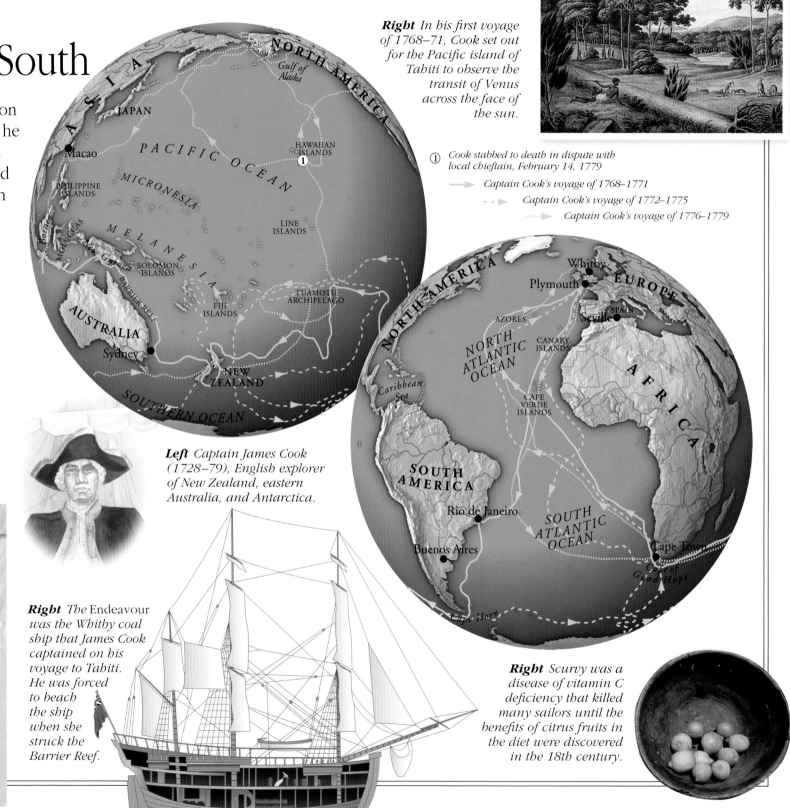

Right In his first voyage of 1768–71, Cook set out for the Pacific island of Tahiti to observe the transit of Venus across the face of the sun.

① *Cook stabbed to death in dispute with local chieftain, February 14, 1779*

→ *Captain Cook's voyage of 1768–1771*

--→ *Captain Cook's voyage of 1772–1775*

····→ *Captain Cook's voyage of 1776–1779*

Left Captain James Cook (1728–79), English explorer of New Zealand, eastern Australia, and Antarctica.

Right The Endeavour was the Whitby coal ship that James Cook captained on his voyage to Tahiti. He was forced to beach the ship when she struck the Barrier Reef.

Right Scurvy was a disease of vitamin C deficiency that killed many sailors until the benefits of citrus fruits in the diet were discovered in the 18th century.

The Red Country

In 1860, after several failed attempts, the citizens of Melbourne sponsored an expedition to traverse the country led by Robert O'Hara Burke and William John Wills. The party of 17 men started out in a blaze of publicity and expectation.

Soon things began to go wrong. Carts ground to a halt in mud. Rats devoured the provisions. Burke decided to form a party of four to press on to the north coast, arranging to meet the main expedition at Cooper's Creek, 400 miles (643 km) into the interior.

Struggling through heat, flies, and sandstorms, and surviving on dried horse and camel meat, the party made it to the mangrove swamps near the northern coast in February 1861. They could not penetrate the swamps and turned back, emaciated and in rags, to Cooper's Creek. No one was there to meet them and Burke and Wills died in June 1861 at Cooper's Creek.

Above Robert Burke (1821–61), Irish explorer who led the trans-Australian expedition.

Above William Wills (1834–61), English explorer who accompanied Burke on his Australian expedition.

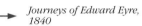

Right Camels were shipped from India for the desert journey, but they fought with each other and with the horses.

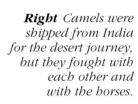

Left European explorers found the Outback harsh and unyielding.

→ Journeys of Edward Eyre, 1840

→ Journeys of Charles Sturt, 1844–1845

→ Journeys of Robert Burke and William Wills, 1860–1861

① Burke and Wills died here on their return journey, 1861

Right Many European expeditions to Australia relied on the bushcraft and hardiness of the Aborigines. They acted as guides, pointing out water sources, and hunting for food.

The Pioneering Dutch

→ *Abel Tasman's Pacific voyage, 1642*

By the early 17th century, the Dutch were dominating the spice trade in the East Indies establishing a commercial empire based in Batavia (Jakarta). The more southerly regions, including the west coast of Australia, had been encountered mainly by accident, when ships were blown off course.

In 1642, a sea captain named Abel Tasman was hired by the governor of Batavia to explore the commercial opportunities of the "Southland." Tasman sailed from Mauritius to the island he called Van Diemen's Land (now Tasmania) at the southern tip of Australia.

Turning east, Tasman was the first European to sight New Zealand. After a violent clash with the Maoris, he sailed northward becoming the first to visit the Pacific islands of Tonga and Fiji.

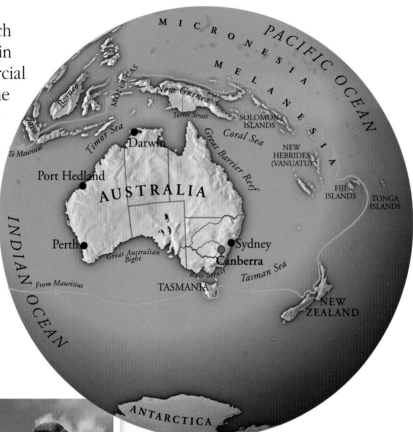

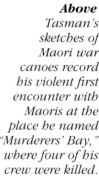

Pobis verstond hem de Moordenaers Bay als gy op 18° ademen daar in geankert zyt

Above
Tasman's sketches of Maori war canoes record his violent first encounter with Maoris at the place he named "Murderers' Bay," where four of his crew were killed.

Right These giant statues of human heads on Easter Island, are four to five times the height of a child.

LANDFALL AT EASTER ISLAND

In 1722, Jacob Roggeveen, still looking for the great "Southland," sailed into the Pacific from the coast of Chile. On Easter Day he struck land, naming it Easter Island, and was amazed by the giant monolithic statues of human heads (moai) he found there, some up to 32 ft (9.75 m) high. Even today, scientists are unsure about the meaning or purpose of the statues and are only able to tell us that they are the work of a neolithic culture that has since disappeared. One theory goes that the culture vanished following an ecological catastrophe on the island.

Above *The Maoris are a Polynesian people who settled in New Zealand in about 1000 AD. The scary expression tattooed on this warrior's face is designed to frighten the enemy in battle.*

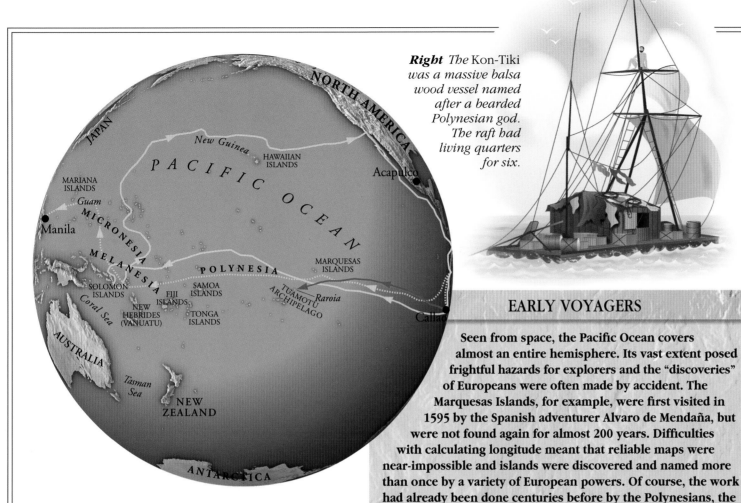

Going West

Voyages of Alvaro de Mendaña, 1567–1569
Voyages of Alvaro de Mendaña, 1595–1596
Kon-Tiki expedition of Thor Heyerdahl

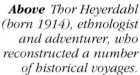

Right The Kon-Tiki was a massive balsa wood vessel named after a bearded Polynesian god. The raft had living quarters for six.

EARLY VOYAGERS

Seen from space, the Pacific Ocean covers almost an entire hemisphere. Its vast extent posed frightful hazards for explorers and the "discoveries" of Europeans were often made by accident. The Marquesas Islands, for example, were first visited in 1595 by the Spanish adventurer Alvaro de Mendaña, but were not found again for almost 200 years. Difficulties with calculating longitude meant that reliable maps were near-impossible and islands were discovered and named more than once by a variety of European powers. Of course, the work had already been done centuries before by the Polynesians, the native peoples of the Pacific, who were highly skilled navigators. Sailing by the stars, voyaging in double-hulled canoes and other smaller craft, they settled the entire hemisphere.

In the late 1930s, Thor Heyerdahl, a Norwegian living in the Marquesas Islands, developed the theory that the islands of the Pacific had originally been populated not from Asia, but from South America. He decided to try and sail from Peru to the Marquesas using only the materials that would have been available to ancient South American peoples.

In Callao Harbor, Peru, he constructed a massive balsa wood vessel, the *Kon-Tiki*, with living quarters for six men to make the 4,000-mile (6,435-km) journey. They took books, provisions, cinema film, scientific instruments, and a parrot.

Within 97 days, they reached an uninhabited island near Raroia in the Tuamotu group. After several weeks they were taken aboard a French schooner and back to a world eager for news. Heyerdahl's book became a bestseller.

Above Thor Heyerdahl (born 1914), ethnologist and adventurer, who reconstructed a number of historical voyages.

Below Thor Heyerdahl argued that similar stone statues found in the Marquesas and Bolivia indicated that South Americans settled the Pacific Islands.

Left Alvaro de Mendaña was the first European to discover the remote Marquesas Islands in 1595, some centuries after the Polynesians.

Arctic Waters

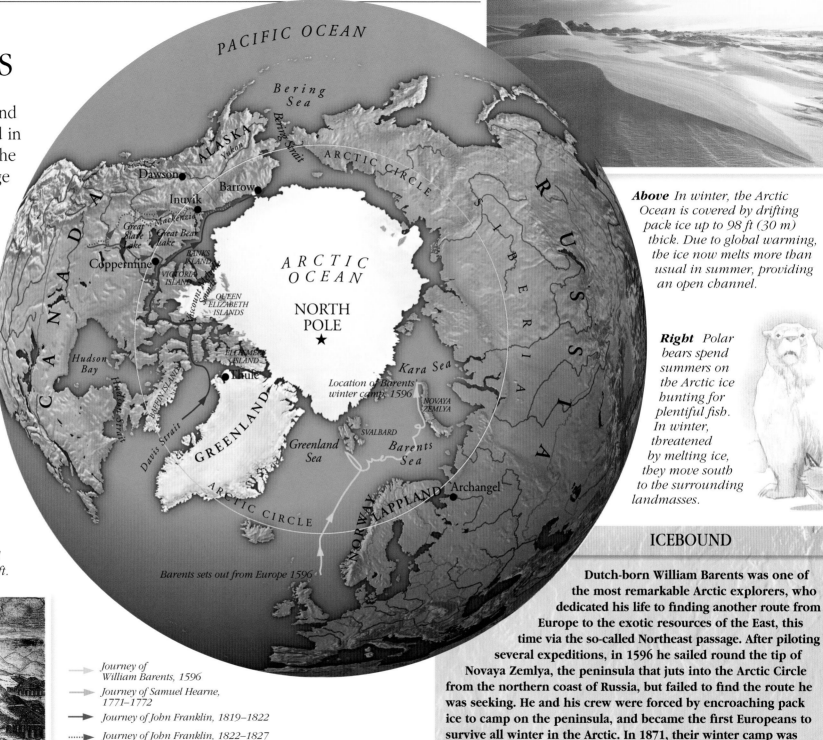

As trade between Europe and the East Indies increased in the 16th and 17th centuries, the search for a northwest passage between the Atlantic and Pacific began. A succession of explorers attempted to find a route through the Arctic waters.

In 1903, the Norwegian explorer, Roald Amundsen, set out in his ship *Gjöa* to navigate a way through the islands north of Canada. It took him two and a half years to negotiate the route to the Pacific, proving that it was not a practical seaway.

Below In 1871, 275 years after his Arctic journey, the winter camp of William Barents was found preserved in the snow, exactly as it had been left.

Above In winter, the Arctic Ocean is covered by drifting pack ice up to 98 ft (30 m) thick. Due to global warming, the ice now melts more than usual in summer, providing an open channel.

Right Polar bears spend summers on the Arctic ice hunting for plentiful fish. In winter, threatened by melting ice, they move south to the surrounding landmasses.

Map labels

PACIFIC OCEAN
Bering Sea
Bering Strait
ALASKA
ARCTIC CIRCLE
Dawson
Barrow
Inuvik
Yukon
Mackenzie
Great Slave Lake
Great Bear Lake
Coppermine
BANKS ISLAND
VICTORIA ISLAND
Viscount Melville Sound
QUEEN ELIZABETH ISLANDS
CANADA
Hudson Bay
Hudson Strait
BAFFIN ISLAND
Davis Strait
ELLESMERE ISLAND
Thule
GREENLAND
ARCTIC CIRCLE
ARCTIC OCEAN
NORTH POLE
Location of Barents' winter camp, 1596
Kara Sea
NOVAYA ZEMLYA
SVALBARD
Greenland Sea
Barents Sea
SIBERIA
RUSSIA
NORWAY
LAPPLAND
Archangel
Barents sets out from Europe 1596

Legend

→ Journey of William Barents, 1596
→ Journey of Samuel Hearne, 1771–1772
→ Journey of John Franklin, 1819–1822
····· Journey of John Franklin, 1822–1827
→ Successful navigation of Northwest Passage by Roald Amundsen, 1903–1906

ICEBOUND

Dutch-born William Barents was one of the most remarkable Arctic explorers, who dedicated his life to finding another route from Europe to the exotic resources of the East, this time via the so-called Northeast passage. After piloting several expeditions, in 1596 he sailed round the tip of Novaya Zemlya, the peninsula that juts into the Arctic Circle from the northern coast of Russia, but failed to find the route he was seeking. He and his crew were forced by encroaching pack ice to camp on the peninsula, and became the first Europeans to survive all winter in the Arctic. In 1871, their winter camp was found preserved, intact, in the snow.

The Race To The North Pole

ARCTIC
OCEAN

★ NORTH
POLE

Cape Columbia

PEARY LAND

Independence Fiord

GREENLAND

Fort Conger

ELLESMERE ISLAND

Kane Basin

Eureka

AXEL HEIBERG ISLAND

Bowdoin Bay

Red Cliff House

Dundas

Baffin Bay

→ *Peary's expedition to the North Pole, 1892*
→ *Peary's expedition to the North Pole, 1895*
→ *Peary's expedition to the North Pole, 1898–1902*
→ *Successful route to the North Pole, 1909*

Above *After several unsuccessful Arctic expeditions, Robert Peary reached the North Pole on April 6, 1909.*

Below *The Inuit have survived the harsh terrain and year-round sub-zero temperatures of the Arctic for thousands of years.*

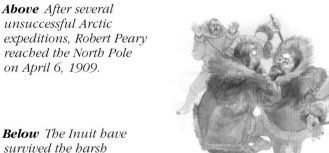

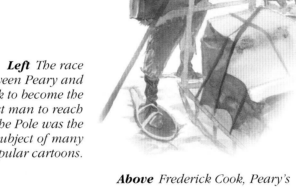

Left *The race between Peary and Cook to become the first man to reach the Pole was the subject of many popular cartoons.*

Above *Frederick Cook, Peary's former assistant, later claimed he had reached the Pole a year earlier.*

At the end of the 19th century, the North Pole was among the few unexplored places on the globe.

A US naval officer called Robert Peary made it his life's goal to be the first man to reach the Pole. He spent decades training and preparing for his goal.

Successive expeditions were dogged by disaster— hurricanes, a tidal wave, and endless quarrels. On the third attempt, a dash for the Pole led to frostbite, and Peary recounted the terrible experience of taking off his boots and leaving parts of his toes behind.

In March 1909 Peary was at last ready to make his final bid for glory, striking out north from Cape Columbia with the loyal support of his Inuit teams. He reached and claimed the North Pole on April 6, 1909.

Above *Robert Peary (1856–1920), the American Arctic explorer, whose obsession with reaching the North Pole was to dominate his life.*

Shackleton And The South Pole

In the 19th century, explorers, such as Thaddeus Bellingshausen, Charles Wilkes, and James Clark Ross, established the astonishing size of Antarctica—about 10 percent of the Earth's surface.

Englishman Ernest Shackleton made two attempts to reach the South Pole but was defeated by frostbite, scurvy, hunger, and exhaustion. In 1914, Shackleton embarked on an attempt to cross the continent. But his ship *Endurance*, entombed by pack ice, was crushed. Taking to lifeboats, the crew reached Elephant Island in the South Shetlands.

Shackleton and five others then made an incredible 700-mile (1,126-km) journey in a lifeboat to South Georgia to find help. Four months later they returned to rescue the remaining crew: all had survived.

Left *Sir Ernest Henry Shackleton (1874–1922), the Antarctic explorer, who attempted to reach the South Pole and cross Antarctica.*

→ *Journey of Thaddeus Bellingshausen, 1819–1821*
→ *Journey of James Ross, 1839–1843*
⋯ *Shackleton's journey towards the South Pole, 1902, 1908–1909*
→ *The voyage of the Endurance, 1914–1916*

Shackleton and rescue party leave by boat for South Georgia, 24 April 1916

SOUTH ATLANTIC OCEAN

Endurance enters pack ice

SOUTH GEORGIA
SOUTH SANDWICH ISLANDS
Scotia Sea

Crew make landfall

Weddell Sea

ELEPHANT ISLAND
SOUTH SHETLAND ISLANDS
JAMES ROSS ISLAND
ANTARCTIC PENINSULA

QUEEN MAUD LAND

MAC ROBERTSON LAND

Endurance destroyed by pack ice

PRINCESS ELIZABETH LAND

SOUTH INDIAN OCEAN

Bellingshausen Sea

SOUTH POLE
★
A N T A R C T I C A

QUEEN MARY LAND

MARIE BYRD LAND

ROSS ICE SHELF

WILKES LAND

SOUTH PACIFIC OCEAN

Amundsen Sea

Ross Sea

ROSS ISLAND

VICTORIA LAND

GEORGE V LAND

SOUTHERN OCEAN

Above *The Endurance, trapped in the ice on the Weddell Sea.*

Below *Shackleton's expedition camped in shelters that were built from materials salvaged from the ship.*

Center Of The Southern Ice

Above *The Norwegian explorer Roald Amundsen who reached the South Pole in 1911.*

Above *The British explorer Robert Scott who reached the South Pole in 1912 but died in the attempt.*

Below *The harsh climate of Antarctica makes it uninhabitable. The continent is covered by an ice sheet 1.2 miles (2 km) thick and the surrounding seas are frozen.*

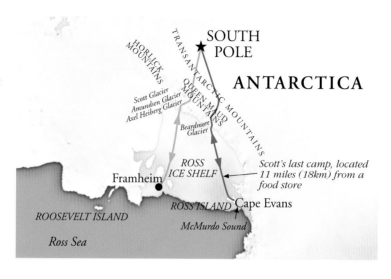

HORLICK MOUNTAINS
TRANSANTARCTIC MOUNTAINS
QUEEN MAUD MOUNTAINS

SOUTH POLE

ANTARCTICA

Scott Glacier
Amundsen Glacier
Axel Heiberg Glacier

Beardmore Glacier

Scott's last camp, located 11 miles (18km) from a food store

ROSS ICE SHELF

Framheim

ROSS ISLAND Cape Evans

ROOSEVELT ISLAND

McMurdo Sound

Ross Sea

→ *Expedition of Roald Amundsen, 1911–1912*

→ *Expedition of Robert Falcon Scott, 1911–1912*

In June 1910, the Norwegian explorer Roald Amundsen set off for Antarctica. His goal was to reach the South Pole. He set up a base (Framheim) on the Ross Ice Shelf and spent the winter laying down supplies. Meanwhile, a rival British expedition, under the command of Robert Falcon Scott, had arrived at the other side of the Ross Ice Shelf at Cape Evans.

In October, Amundsen started off on an unexplored route over difficult country scarred with crevasses. After a 1,400-mile (2,250-km) journey the five-man team reached the Pole on December 14, 1911.

Meanwhile, Scott struggled to the Pole, reaching it on January 17, 1912. On the return journey the party was delayed by bad weather and the sickness of two of the men, Lawrence Oates and Edgar Evans. Oates sacrificed his life by walking into the blizzard, but in vain. The remaining four died near One Ton Depot at the end of March.

Above *Amundsen's two-month dash to the South Pole, by dog sleds and skis, involved pioneering a route up the Axel Heiberg glacier to the polar plateau.*

First Man In Space

People have long dreamed of voyaging to the stars but it was not until October 4, 1957, when the Soviet Union launched the first satellite, *Sputnik 1*, to orbit the Earth, that the space age actually began.

Then came the sensational news that Yuri Gagarin, a 27-year-old Soviet cosmonaut, was the first man in space. His flight around the Earth, on April 12, 1961, lasted 108 minutes reaching a maximum altitude of 187 miles (300 km). He landed back in the Soviet Union to a hero's welcome.

Right Sputnik 1, *launched in October 1957, was a small sphere, weighing only 183 lb (83 kg) and 22 inches (560 mm) in diameter. Sputnik 2 launched a dog, Laika, into orbit but it died after a week.*

Below *In April 1961 an R-7 rocket lifted off from the Baikonur Space Center in Kazakhstan and put the spaceship Vostok 1 into orbit. Inside was Gagarin.*

12
АПРЕЛЯ
1961

Above *Yuri Gagarin (1934–68), the Russian cosmonaut and first man in space.*

Man On The Moon

Right *Armstrong and Aldrin spent two hours on the Moon's surface, collecting samples of dust and rock, and taking photographs. These samples have been invaluable scientific research.*

Left *A space shuttle is an aircraft that can make repeated flights in space. The American space shuttle uses huge booster rockets to launch it into orbit.*

President Kennedy committed the United States to putting a man on the Moon by the end of the 1960s.

On July 16, 1969, a Saturn rocket took off from Florida at the start of a 240,000-mile (386,000-km) journey. At 120 miles (193 km) above the Earth, the command module *Columbia* was thrust out of the Earth's gravitational pull and was on course for the moon.

On July 20, Neil Armstrong and Edwin (Buzz) Aldrin entered the lunar module, *Apollo 11*. When the module touched down Armstrong became the first man on the Moon, saying "That's one small step for man, one giant leap for mankind."

SPACE: THE FINAL FRONTIER

Humans are continually seeking new frontiers, and the exploration of space is no exception. Who knows, science fiction may well become fact in the 21st century, as technology, experience, and scientific knowledge grow.

Robotic missions equipped with cameras and sensors already collect information about the Solar System and beam it back to earth by radio. The Pathfinder investigations and the discovery of possible ancient life on Mars mean the world's attention is now focused on space once more.

Left *Neil Armstrong climbed down from the* Apollo 11 *lunar module in July 20, 1969—the first person on the Moon.*

Right *Human missions to the Moon and Mars may soon become a reality. Space colonies may cease to be science fiction.*

Chapter 5:
The World Today

People around the world have contrasting lifestyles. For example, they speak many different languages and follow a variety of religions. The differences between people have often led to conflict and wars. However, easier forms of long-distance travel and modern technology are drawing people closer together, reducing the differences between them.

Hot, Cold, Wet, Dry

Central heating and air conditioning have made it possible for people to live anywhere in the world, even in the coldest and hottest places. However, regions where it is too cold for most plants to grow contain few people. Most of the continent of Antarctica is buried under the world's biggest ice sheet and it has no permanent population. A few scientists do live there comfortably for short periods of time, doing research to find out more about this frozen land, but they have to get all their food and other supplies from the outside world.

Egypt has a hot, dry climate. Windswept desert covers most of the land. The River Nile, whose water comes from the highlands of northeast Africa, flows through the country from south to north. Its valley provided a home for ancient Egypt, a great early civilization, and most Egyptians today live along its banks. Many other desert countries are thinly populated, because they lack the water needed to grow crops.

Below The continent of Antarctica is too cold for plants to grow and support a permenant population.

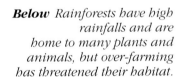

Above The majority of the world's people live in areas where land can be farmed and used to grow crops.

Left Only about a tenth of the world can be used to grow crops.

Only about a tenth of the world can be used to grow crops and it is here where most of the world's people live. Pasture, which can be used to graze farm animals, covers a larger area—about a fifth of the world's land. These regions also support people, but fewer than farming areas. Many people in dry grassland regions are nomads, who wander from place to place in search of pasture. The natural vegetation of the hot and wet regions around the Equator is rainforest. These dense forests were once the home of people who lived mainly by hunting and gathering. Today, large areas of forest have been removed and the land used for farming. But forest destruction is contributing to global warming, the most serious threat now facing the human race.

Below Rainforests have high rainfalls and are home to many plants and animals, but over-farming has threatened their habitat.

Above In the hot, dry climate of Egypt, people use camels as transport over the desert.

The Living World

The cold, treeless areas in polar regions, where plants grow during the short summer, are called tundra.

Mountains contain zones of different plants according to height, including forests, pasture, and ice fields.

Evergreen coniferous forests, with trees such as fir, pine, and spruce, grow in places with cold, snowy climates.

Temperate forests, with trees that shed their leaves in autumn, grow in places with warm temperate climates.

Climate largely determines the plants and animals in any region. For example, the cold, frozen tundra is treeless, and only animals can survive the cold and live in polar regions.

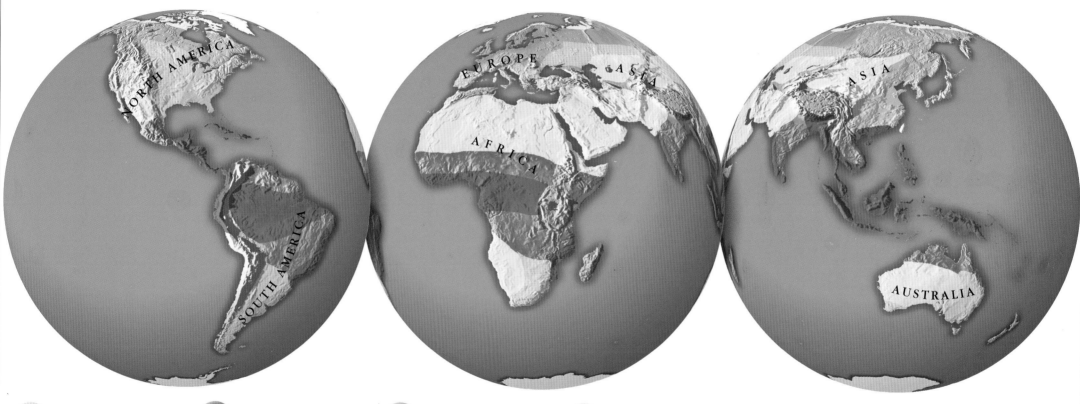

Temperate, mainly treeless grasslands occur in places with dry climates. They include prairie and steppe.

Tropical rainforests grow in regions with tropical climates, with plenty of rainfall, often throughout the year.

Savannah, tropical grassland with scattered trees, occurs in tropical rainy regions with a marked dry season.

Deserts have little rainfall. No rain may fall for several years, but then one cloudburst may flood large areas.

Animals and plants thrive in warm temperate forests, but these have been largely cut down to make space for farming. Today, tropical rainforests are also being cut down. These forests contain more than half of the world's living things. Scientists regard their destruction as a major disaster.

Population

In 1999, the world's population passed the six billion mark. Large areas are too dry or too cold to support more than a few people, while in other areas people are crowded together.

Areas with good soils and a pleasant climate contain large numbers of people, especially in cities. For example, about two-thirds of the land in Australia is almost empty of people, because it is too dry. More than 60 percent of Australians live in five cities: Sydney, Melbourne, Brisbane, Perth, and Adelaide. From space, cities show up as sparkling dots of light at night.

Hong Kong is a thriving island city off the coast of South China, with a population of over six million people. With only limited land available for the growing population, most people live in high-rise buildings. Many Asian cities have populations of over a million. The majority of the world's most rapidly growing cities are in this region.

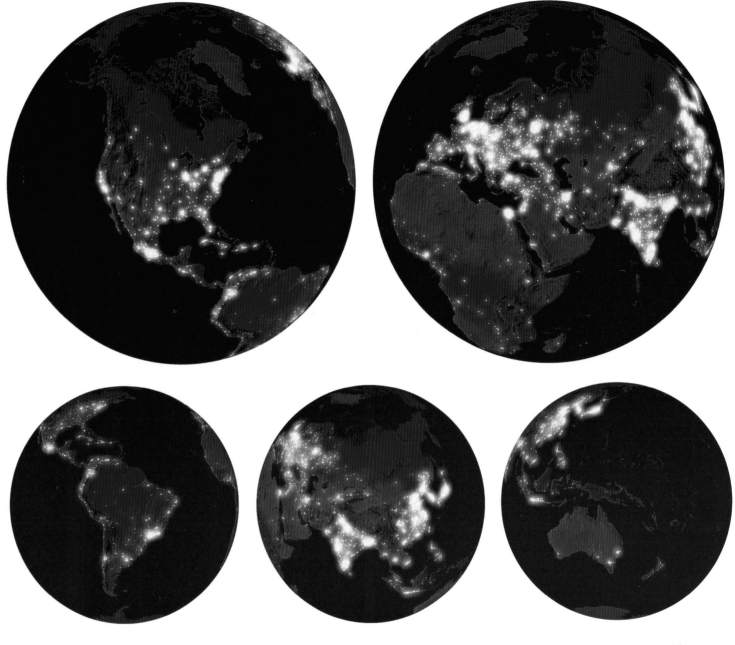

Imagine looking down from space on Earth at night. If everyone on Earth stood in the open holding a lit candle, thickly populated areas of the world would appear as bright points of light. Thinly populated areas would look dark and empty.

The darkened globes shown above reveal brightly lit areas where people are crowded together. You can see how the northeastern United States and west-central Europe are thickly populated. But most of northern Africa, which is desert, looks empty of people.

Asia contains some of the world's most thickly populated areas, especially in India, Bangladesh, eastern China, and Southeast Asia. China and India have more people than any other country. In contrast, most of South America and Australia are thinly populated.

*The shortest distance between two points is a straight line. But straight lines drawn on many world maps are not the shortest distances. This is because the Earth is round and not flat. To find the shortest distance between places on Earth, take a piece of string and stretch it across a globe between any two places. The line followed by the string is called a great-circle route, (a great circle divides the Earth into two equal halves). The globes, **right** and **below**, show some great-circle routes between cities.*

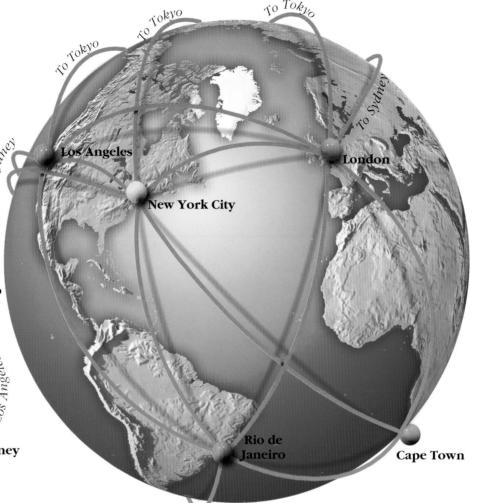

*Modern canals save ships long sea journeys. **Right** the globe shows that before the Panama Canal was completed in 1914, the sea journey from New York City to San Francisco around South America was more than 13,000 miles (20,900 km). The canal reduced the journey to about 5,200 miles (less than 8,300 km). **Center right** the Suez Canal, Egypt, connects the Mediterranean and Red Seas. It saves oil tankers from the Gulf region having to sail around Africa to reach western Europe. **Far right** Greece's Corinth Canal, is a shortcut for ships sailing from the Aegean to the Ionian Seas.*

Getting Around

Around 200 years ago, people seldom went far from their homes. Most of them lived by farming and the longest journey many of them took was a walk to the nearest town on market day. But the invention of engine-powered machines from the late 18th century caused a rapid revolution in transportation. Today, heavy raw materials for industry are shipped around the world by road and sea, while people fly in jet airliners to countries on the other side of the globe. Some experts predict that, before long, tourists will be taking trips in space!

Transportation takes three main forms: land, water, and air. Land transportation includes cars, trains, and huge trucks that carry heavy goods. Water transportation includes the movement of bulky goods in cargo ships, such as the huge tankers that carry oil to industrial countries. Air transportation is suited to moving expensive, lightweight, and perishable goods, as well as passengers. Faster, cheaper means of transportation have helped to increase international trade, raising the living standards of developing countries.

Canada And Greenland

Let's take a trip to Canada. From space, we can see that Canada borders the icy Arctic Ocean. East of Canada is Greenland, the world's largest island. Most of Greenland is buried by ice.

Canada is the world's second largest country, after Russia. But it has only about 30 million people. The United States has over nine times as many people as Canada. The far north is too cold even for trees. But vast forests of evergreen trees cover central Canada and the western mountains. Animals such as bears, beavers, moose and wolves live in the northern forests.

Mount Logan, Canada's highest peak, lies near the border with Alaska. Most Canadians live within about 200 miles (320 km) of the United States border. This region contains most of Canada's fertile farmland and its largest cities, including the capital, Ottawa.

Above Wheat is the chief crop on the prairies east of the Rocky Mountains.

Below The Inuit in northern Canada use sledges pulled by huskies.

Right A Native American totem pole from western Canada.

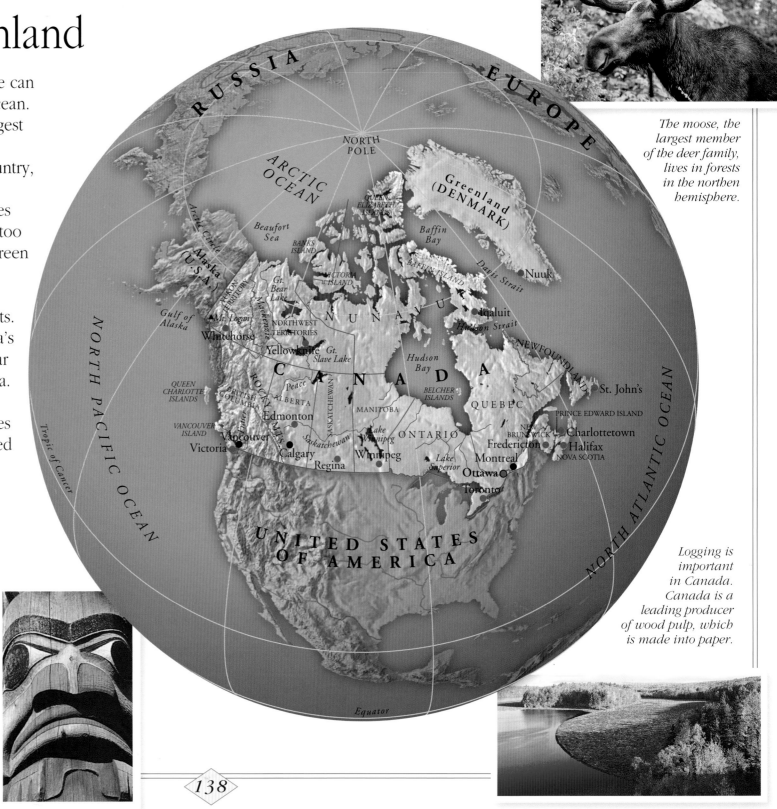

The moose, the largest member of the deer family, lives in forests in the northern hemisphere.

Logging is important in Canada. Canada is a leading producer of wood pulp, which is made into paper.

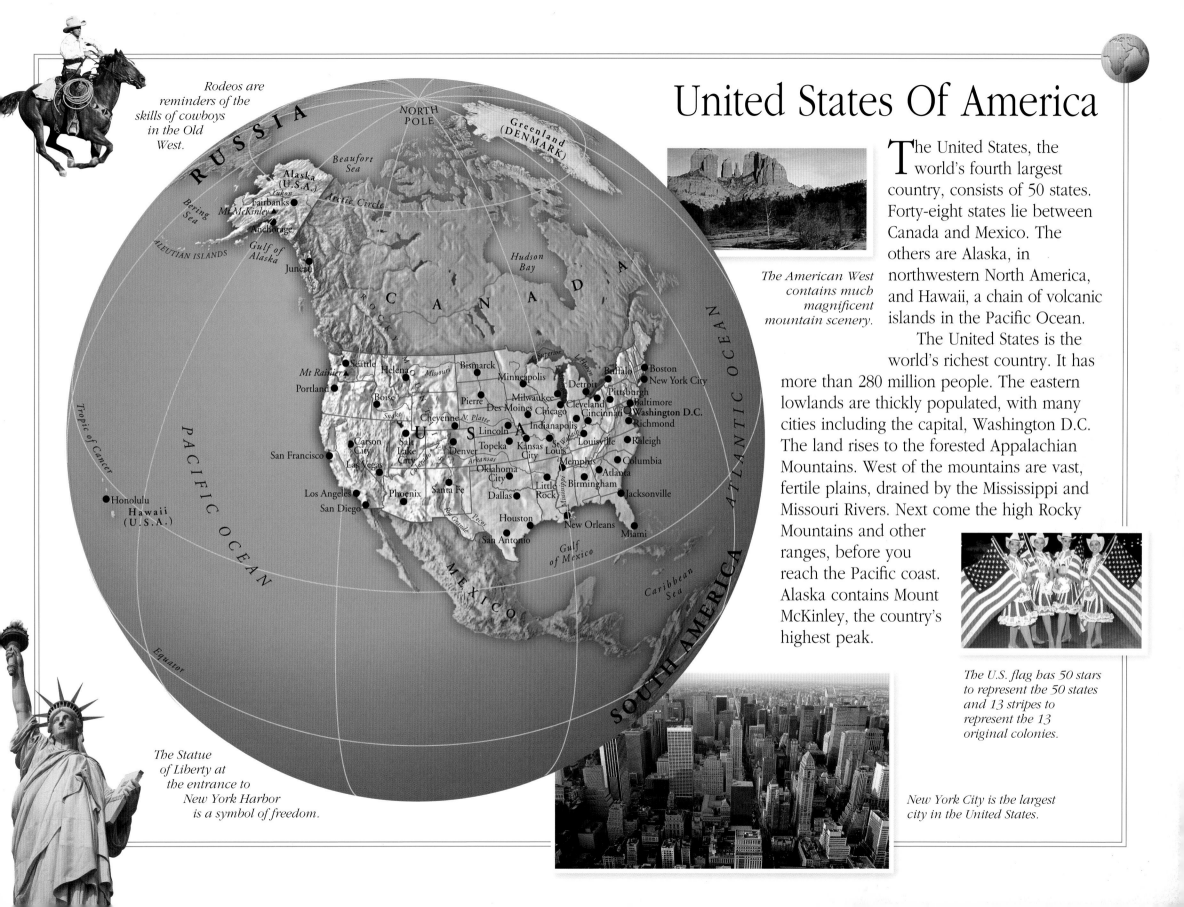

United States Of America

Rodeos are reminders of the skills of cowboys in the Old West.

The American West contains much magnificent mountain scenery.

Tthe United States, the world's fourth largest country, consists of 50 states. Forty-eight states lie between Canada and Mexico. The others are Alaska, in northwestern North America, and Hawaii, a chain of volcanic islands in the Pacific Ocean.

The United States is the world's richest country. It has more than 280 million people. The eastern lowlands are thickly populated, with many cities including the capital, Washington D.C. The land rises to the forested Appalachian Mountains. West of the mountains are vast, fertile plains, drained by the Mississippi and Missouri Rivers. Next come the high Rocky Mountains and other ranges, before you reach the Pacific coast. Alaska contains Mount McKinley, the country's highest peak.

The U.S. flag has 50 stars to represent the 50 states and 13 stripes to represent the 13 original colonies.

The Statue of Liberty at the entrance to New York Harbor is a symbol of freedom.

New York City is the largest city in the United States.

Map labels

RUSSIA
NORTH POLE
Greenland (DENMARK)
Beaufort Sea
Alaska (U.S.A.)
Yukon
Fairbanks
Mt McKinley
Anchorage
Bering Sea
ALEUTIAN ISLANDS
Gulf of Alaska
Arctic Circle
Juneau
CANADA
Hudson Bay
ROCKY
Mt Rainier
Seattle
Helena
Missouri
Bismarck
Minneapolis
Superior
Buffalo
Boston
New York City
Portland
Detroit
Pittsburgh
Boise
Pierre
Milwaukee
Cleveland
Cincinnati
Baltimore
Washington D.C.
Snake
Cheyenne
N. Platte
Des Moines
Chicago
Indianapolis
Richmond
Carson City
Salt Lake City
U S A
Lincoln
St Wabash
Louisville
Raleigh
San Francisco
Colorado
Denver
Topeka
Kansas City
St Louis
Arkansas
Memphis
Columbia
Las Vegas
Oklahoma City
Atlanta
Los Angeles
Phoenix
Santa Fe
Dallas
Little Rock
Birmingham
Mississippi
Jacksonville
San Diego
Rio Grande
Pecos
Houston
New Orleans
Miami
San Antonio
Gulf of Mexico
MEXICO
Caribbean Sea
PACIFIC OCEAN
Tropic of Cancer
Honolulu
Hawaii (U.S.A.)
ATLANTIC OCEAN
SOUTH AMERICA
Equator

Southern North America

North America is the third largest continent after Asia and Africa. It contains not only Canada and the United States, but also Mexico, the seven countries of Central America, and the island countries in the Caribbean Sea.

Mexico is the largest country in southern North America. If you take a look at Mexico from space, you will see that it contains mountain ranges, a central plateau dotted with smoking volcanoes, and some coastal lowlands. South of Mexico, the countries of Central America form a bridge, linking North and South America. The Panama Canal cuts through this bridge, providing a shortcut for ships sailing from the Atlantic to the Pacific oceans.

The Caribbean Islands have beautiful beaches which attract many tourists. But danger sometimes lurks in the Caribbean. Great hurricanes often batter the coasts, and volcanoes occasionally erupt, driving people from their homes.

Above *Many tourists visit island resorts in the Caribbean Sea.*

Below *Most Mexicans are of mixed white and Native American origin.*

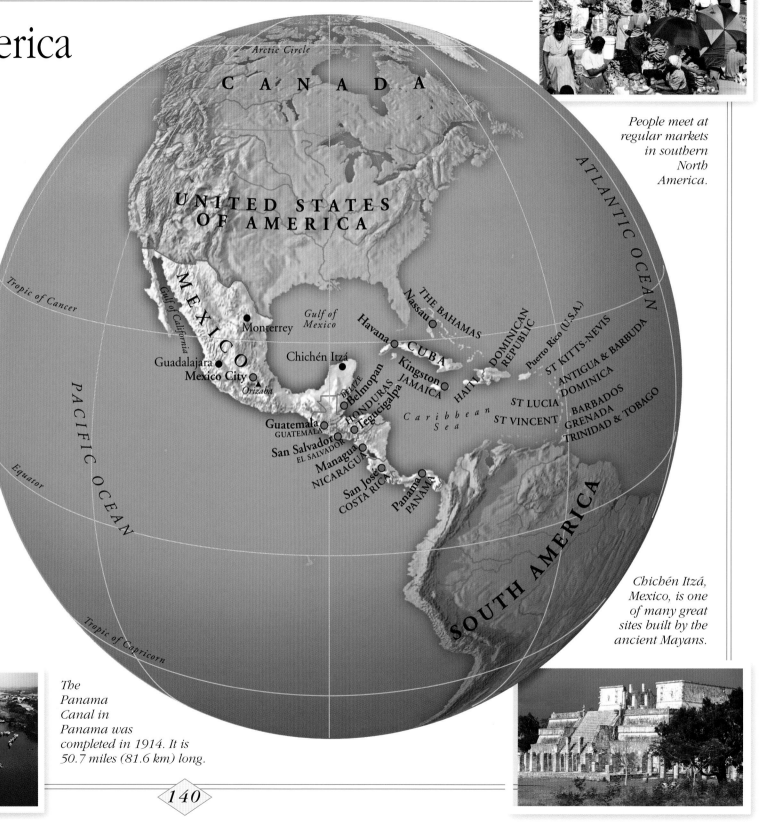

People meet at regular markets in southern North America.

Chichén Itzá, Mexico, is one of many great sites built by the ancient Mayans.

The Panama Canal in Panama was completed in 1914. It is 50.7 miles (81.6 km) long.

South America

South America is the world's fourth largest continent. It consists of 12 independent countries and two territories. The territories are French Guiana and the British-ruled Falkland Islands. The globe shows that Brazil, the world's fifth largest country, occupies nearly half of South America. The mighty Amazon River flows across northern Brazil. Many rivers that feed the Amazon rise in the Andes, the world's longest mountain range.

From space, you might think that northern Brazil is covered by a huge green carpet. This is a vast rainforest made up of closely packed trees. It contains many kinds of plants and animals. Not all of South America is wet and hot. Northern Chile contains the Atacama Desert, one of the world's driest places.

Many people in South America are descendants of Native Americans and Europeans.

The Iguassu Falls lie between Argentina and Brazil.

Dense rainforests cover much of northern South America.

Machu Picchu, Peru, is an ancient Inca city. The Incas once ruled a great empire in the Andes Mountains.

Map Labels

Tropic of Cancer
ATLANTIC OCEAN
Caribbean Sea
Caracas
VENEZUELA
GUYANA
Georgetown
SURINAM
Paramaribo
French Guiana
Medellín
Ciudad Bolívar
Cayenne
Bogotá
COLOMBIA
Cali
Orinoco
Quito
Cotopaxi
Negro
Amazon
Manaus
Amazon
ISLA DE MARAJO
Belém
ECUADOR
Putumayo
Equator
GALAPAGOS IS. (ECUADOR)
Jurúa
Madeira
Tapajós
Fortaleza
PERU
Purus
Xingu
Araguaia
São Francisco
Tocantins
Huascarán
B R A Z I L
Recife
Machu Picchu
Guaporé
Lima
MATO GROSSO PLATEAU
Salvador
Cuzco
BOLIVIA
La Paz
Brasília
Arequipa
Mt Illimani
PACIFIC OCEAN
PARAGUAY
Paraná
Antofagasta
ATACAMA DESERT
Pilcomayo
Asunción
Rio de Janeiro
Tropic of Capricorn
Rio Salado
Iguassu Falls
São Paulo
CHILE
ANDES
Córdoba
Pôrto Alegre
Aconcagua
PAMPAS
Valparaíso
URUGUAY
ATLANTIC OCEAN
Santiago
Buenos Aires
Montevideo
Concepción
ARGENTINA
Bahía Blanca
PATAGONIA
FALKLAND IS. (U.K.) ISLAS MALVINAS
SOUTH GEORGIA IS. (U.K.)
Scotia Sea
Drake Passage
Antarctic Circle
ANTARCTICA

Europe

Europe is the sixth largest continent, but it is densely populated with many cities. It contains 43 complete countries, containing about 700 million people. It also includes a quarter of Russia. But European Russia has about four-fifths of Russia's population, about 115 million people.

Northern Europe borders the icy Arctic Ocean. Evergreen forests in the north are the home of such animals as brown bears, reindeer, and wolves. The forests of central and southern Europe have been largely cut down to make way for farmland and cities. The chief mountain range in western Europe is the Alps. South of the Alps lie Europe's Mediterranean countries, which have hot, dry summers.

Tulips are famous products of the Netherlands.

The Matterhorn is one of the magnificent peaks in the Alps.

Above *Stonehenge in southern England is one of Europe's best known ancient sites. Europe has a long history, with many monuments dating back 2,000 years and more.*

Right *Europe has several small countries which are hard to find on the map. On this globe, 15 small countries are shown by numbers. Can you find the 15 countries listed below on the globe?*

1 Andorra	7 Luxembourg
2 Bosnia & Herzegovina	8 Macedonia
3 Croatia	9 Moldova
4 Gibraltar (UK)	10 Monaco
5 Kaliningrad (Russia)	11 San Marino
6 Liechtenstein	12 Slovenia
	13 Vatican City
	14 Serbia
	15 Montenegro

A church in Bavaria, Germany, is a reminder that Christianity is the chief religion of Europe.

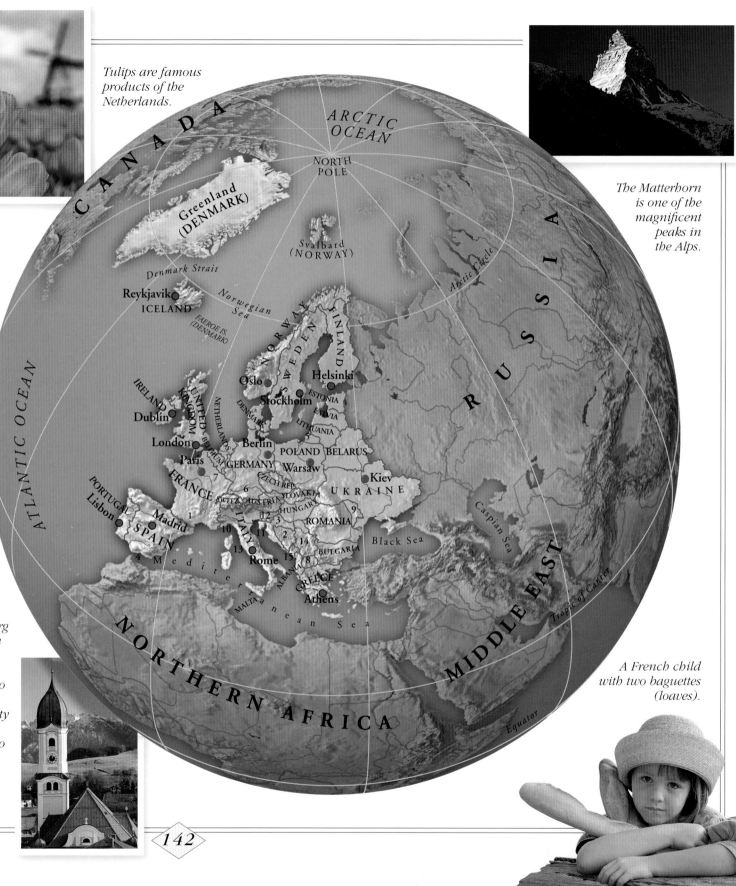

ARCTIC OCEAN

CANADA

NORTH POLE

Greenland (DENMARK)

Svalbard (NORWAY)

Denmark Strait

RUSSIA

Arctic Circle

Norwegian Sea

Reykjavik
ICELAND

FAEROE IS. (DENMARK)

NORWAY
SWEDEN
FINLAND

ATLANTIC OCEAN

Oslo
Helsinki
ESTONIA
Stockholm
LATVIA
LITHUANIA

IRELAND
UNITED KINGDOM
Dublin
NETHERLANDS
DENMARK

London
BELGIUM
Berlin
POLAND
BELARUS

Paris
GERMANY
Warsaw

FRANCE
CZECH REP.
SLOVAKIA
UKRAINE
Kiev

PORTUGAL
SWITZ. AUSTRIA
HUNGARY

Lisbon
Madrid
SPAIN
ITALY
ROMANIA

Caspian Sea

Rome
BULGARIA
Black Sea

ALBANIA
GREECE

MALTA
Athens
Mediterranean Sea

MIDDLE EAST

NORTHERN AFRICA

Equator
Tropic of Cancer

A French child with two baguettes (loaves).

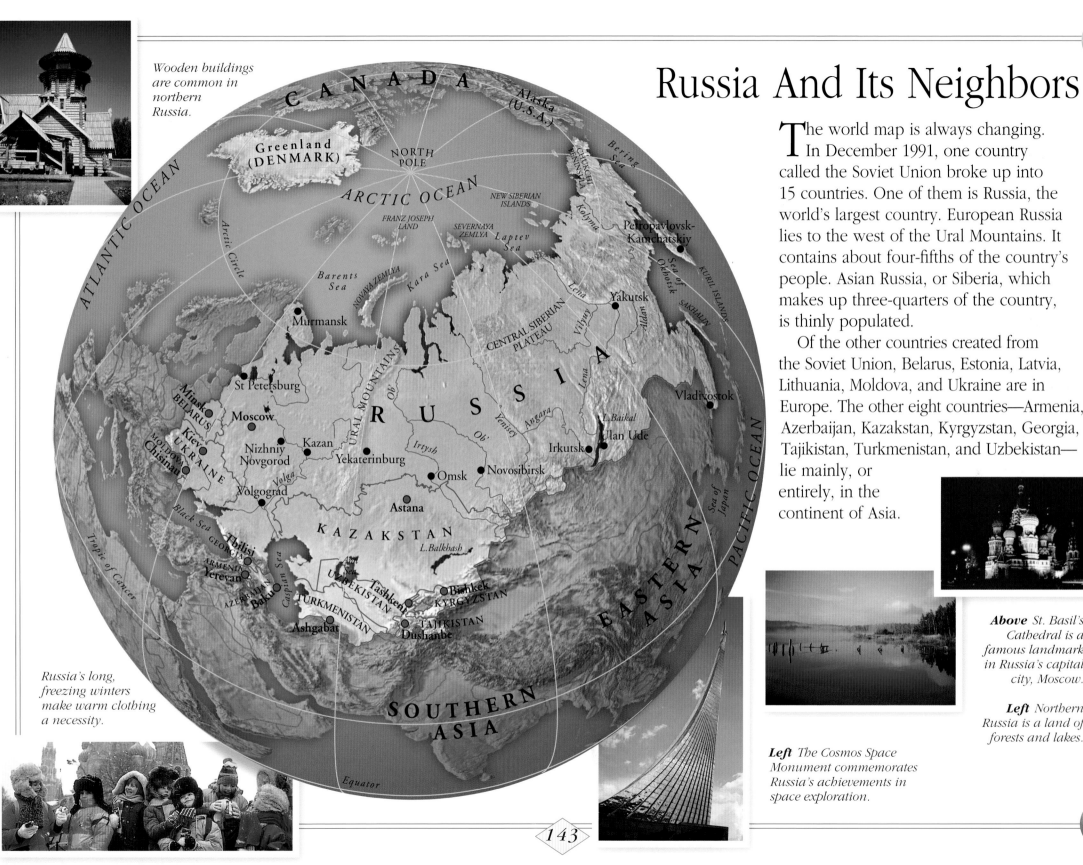

Russia And Its Neighbors

Wooden buildings are common in northern Russia.

The world map is always changing. In December 1991, one country called the Soviet Union broke up into 15 countries. One of them is Russia, the world's largest country. European Russia lies to the west of the Ural Mountains. It contains about four-fifths of the country's people. Asian Russia, or Siberia, which makes up three-quarters of the country, is thinly populated.

Of the other countries created from the Soviet Union, Belarus, Estonia, Latvia, Lithuania, Moldova, and Ukraine are in Europe. The other eight countries—Armenia, Azerbaijan, Kazakstan, Kyrgyzstan, Georgia, Tajikistan, Turkmenistan, and Uzbekistan— lie mainly, or entirely, in the continent of Asia.

CANADA

Alaska (U.S.A.)

Greenland (DENMARK)

NORTH POLE

ATLANTIC OCEAN

ARCTIC OCEAN

Arctic Circle

NEW SIBERIAN ISLANDS

FRANZ JOSEPH LAND

SEVERNAYA ZEMLYA

Barents Sea

NOVAYA ZEMLYA

Kara Sea

Laptev Sea

CHUKCHI PENINSULA

Bering Sea

Kolyma

Petropavlovsk-Kamchatskiy

Sea of Okhotsk

KURIL ISLANDS

SAKHALIN

Lena

Yakutsk

CENTRAL SIBERIAN PLATEAU

Vilyuy

Aldan

Murmansk

St Petersburg

Minsk
BELARUS

Moscow

Kiev
UKRAINE

MOLDOVA
Chisinau

Nizhniy Novgorod

Kazan

Volga

Volgograd

Black Sea

URAL MOUNTAINS

Ob

Yekaterinburg

Irtysh

Omsk

R U S S I A

Ob'

Yenisey

Angara

Novosibirsk

Astana

K A Z A K S T A N

L.Balkhash

L.Baikal

Ulan Ude

Irkutsk

Lena

Vladivostok

Sea of Japan

EASTERN ASIA

PACIFIC OCEAN

Tropic of Cancer

Tbilisi
GEORGIA

ARMENIA
Yerevan

AZERBAIJAN
Baku

Caspian Sea

Aral Sea

UZBEKISTAN

TURKMENISTAN

Ashgabat

Tashkent

Dushanbe
TAJIKISTAN

Bishkek
KYRGYZSTAN

SOUTHERN ASIA

Equator

Russia's long, freezing winters make warm clothing a necessity.

Above St. Basil's Cathedral is a famous landmark in Russia's capital city, Moscow.

Left Northern Russia is a land of forests and lakes.

Left The Cosmos Space Monument commemorates Russia's achievements in space exploration.

Northern Africa

Imagine flying across the middle of North Africa from the Atlantic Ocean to the Red Sea. Your journey would take you across the Sahara, the world's largest desert. You would see very few signs of life until you reach the well-cultivated Nile Valley in Egypt and Sudan. The Nile is the world's longest river. Its water comes from the rainy highlands to the south.

Some areas in the north, where the Mediterranean Sea separates Africa from Europe, have enough rain for farming. Northern North Africa is the land of the Arabs, who believe in Islam. South of the Sahara, the land merges into grassland with scattered trees, called savannah. The far south is hot and rainy, but most of the former forests have been cut down by farmers.

Camels are used as "beasts of burden" throughout northern Africa.

Date palms are common plants in the dry countries of North Africa.

*Ancient Egypt grew up in the Nile Valley around 5,000 years ago. Farmers used river water to grow crops. Great ancient Egyptian monuments, including the pyramids, **above**, and the sphinx, **right**, can be seen near Cairo.*

NORTH ATLANTIC OCEAN

EUROPE

ASIA

Arctic Circle

Mediterranean Sea

Rabat
Casablanca
Algiers
Tunis
TUNISIA
Tripoli
Cairo

CANARY ISLANDS (SPAIN)
MOROCCO
ATLAS MOUNTAINS

WESTERN SAHARA

ALGERIA
LIBYA
EGYPT

Tropic of Cancer

LIBYAN DESERT

Red Sea

CAPE VERDE ISLANDS

MAURITANIA
Nouakchott

SAHARA DESERT

AHAGGAR MOUNTAINS

NUBIAN DESERT

MALI

TIBESTI MOUNTAINS

ERITREA
Asmara

Gulf of Aden

Dakar
SENEGAL
Senegal
GAMBIA
Banjul
Bissau
GUINEA-BISSAU
GUINEA
Bamako
BURKINA FASO
Niamey

NIGER

CHAD

L.Chad

Khartoum

Blue Nile

DJIBOUTI
Djibouti

Niger

SUDAN

Nile

White Nile

Addis Ababa

Conakry
Freetown
SIERRA LEONE
Ouagadougou
NIGERIA
N'Djamena
ETHIOPIA

Monrovia
LIBERIA
CÔTE D'IVOIRE
GHANA
TOGO
BENIN
Abuja
Niger
Benue
SOMALIA
Mogadishu

Yamoussoukro
Abidjan
Accra
Lomé
Porto-Novo
Lagos

Equator

SOUTH ATLANTIC OCEAN

SOUTHERN AFRICA

INDIAN OCEAN

Tropic of Capricorn

Many soldiers in Morocco are skilled horsemen.

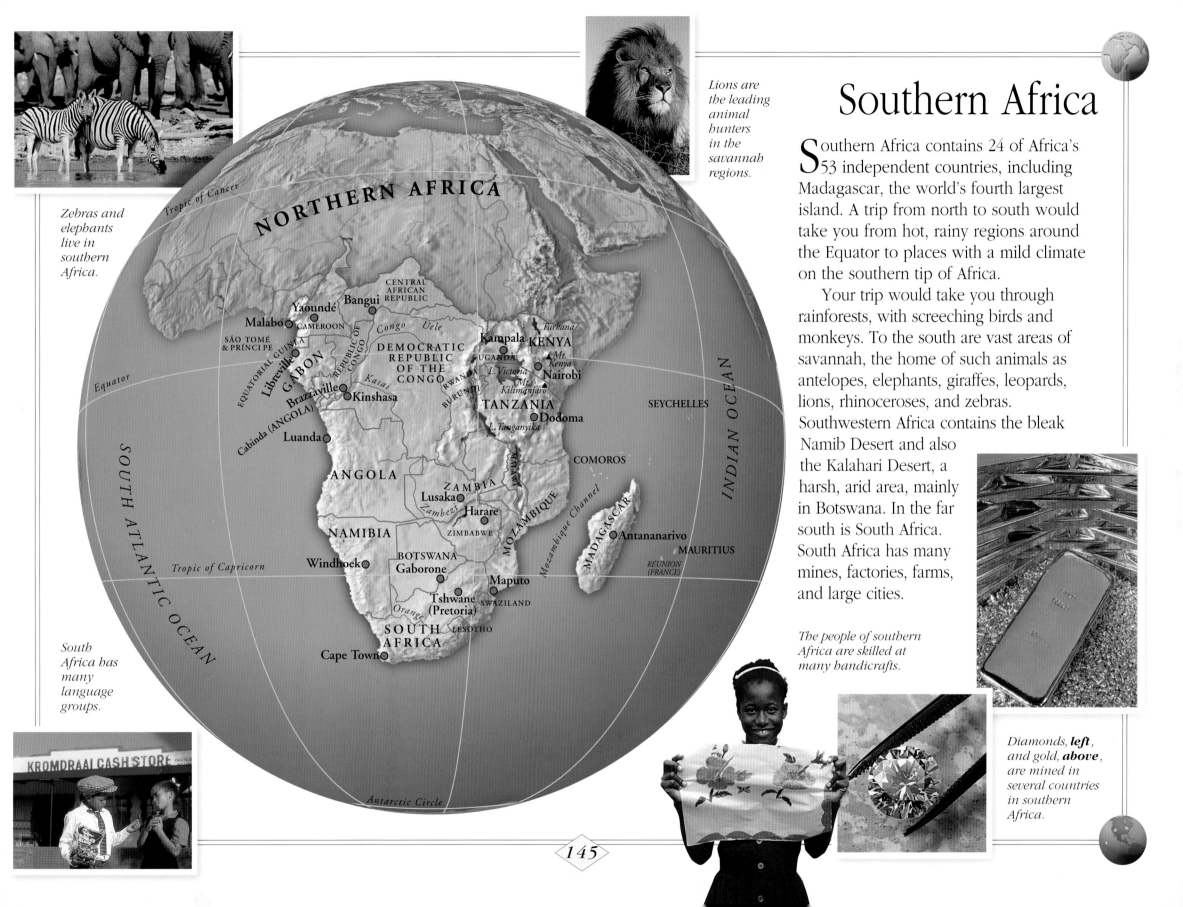

Southern Africa

Southern Africa contains 24 of Africa's 53 independent countries, including Madagascar, the world's fourth largest island. A trip from north to south would take you from hot, rainy regions around the Equator to places with a mild climate on the southern tip of Africa.

Your trip would take you through rainforests, with screeching birds and monkeys. To the south are vast areas of savannah, the home of such animals as antelopes, elephants, giraffes, leopards, lions, rhinoceroses, and zebras. Southwestern Africa contains the bleak Namib Desert and also the Kalahari Desert, a harsh, arid area, mainly in Botswana. In the far south is South Africa. South Africa has many mines, factories, farms, and large cities.

Lions are the leading animal hunters in the savannah regions.

Zebras and elephants live in southern Africa.

South Africa has many language groups.

The people of southern Africa are skilled at many handicrafts.

*Diamonds, **left**, and gold, **above**, are mined in several countries in southern Africa.*

Map labels

NORTHERN AFRICA

Tropic of Cancer

Equator

Tropic of Capricorn

Antarctic Circle

SOUTH ATLANTIC OCEAN

INDIAN OCEAN

CENTRAL AFRICAN REPUBLIC — Bangui
CAMEROON — Yaoundé
Malabo
SÃO TOMÉ & PRÍNCIPE
EQUATORIAL GUINEA
GABON — Libreville
REPUBLIC OF CONGO — Brazzaville
Congo
Uele
DEMOCRATIC REPUBLIC OF THE CONGO
Kasai
Kinshasa
Cabinda (ANGOLA)
Luanda
ANGOLA
L. Turkana
KENYA — Nairobi
Kampala
UGANDA
Mt. Kenya
L. Victoria
RWANDA
BURUNDI
Mt. Kilimanjaro
TANZANIA — Dodoma
L. Tanganyika
SEYCHELLES
COMOROS
ZAMBIA — Lusaka
Zambezi
MALAWI
Harare
ZIMBABWE
MOZAMBIQUE
Mozambique Channel
MADAGASCAR — Antananarivo
MAURITIUS
RÉUNION (FRANCE)
NAMIBIA
Windhoek
BOTSWANA — Gaborone
Maputo
SWAZILAND
Orange
Tshwane (Pretoria)
LESOTHO
SOUTH AFRICA
Cape Town

KROMDRAAL CASH STORE

Middle East

Asia, the world's largest continent, is divided into four main regions. One of them is called the Middle East, or Southwestern Asia. A view from space shows that most of the Middle East consists of empty desert or parched grassland, where water is scarce. Farmland occurs in the northern uplands and along rivers, especially the Tigris and Euphrates in Turkey and Iraq. Other farms are irrigated, or artificially watered. Some countries have rich reserves of oil and natural gas. These fuels have brought great wealth to some nations. From 2000 onwards, wars have occurred in the Middle East. In 2001, forces led by the United States attacked Afghanistan, while in 2003, forces overthrew Iraq's dictator, Saddam Hussein.

The Middle East is the home of three great religions: Judaism, the chief religion of Israel; Christianity; and Islam. More than four out of every five people in the Middle East are Muslims (followers of Islam).

Camels can go for several days without water.

Jerusalem is a holy city for Jews, Christians, and Muslims.

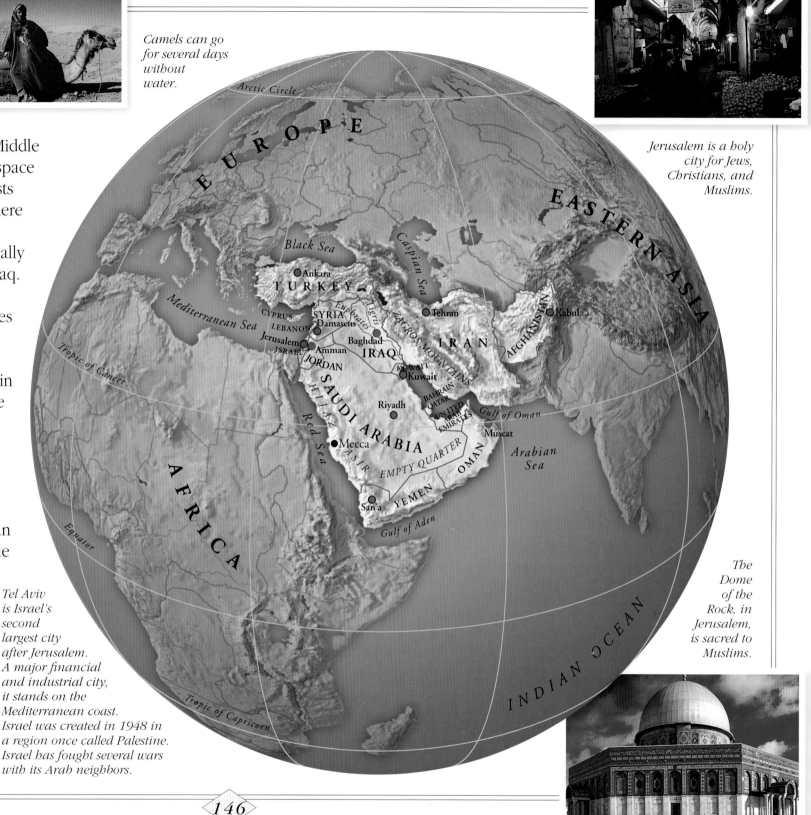

Tel Aviv is Israel's second largest city after Jerusalem. A major financial and industrial city, it stands on the Mediterranean coast. Israel was created in 1948 in a region once called Palestine. Israel has fought several wars with its Arab neighbors.

The Dome of the Rock, in Jerusalem, is sacred to Muslims.

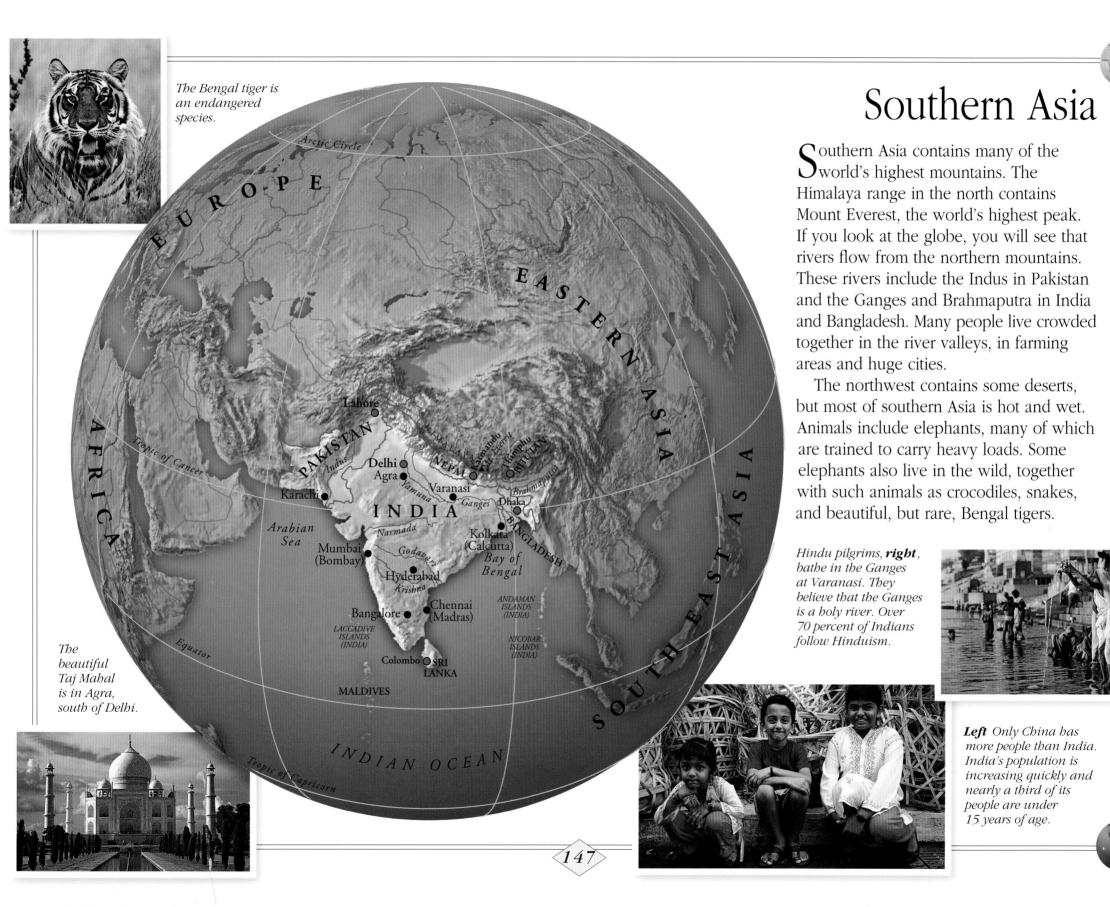

Southern Asia

Southern Asia contains many of the world's highest mountains. The Himalaya range in the north contains Mount Everest, the world's highest peak. If you look at the globe, you will see that rivers flow from the northern mountains. These rivers include the Indus in Pakistan and the Ganges and Brahmaputra in India and Bangladesh. Many people live crowded together in the river valleys, in farming areas and huge cities.

The northwest contains some deserts, but most of southern Asia is hot and wet. Animals include elephants, many of which are trained to carry heavy loads. Some elephants also live in the wild, together with such animals as crocodiles, snakes, and beautiful, but rare, Bengal tigers.

The Bengal tiger is an endangered species.

The beautiful Taj Mahal is in Agra, south of Delhi.

*Hindu pilgrims, **right**, bathe in the Ganges at Varanasi. They believe that the Ganges is a holy river. Over 70 percent of Indians follow Hinduism.*

Left *Only China has more people than India. India's population is increasing quickly and nearly a third of its people are under 15 years of age.*

147

Eastern Asia

Eastern Asia includes China, the world's third largest country. With a population of more than one billion people, it has more than any other country. Asia also includes the rich country of Japan.

On the globe, you will see that western China has many mountain ranges. It also includes the windswept plateau (tableland) of Tibet, and several deserts, including the cold Gobi Desert in northern China and Mongolia. Most Chinese people live in the east, especially in the valleys of rivers such as the Huang He, the Chang Jiang, and the Xi Jiang. Eastern Asia contains many great cities, including Tokyo, capital of Japan, together with Shanghai, on the east coast of China, and Beijing, the Chinese capital.

Above *Japanese geishas are entertainers. They are trained in the arts of dance, music, and conversation.*

Above right *The former British territory of Hong Kong is a port and a leading financial and industrial center. Britain returned Hong Kong to China in 1997.*

The Great Wall of China.

Japan has high-speed, bullet-shaped electric trains.

South Korean children on their way to school.

Chinese children in Tiananmen Square, in China's capital Beijing.

Southeast Asia

Southeast Asia consists of some countries on the southern Asian mainland, together with many islands. Much of the land is mountainous, with active volcanoes on some of the islands. The climate is hot and rainy, and forests and swamps cover large areas. But many forests have been cut down or burned to create farms. The number of wild animals has decreased, although monkeys, gibbons, and orangutans still live in the forests. One animal found in Indonesia is called the Komodo dragon. It is the world's largest lizard.

Farming is the main activity in Southeast Asia and rice is the chief crop and staple food. But the region also has large cities, with many factories.

Elephants are used as "beasts of burden" in Southeast Asia.

Rice is grown on step-like terraces cut into slopes.

Children in northern Thailand wear traditional dress.

Many people in Bali worship at Hindu temples.

Left *A Buddhist temple in Myanmar (Burma).*

Below *Singapore is a busy center of industry and trade.*

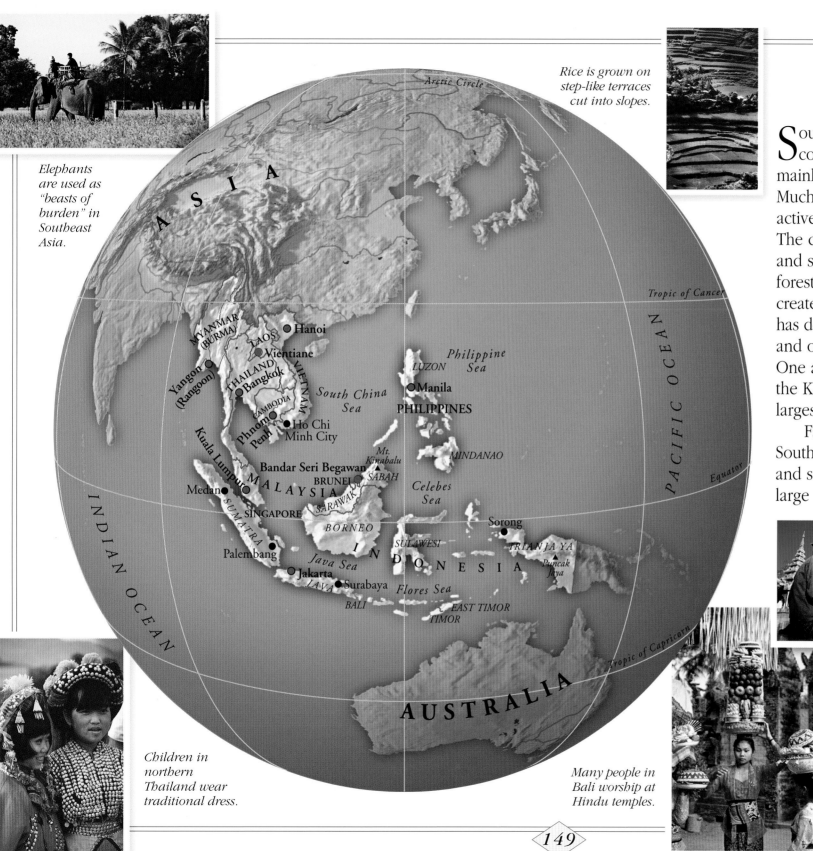

ASIA

MYANMAR (BURMA)

LAOS

Hanoi

Vientiane

Yangon (Rangoon)

THAILAND
Bangkok

VIETNAM

CAMBODIA

Phnom Penh

Ho Chi Minh City

South China Sea

Philippine Sea

LUZON

Manila

PHILIPPINES

MINDANAO

Mt. Kinabalu

Bandar Seri Begawan

BRUNEI

SABAH

Kuala Lumpur

MALAYSIA

SARAWAK

Medan

SINGAPORE

SUMATRA

BORNEO

Celebes Sea

SULAWESI

Sorong

IRIAN JAYA

Puncak Jaya

Palembang

Java Sea

INDONESIA

Jakarta

JAVA

Surabaya

Flores Sea

BALI

EAST TIMOR

TIMOR

PACIFIC OCEAN

INDIAN OCEAN

AUSTRALIA

Arctic Circle

Tropic of Cancer

Equator

Tropic of Capricorn

Australia And New Zealand

Australia, the smallest of the world's seven continents, and the island country of New Zealand lie in the Southern Hemisphere. Australia is the flattest continent. If you fly from east to west across Australia, you will see that the Great Dividing Range separates the east coast from the rest of the country. The Great Dividing Range is Australia's main upland area. It contains Australia's highest peak, Mount Kosciuszko. Beyond the Great Dividing Range lie the flat central lowlands, where farmers raise cattle and sheep.

To the west is a huge plateau, or flat tableland, broken by some low mountains. The west is mainly desert and few people live there.

New Zealand has more varied scenery. North Island has active volcanoes and South Island contains a mountain range called the Southern Alps. Its highest peak is Mount Cook.

Koalas live in trees in Australia.

Lamb and wool are major exports from New Zealand.

Above *Maoris were the original people of New Zealand.*

Right *Uluru (Ayers Rock) in central Australia is regarded as a sacred place by Aboriginal people of Australia.*

Left *Sydney is Australia's largest city. Its famous Opera House consists of white concrete shells that look like huge sails.*

Kangaroos are now protected in Australia.

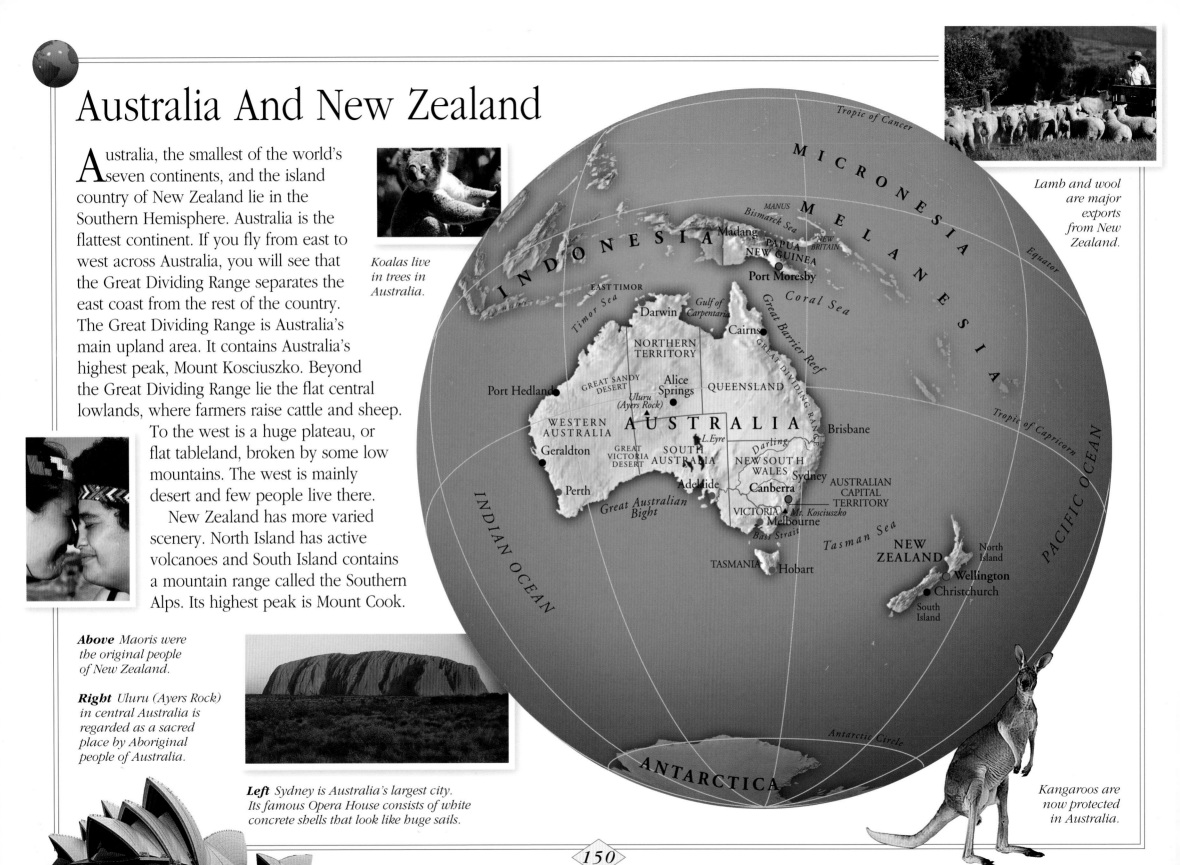

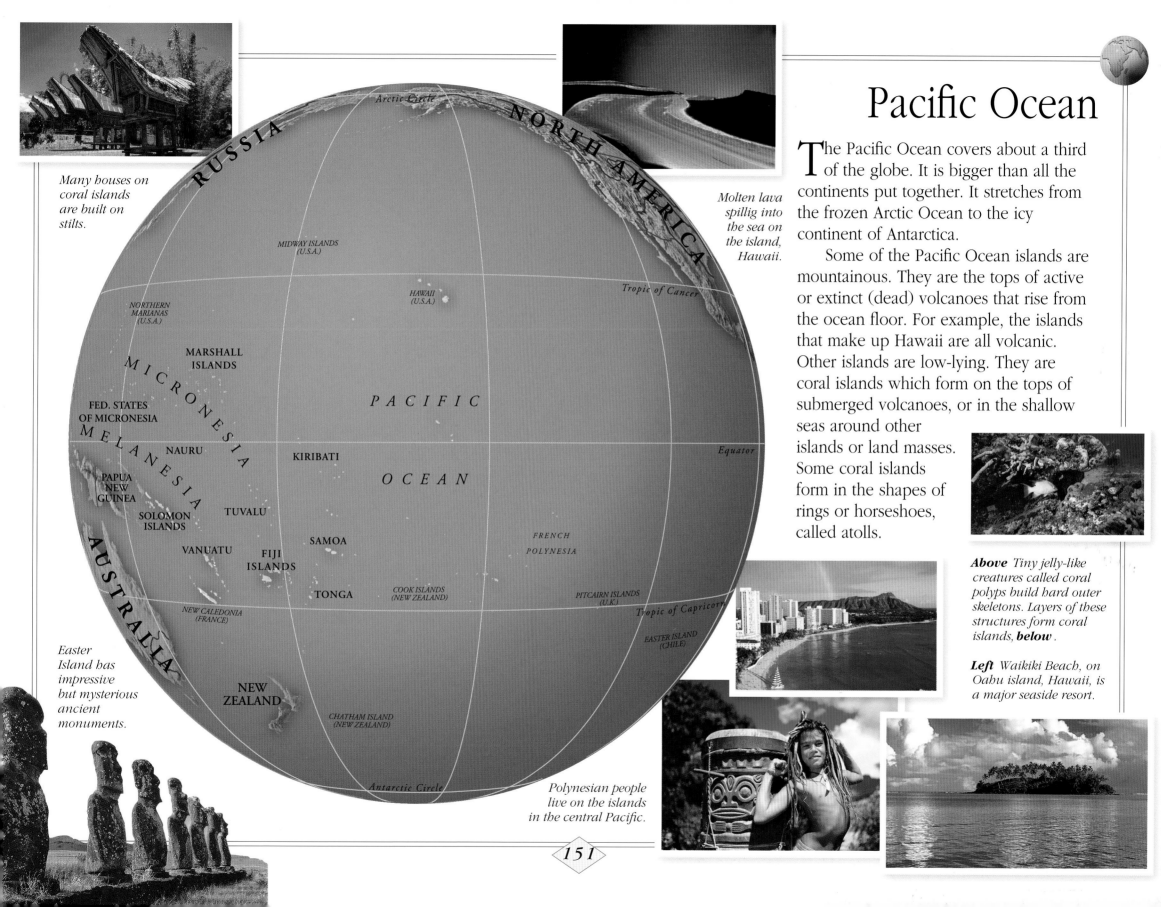

Pacific Ocean

The Pacific Ocean covers about a third of the globe. It is bigger than all the continents put together. It stretches from the frozen Arctic Ocean to the icy continent of Antarctica.

Some of the Pacific Ocean islands are mountainous. They are the tops of active or extinct (dead) volcanoes that rise from the ocean floor. For example, the islands that make up Hawaii are all volcanic. Other islands are low-lying. They are coral islands which form on the tops of submerged volcanoes, or in the shallow seas around other islands or land masses. Some coral islands form in the shapes of rings or horseshoes, called atolls.

Many houses on coral islands are built on stilts.

Molten lava spillig into the sea on the island, Hawaii.

Above Tiny jelly-like creatures called coral polyps build hard outer skeletons. Layers of these structures form coral islands, **below** *.*

Left Waikiki Beach, on Oahu island, Hawaii, is a major seaside resort.

Easter Island has impressive but mysterious ancient monuments.

Polynesian people live on the islands in the central Pacific.

RUSSIA
NORTH AMERICA
Arctic Circle
MIDWAY ISLANDS
(U.S.A.)
NORTHERN
MARIANAS
(U.S.A.)
HAWAII
(U.S.A.)
Tropic of Cancer
MICRONESIA
MARSHALL
ISLANDS
FED. STATES
OF MICRONESIA
PACIFIC
MELANESIA
NAURU
KIRIBATI
Equator
PAPUA
NEW
GUINEA
OCEAN
SOLOMON
ISLANDS
TUVALU
VANUATU
FIJI
ISLANDS
SAMOA
FRENCH
POLYNESIA
AUSTRALIA
TONGA
COOK ISLANDS
(NEW ZEALAND)
PITCAIRN ISLANDS
(U.K.)
NEW CALEDONIA
(FRANCE)
Tropic of Capricorn
EASTER ISLAND
(CHILE)
NEW
ZEALAND
CHATHAM ISLAND
(NEW ZEALAND)
Antarctic Circle

Atlantic Ocean

The Atlantic is the world's second largest ocean. It is a busy ocean, with ships crisscrossing its waters, carrying goods from one continent to another. It also contains large fishing grounds, although overfishing has caused fish stocks to drop to low levels.

The ocean's chief feature is mainly hidden from view. This is the mid-Atlantic Ridge, a huge mountain range rising from the deep ocean floor and running north-south through the ocean. The ridge is the place where plates are moving apart and where molten lava is rising to the surface to form new crustal rock. As a result, the Atlantic Ocean is becoming wider by about 1 inch (2.5 cm) a year. The volcanic island of Iceland rises from the ridge. It, too, is becoming wider as the plates on either side move apart. Newfoundland, in eastern Canada, the British Isles, and the sunny islands of the Caribbean Sea are also Atlantic islands.

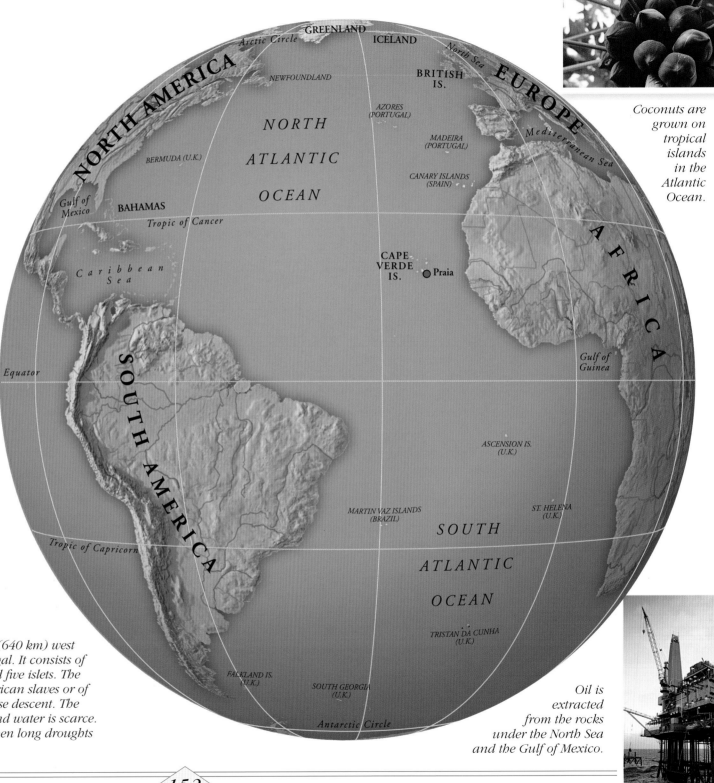

Cape Verde is a republic in the North Atlantic Ocean. It is located about 400 miles (640 km) west of Dakar, the capital of Senegal. It consists of 10 large volcanic islands and five islets. The people are descendants of African slaves or of mixed African and Portuguese descent. The islands have a dry climate and water is scarce. Most people are poor and, when long droughts occur, many people starve.

Coconuts are grown on tropical islands in the Atlantic Ocean.

Oil is extracted from the rocks under the North Sea and the Gulf of Mexico.

Indian Ocean

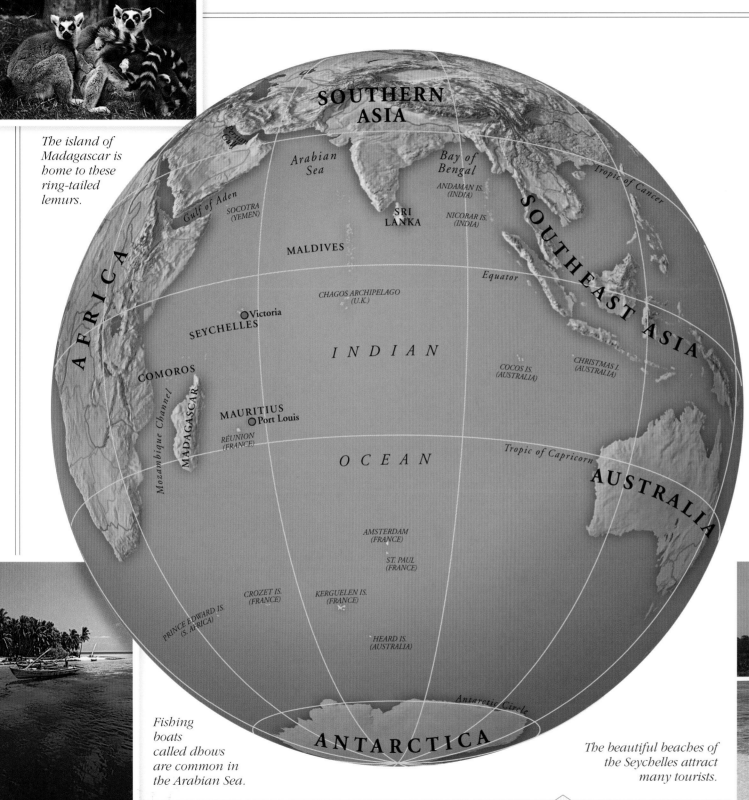

The island of Madagascar is home to these ring-tailed lemurs.

SOUTHERN ASIA

Persian Gulf

Arabian Sea

Gulf of Aden

SOCOTRA (YEMEN)

SRI LANKA

Bay of Bengal

ANDAMAN IS. (INDIA)

NICOBAR IS. (INDIA)

Tropic of Cancer

SOUTHEAST ASIA

MALDIVES

Equator

CHAGOS ARCHIPELAGO (U.K.)

○ Victoria
SEYCHELLES

COMOROS

I N D I A N

COCOS IS. (AUSTRALIA)

CHRISTMAS I. (AUSTRALIA)

Mozambique Channel

MADAGASCAR

MAURITIUS
○ Port Louis

RÉUNION (FRANCE)

O C E A N

Tropic of Capricorn

AUSTRALIA

AMSTERDAM (FRANCE)

ST. PAUL (FRANCE)

CROZET IS. (FRANCE)

KERGUELEN IS. (FRANCE)

PRINCE EDWARD IS. (S. AFRICA)

HEARD IS. (AUSTRALIA)

Antarctic Circle

ANTARCTICA

AFRICA

Fishing boats called dhows are common in the Arabian Sea.

The beautiful beaches of the Seychelles attract many tourists.

The Indian Ocean, the world's third largest ocean, extends from Southern Asia to Antarctica. The northern part of the ocean contains busy shipping lanes. Huge tankers, for example, cross the ocean to transport oil from the Persian Gulf to many parts of the world. Fishing vessels also sail the ocean, especially off the west coast of India. But fish spoils quickly in the hot weather in the northern and central parts of the Indian Ocean.

Hidden beneath the waves are long ocean ridges and deep trenches. These features are the edges of plates that form the Earth's hard outer layers. Around 180 million years ago, India was located near Antarctica. But a plate carrying India broke away and moved north, colliding with Asia around 50 million years ago. These plate movements created the modern Indian Ocean.

The Arctic

The Arctic Ocean, the smallest of the world's five oceans, lies around the North Pole on the top of the world. Ice covers much of the ocean for most of the year. Ships carrying goods must be accompanied by ice breakers that cut paths through the ice.

The region called the Arctic also includes the northern parts of Asia, Europe, and North America that surround the Arctic Ocean. Ice sheets cover some areas. Greenland, for example, is blanketed by the world's second largest ice sheet. However, in parts of the Arctic, the snow and ice melt in summer and plants grow. Various peoples, such as the Inuit of North America, live in the Arctic. Their traditional way of life depended mainly on hunting animals, such as polar bears, and fishing.

The Hare people of the Canadian Arctic are so called because they make their clothes from hare skins.

A small iceberg at Ellesmere Island, in northern Canada.

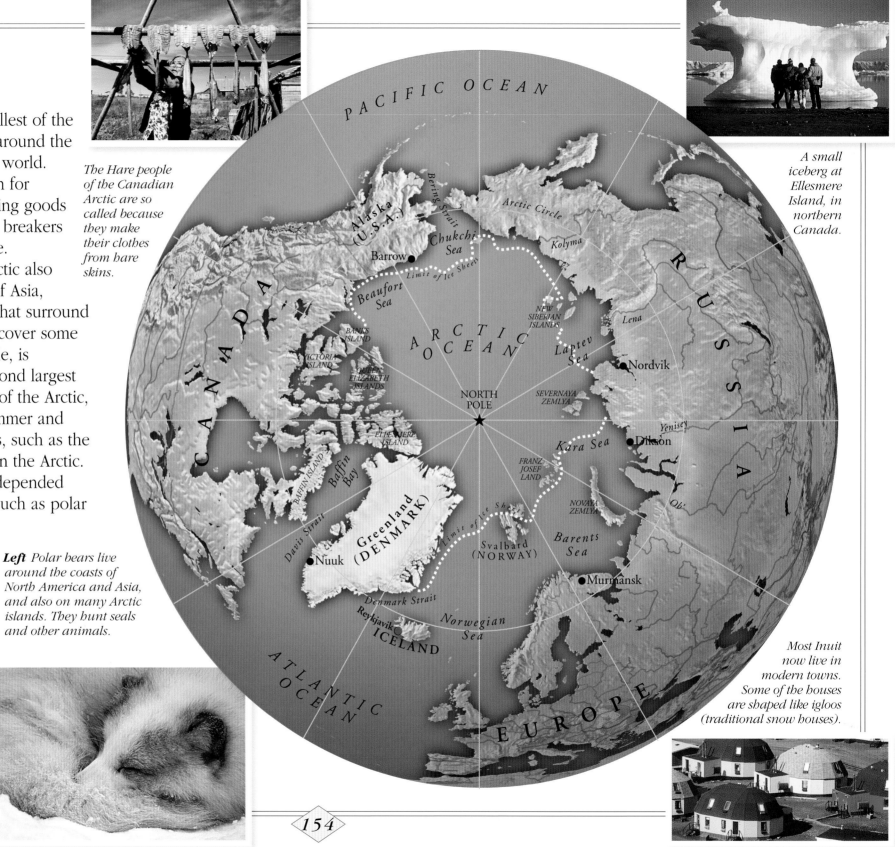

A small iceberg at Ellesmere Island, in northern Canada.

Left *Polar bears live around the coasts of North America and Asia, and also on many Arctic islands. They hunt seals and other animals.*

Right *The Arctic fox uses camouflage to help it catch its prey. Its coat changes from gray or brown in summer to white in winter, when snow covers the land.*

Most Inuit now live in modern towns. Some of the houses are shaped like igloos (traditional snow houses).

The Antarctic

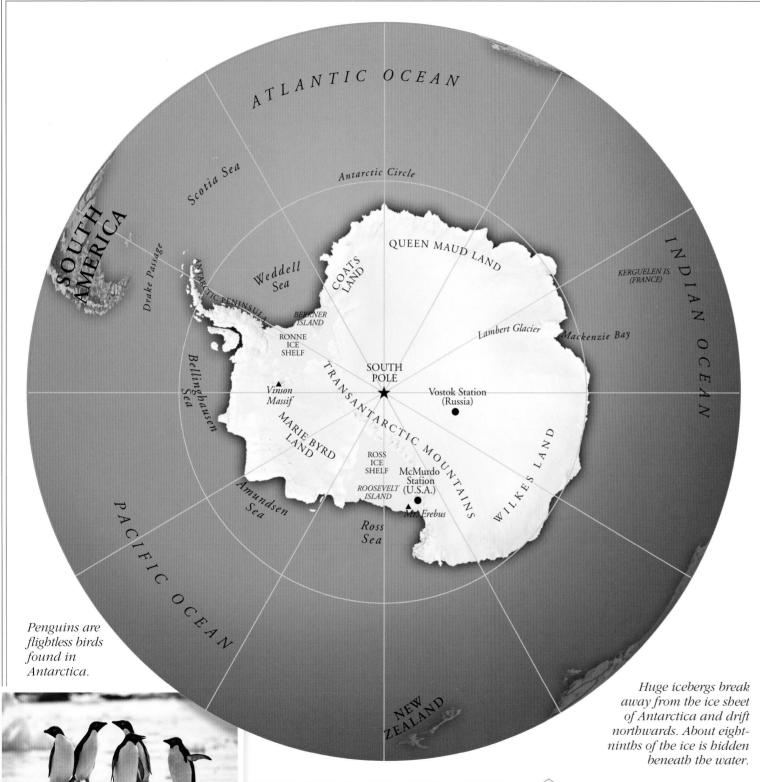

ATLANTIC OCEAN

Scotia Sea

SOUTH AMERICA

Antarctic Circle

Drake Passage

Weddell Sea

COATS LAND

QUEEN MAUD LAND

INDIAN OCEAN

KERGUELEN IS. (FRANCE)

ANTARCTIC PENINSULA

BERKNER ISLAND

RONNE ICE SHELF

Lambert Glacier

Mackenzie Bay

Bellingshausen Sea

SOUTH POLE

Vinson Massif

TRANSANTARCTIC MOUNTAINS

Vostok Station (Russia)

MARIE BYRD LAND

WILKES LAND

ROSS ICE SHELF

McMurdo Station (U.S.A.)

Amundsen Sea

ROOSEVELT ISLAND

Mt Erebus

Ross Sea

PACIFIC OCEAN

NEW ZEALAND

Penguins are flightless birds found in Antarctica.

Antarctica, the world's fifth largest continent, lies around the South Pole at the bottom of the globe. From space, you would see that it is mainly covered by the world's largest ice sheet, and surrounded by frozen seas. But you would also see high mountains jutting through the ice in places. In some parts of the continent, the ice is 15,700 ft (4,800 m) thick.

This frozen land is the world's coldest place. It is swept by strong winds that blow loose snow across the surface, causing blinding blizzards. Some scientists go there to study the continent and its weather, and some tourists now visit the continent. But no-one lives in Antarctica all the time.

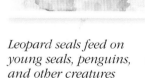

Leopard seals feed on young seals, penguins, and other creatures around Antarctica.

Huge icebergs break away from the ice sheet of Antarctica and drift northwards. About eight-ninths of the ice is hidden beneath the water.

Index

Acknowledgments

Picture Researcher: Lynda Marshall

Maps: Mountain High Maps © Digital Wisdom

Icons: Alex Charles

Illustrations: JB Illustrations (Julian Baker); Trevor Bounford; Alastair Campbell; Eikon Illustrations (Tony Dale & Robert Calow); Rebecca Johns; Kevin Jones Associates; Sally Launder; Nicholas Rowland; John Woodcock

Photographs: Ancient Art & Architecture Collection Limited; Ardea London (Kennith W. Fink, Francois Gohier, P. J. Green & Adrian Warren); Aztec New Media Corp.; Biblioteca Del ICI, Madrid, 115; Biblioteca Nazionale Centrale, Florence; Bridgeman Art Library: Private Collection, 104BR; British Antarctic Survey Photo Library; British Library, London, 124TR & 126; British Museum, London, 121BL; CASELLA CEL Limited, UK; Christies Images, London, 118; Corel Photo Disk; Corbis, 16, 79, 80, 82, 83, 86R, 88B, 89L, 90TR & BR, 95, 96, 97, 98, 99T & R, 101B; Digital Vision; Frank Lane Picture Agency Limited (Peter Dean); GeoScience Features Picture Library; GettyOneStone, 78BL & TR, 81, 82BR, 83BR, 84R, 86L, 87B, 89R, 92T, 94BR, 101TL; International Weather Productions Ltd; istock 6, 11, 81CL, 92; Kon Tiki Museum, Oslo, 125BL; Meteorological Office/Her Majesty's Stationery Office, London; Museum of Mankind, London; National Library of Australia, Canberra, 122TR; National Meteorological Library and Archive, UK (G. A. Robinson); National Oceanic and Atmospheric Administration/Department of Commerce, USA; The Natural History Museum, London; NASA, 9, 10, 11, 12, 13, 130 &131; PhotoDisc; Railways Collection, National Archives, New Zealand; Rex Features, 91; Science Photo Library (Carlos Goldin, Jerry Mason & Sam Ogden); Stapleton Collection, 110B, 113; Tangiwai Memorial, 100BR; Topham Picture-point; Vaisala (UK) Limited.